بسم الله الرحمن الرحيم

Shaykhu'l-Islām
Aḥmad ibn 'Abdu'l-Ḥalīm ibn Taymiyyah

The RELIEF from DISTRESS

An explanation to the *du'ā* of Prophet Yūnus

being a translation of his

'Tafrīj al-Kurūb: Sharḥ ḥadīth da'wah akhi Dhū-n-Nūn...'

دار السنة

THE MESSENGER OF ALLĀH (ﷺ) SAID,

"...none who is experiencing difficulty employs it except that Allāh would relieve him of his difficulty."

at-Tirmidhī [#3505] and an-Nasā'ī, *'Amal* [#606]

The Relief From Distress

An explanation to the *du'ā* of Yūnus

Shaykh al-Islām ibn Taymiyyah

Translated from the original Arabic by
Abū Rumaysah

دار السنة
Dār as-Sunnah Publishers
BIRMINGHAM

Second Edition Published in Great Britain, July 2012^CE / Sha'ban 1433^AH
by Dār as-Sunnah Publishers

DĀR AS-SUNNAH PUBLISHERS
P.O. Box 9818, Birmingham, B11 4WA, United Kingdom

W: www.darassunnah.com
E: info@darassunnah.com
E: daar-us-sunnah@mail.com

British Library Cataloguing in publication Data.
A catalogue record for this book is available from the British Library.

Title: The Relief from Distress - An explanation to the *du'ā* of Yūnus
by Shaykhu'l-Islām Aḥmad ibn 'Abdu'l-Ḥalīm ibn Taymiyyah
Translated from the original Arabic by Abū Rumaysah

ISBN 1-904336-13-2
Paper-back

First Edition, 1425 AH/2006 CE
Second Edition, 1433 AH/2012 CE
Typeset by: Dār as-Sunnah Publishers

CONTENTS

THE LIFE OF IBN TAYMIYYAH 12
His Teachers 16
His Students 17
The Praise of the Scholars for him 18
His Sayings 24
His Death 27
His Works 28

INTRODUCTION TO PROPHET YŪNUS 32
Methodology of Translation 37

THE RELIEF FROM DISTRESS 38
An explanation to the *duʿā* of Yūnus

CHAPTER ONE
'What is the meaning of this supplication?' 40

[1.1 The meaning of *duʿā*] 40
[1.2 The condition of the supplicant] 45
[1.3 The supplication of Yūnus] 47

[1.4 The condition of Yūnus] 54
[1.5 Allāh does not wrong anyone] 55
[1.6 The meaning of *Lā ilāha illAllāh* and *SubḥānAllāh*] 57
[1.7 *Tahlīl* and *tasbīḥ* in the supplication] 60
[1.8 Summary of the meaning of the supplication] 66

CHAPTER TWO:
'Why does this supplication remove harm?' 68

[2.1 Reliance, hope and fear is to be placed in Allāh alone] 68
[2.2 Avarice and Begging] 77
[2.3 Sincerity in testifying to *Tawḥīd*] 79
[2.4 The wisdom in mentioning *Tawḥīd* alongside forgiveness] 82
[2.5 The correct understanding of *Tawḥīd*] 87
[2.6 The obligation to obey the Prophet (ﷺ)] 92
[2.7 The explanation of *Īmān*] 94
[2.8 The foundation of worship] 104
[2.9 Misdirected intentions] 108
[2.10 Ostentation and conceit] 110
[2.11 The Messenger-Servant and Prophet-King] 113
[2.12 *ar-Rubūbiyyah* and *al-Ilāhiyyah*] 123
[2.13 The Infallibility of Prophets] 127
[2.14 Repentance] 130
[2.15 Deeds are by their conclusion] 141
[2.16 Allāh loves those who repent] 145
[2.17 True repentance involves a person changing himself] 152

CHAPTER THREE:
'Does the mere acknowledgement of sin combined with *tawḥīd* lead to its forgiveness and the alleviation of difficulty, or is something else required?' 163

CHAPTER FOUR:
'Does the acknowledgment of one sins lead to the elimination of the evil of many sins that may have been committed, or must that person bring to mind all sins in order for this to occur?' 169

The First Principle 169
The Second Principle 174
The Third Principle 177

CHAPTER FIVE:
'Why is it that relief comes after a person has given up all hope in creation and how can one make his heart dependant on Allāh alone?' 181

APPENDIX ONE:
Digression: Hope and Fear as Understood by the *Ṣūfis* and *Ahlu-l-Kalām* 188

APPENDIX TWO:
Digression: The Different Usages of the Word *Īmān* 194

APPENDIX THREE:
Digression: Examples of Word-Pairs in the Qur'ān 198

APPENDIX FOUR:
Digression: *Fiqh* of War Booty 201

APPENDIX FIVE:
Digression: The incident of the 'Satanic Verses' 206

APPENDIX SIX:
Digression: *Ta'wīl* of those who held the Prophets were sinless 210

APPENDIX SEVEN:
Digression: Emotions in the view of the Philosophers 216

INDEX OF QUR'ĀNIC QUOTATIONS 219
INDEX OF AḤĀDITH QUOTATIONS 226
BIOGRAPHICAL NOTES 229
GENERAL INDEX 242
INDEX OF SECT 249
GLOSSARY OF ARABIC TERMS 250-256

تفريج الكروب

شرح حديث:

«دعوة أخي ذي النون: لا إله إلا أنت سبحانك إني كنت من الظالمين.
ما دعا بها مكروب إلا فرج الله كربته».

IBN TAYMIYYAH

May Allāh have mercy upon him

HE IS AḤMAD bin 'Abdu-l-Ḥalīm bin 'Abdu-s-Salām bin 'Abdullāh bin Abū Qāsim ibn Taymiyyah al-Ḥarrānī Taqī ad-Dīn Abū al-'Abbās bin Shihāb ad-Dīn. He was born in Ḥarrān, an old city within the Arabian Peninsula between Syria[1] and Iraq, on the tenth or the twelfth of the month *Rabī'u-l-Awwal* in the year 661H. He and his family were later forced to flee to Damascus due to the occupation by the Tartars.

He came from a family of scholars, his father and grandfather were both scholars as were three of his brothers: 'Abdu-r-Raḥmān, 'Abdullāh and his half-brother, Muḥammad.

During his early studies of Islām, he never ceased to amaze his teachers at the strength of his memory, keen intelligence and depth of understanding. It is said that he was first allowed to give legal verdicts at the age of nineteen and he began teaching at *Dār al-Ḥadīth as-Sukriyyah* at the age of twenty-two.

He became famous for his knowledge of ḥadīth, indeed he was a

[1] Ar. *Shām*, in those days represented the areas of Syria, Jordan and Palestine.

Ḥāfiẓ (Ḥadīth Master), and for his knowledge of the Qur'ān and its related sciences, he impressed all with his circles on *tafsīr*. He also attained expertise in *Usūl al-Fiqh* and *Fiqh*, knowledge of the differences of opinions present amongst the scholars, writing, mathematics, history, astronomy and medicine. Many of the scholars of his time testified that he had attained the rank of *Mujtahid*.

He always showed a great concern for the affairs and welfare of the Muslims and this manifested itself greatly in his efforts during the *Jihād* against the Tartars, Christians and *Rawāfiḍah* wherein his displays of bravery, courage and inspiring talks were one of the most important factors in the Muslims victory against their enemies. These efforts won the praise and admiration of many scholars and indeed the ensuing generations of Muslims to this very day.

Aside from the physical *Jihād*, ibn Taymiyyah launched an intellectual struggle against the various deviant sects and heretical ideas of his day. He refuted the *Shī'a*, the People of Theological Rhetoric (*Ahl al-Kalām*) - such as the *Jahmiyyah*, *Mu'tazilah* and many of *Ashā'irah*, the philosophers who promoted the school of the early Greeks (*falāsifa*), the majority of *Ṣūfi* sects and paths and the adherents of other religions. His criticisms were not based on a lack of understanding, rather he first gained an in-depth knowledge of each of these schools and as such his critique of them was systematic, acute and valid. For example it is said that his refutation of Greek philosophy was one of the most devastating attacks ever leveled against them. His refutation of Christianity was outstanding and his rebuttal of the *Shī'a* completely demolished their beliefs and innovations from root to branch.[2]

Needless to say, these refutations, and his very direct methods of

[2] When this is understood, the critique levelled against him by some that 'his learning exceeded his intellect' can safely be relegated to the trash bin.

refuting, made him many enemies and as a result his life was full of trials and persecutions. His enemies were careful to look for anything by which they could attack him and they eventually found what they were looking for in his works of belief entitled *'Aqīdah al-Wāsiṭiyyah* and *'Aqīdah al-Ḥamawiyyah*. Due to their total misunderstanding of what he wrote, they accused him of anthropomorphism and had him imprisoned on more than one occasion. Ibn Kathīr mentions that some scholars sat with ibn Taymiyyah to debate with him concerning his *'Aqīdah al-Wāsiṭiyyah* and the debate ending with their agreeing with him in what he had written.[3] Similarly ibn Kathīr mentions that some scholars debated with him concerning *'Aqīdah al-Ḥamawiyyah* and his replies to their accusations could not be rebutted.[4] Ibn Taymiyyah was again imprisoned because of a legal ruling he gave concerning divorce, and yet again he was later imprisoned for a legal verdict he issued prohibiting making journeys for the purpose of visiting graves. It was during this imprisonment that he passed away.

With regards his personality and worship, he exerted a huge and lasting influence on all who met him and he was known for his worship and glorification of the Islāmic laws, both inwardly and outwardly. His complete reliance upon Allāh can be best summed up in what his student, ibn al-Qayyim, relates from him when he was told that his enemies had plotted to kill him or imprison him,

> If they kill me it will be martyrdom for me. If they expel me, it will be migration for me; if they expel me to Cyprus, I will call its people to Allāh so that they answer me. If they imprison me, it will be a place of worship for

---

[3] Ibn Kathīr, *Bidāyah wa an-Nihāyah* [Vol. 14, under the heading *'Aqd Majālis ath-Thalātha*].

[4] Ibn Kathīr [14/5].

me.[5]

Ibn al-Qayyim himself said,

> Allāh knows, I have never seen anyone who had a better life than his. Despite the difficulties and all that expunges comfort and luxury, nay, things completely opposite to them; despite imprisonment, intimidation and oppression, ibn Taymiyyah had a purer life than anyone could. He was the most generous, the strongest of heart and the most joyful of souls, with the radiance of bliss in his face. When we were seized with fear and our thoughts turned negative, and the earth grew narrow for us, we would go to him. No sooner did we look at him and hear his words, all these feelings would leave us to be replaced by relief, strength, certainty and tranquillity.[6]

Al-Bazzār said,

> I was of those who knew well his habits, he would not talk to anyone unnecessarily after the prayer of Fajr and would remain performing the *dhikr* of Allāh in a low voice which perhaps could just be heard by one sitting next to him; and frequently would he direct his gaze to the sky. This he would do until the Sun had risen high and the time in which it is prohibited to pray was over.[7]

He also said,

> I have not seen him mention any of the pleasures and

[5] *Nāhiyah min Ḥayāh Shaykh al-Islām* [p. 30].

[6] Ibn al-Qayyim, *Al-Wābil as-Ṣayyib* [p. 69].

[7] al-Bazzār, *al-A'lām al-'Aliyyah* [p. 40]

> attractions of this world, he did not delve into worldly conversations and he never asked for any of its livelihood. Instead he directed his attentions and conversations to seeking the Hereafter and what could get him closer to Allāh.[8]

Once, the ruler Muḥammad bin Qalāwūn accused him of wanting to wrench kingship from him due to his large following to which he replied,

> I would do that! By Allāh, your kingship and the kingship of Moghul is not even worth two meagre coins in my eyes![9]

His Teachers[10]

He studied under a great number of scholars and he himself mentioned a number of them as related by adh-Dhahabī directly from him.[11] This particular chronicle of teachers includes forty-one male scholars and four female scholars. The total number of scholars whom he took knowledge from exceeds two hundred.[12]

The following is a selection of some of his teachers:

---

[8] al-Bazzār [p.52].

[9] al-Bazzār [p. 74].

[10] Refer to: *Majmū' Fatāwā Shaykh al-Islām* [18/76-121]; *Dhayl ibn Rajab* [2/387]; Ibn Kathīr [14/136-137]; adh-Dhahabī, *Tadhkirah al-Ḥuffāẓ* [3/1496]; Ibn Ḥajr al-'Asqalānī, *ad-Durar al-Kāminah fī A'yān al-Mi'ah ath-Thāminah* [1/154].

[11] *Majmū' al-Fatāwā* [18/76-121].

[12] *Al-'Uqūd ad-Durriyyah* [p. 3]; *al-Kawākib ad-Durriyyah* [p. 52].

- Abū al-'Abbās Aḥmad ibn 'Abdu-l-Dā'im al-Maqdasī
- Abū Naṣr 'Abdu-l-'Azīz ibn 'Abdu-l-Mun'im
- Abū Muḥammad Ismā'īl ibn Ibrāhīm at-Tanūkhī
- Al-Manjā ibn 'Uthmān at-Tanūkhī ad-Dimashqī
- Abu al-'Abbās al-Mu'ammil ibn Muḥammad al-Bālisī
- Abū 'Abdullāh Muḥammad ibn Abū Bakr ibn Sulaymān al-Āmirī
- Abū al-Faraj 'Abdur-Raḥmān ibn Sulaymān al-Baghdādī
- Sharaf ad-Dīn al-Maqdasī, Aḥmad ibn Aḥmad ash-Shāfi'ī
- Muḥammad ibn 'Abdu-l-Qawī al-Maqdasī
- Taqī ad-Dīn al-Wāsiṭī, Ibrāhīm ibn 'Alī as-Ṣāliḥī al-Ḥanbalī
- His paternal aunt, Sitt ad-Dār bint 'Abdu-s-Salām ibn Taymiyyah

His Students

He had many students and those who were affected by him are many, some of his students were:

- Ibn al-Qayyim al-Jawziyyah, Muḥammad ibn Abū Bakr.
- Adh-Dhahabī, Muḥammad ibn Aḥmad.
- Al-Mizzī, Yūsuf ibn 'Abdur-Raḥmān.
- Ibn Kathīr, Ismā'īl ibn 'Umar.
- Ibn 'Abdu-l-Hādī, Muḥammad ibn Aḥmad.
- Al-Bazzār, 'Umar ibn 'Alī.
- Ibn Qāḍī al-Jabal, Aḥmad ibn Ḥusain.
- Ibn Faḍlillāh al-Amrī, Aḥmad ibn Yaḥyā.
- Muḥammad ibn al-Manj, ibn 'Uthmān at-Tanūkhī.
- Yūsuf ibn 'Abdu-l-Maḥmūd ibn 'Abdu-s-Salām al-Battī.
- Ibn al-Wardī, Zayn ad-Dīn 'Umar.
- 'Umar al-Ḥarrānī, Zayn ad-Dīn Abū Ḥafs.
- Ibn Mufliḥ, Shams ad-Dīn Abū 'Abdullāh.

The Praise of the Scholars for him

Many scholars praised ibn Taymiyyah, not only for his scholarly achievements but also for his active participation in *Jihād* and the affairs relating to public welfare, his abundant concern for others and his worship. Below is a selection of some of these statements:

1. Al-Ḥāfiẓ adh-Dhahabī said,

> It was amazing when he mentioned an issue over which there was a difference of opinion and when he gave evidence and decided the strongest opinion - he could perform *ijtihād* due to his fulfilling its conditions. I have not seen one who was quicker than he at recalling a verse which pertained to the issue that he derived from it, nor a man who was stronger in recalling texts and referring them to their sources. The *Sunnah* was in front of his eyes and upon the tip of his tongue with eloquent phrases and an open eye.
>
> He was a sign from the signs of Allāh in *tafsīr* and expounding upon it. With regards to the foundation of the religion and knowledge of the differing opinions [on an issue], he was unequalled - this alongside his generosity, courage and lack of attention to the joys of the soul.
>
> Quite possibly his legal rulings in the various sciences reached three hundred volumes, indeed more and he was always saying the truth for the sake of Allāh, not caring for the blame that came to him.
>
> Whosoever associates with him and knows him well accuses me of falling short with regards to him. Whosoever opposes him and differs with him accuses me of exaggeration, and I have been wronged by both parties -

his companions and his opponents.

He was white skinned with black hair and a black beard with a few grey hairs. His hair reached his earlobes and his eyes were eloquent tongues. He had broad shoulders and a loud, clear voice with a fast recitation. He was quick to anger but overcame it with patience and forbearance.

I have not seen his like for supplications [to Allāh], his seeking succour with Him and his abundant concern for others. However I do not believe him to be infallible, rather I differ with him on both fundamental and subsidiary matters, for he - despite his vast learning, extreme courage, fluid mind and regard for the sanctity of the religion - was a man from amongst men. He could be overcome with sharpness and anger in discussion, and attack his opponents [verbally] hence planting enmity in their souls towards him.

If only he were gentle to his opponents then there would have been a word of agreement over him - for indeed their great scholars bowed to his learning, acknowledged his ability, lack of mistakes and conceded that he was an ocean having no limits and a treasure having no equivalent...

He used to preserve the prayers and fasts, glorifying the laws outwardly and inwardly. He did not give legal rulings out of poor understanding for he was extremely intelligent, nor out of lack of knowledge for he was an overflowing ocean. Neither did he play with the religion but derived evidence from the Qur'ān, *Sunnah* and *Qiyās* (analogy), he proved [his stances] and argued following the footsteps of the *Imāms* who preceded him, so he has a reward if he erred and two rewards if he was correct.

> He fell ill in the castle [wherein he was imprisoned] with a serious disease until he died on the night of Monday 20th *Dhū-l-Qaʿdah*, and they prayed over him in the *Masjid* of Damascus. Afterwards many talked about the number that attended his funeral prayer, and the least number given was fifty thousand.[13]

2. Ibn Ḥajr al-ʿAsqalānī said,

> The *Shaykh* of our *Shaykhs*, *al-Ḥāfiẓ* Abū al-Yuʿmarī [ibn Sayyid an-Nās] said in his biography of ibn Taymiyyah, 'al-Mizzī encouraged me to express my opinion on *Shaykh al-Islām* Taqī ad-Dīn. I found him to be from those who had acquired a fortune of knowledge in the sciences that he had. He used to completely memorise and implement the *Sunan* and *Āthār* (narrations). Should he speak about *tafsīr*, he would carry its flag, and should he pass a legal ruling in *fiqh*, he knew its limits. Should he speak about a ḥadīth, he was the seat of its knowledge and fully cognisant of its narrations. Should he give a lecture on religions and sects, none was seen who was more comprehensive or meticulous than he. He surpassed his contemporaries in every science, you would not see one like him and his own eye did not see one like himself...' [14]

3. Ibn Ḥajr also said,

> The acclaim of Taqī ad-Dīn is more renown then that of the Sun and titling him *Shaykh al-Islām* of his era remains until our time upon the virtuous tongues. It will continue tomorrow just as it was yesterday. No one refutes this but a person who is ignorant of his prestige or one who

[13] Ibn Ḥajr, [under the biography of ibn Taymiyyah].

[14] Ibid.

turns away from justice...

...those of his stances that were rejected from him were not said by him due to mere whims and desires and neither did he obstinately and deliberately persist in them after the evidence was established against him. Here are his works overflowing with refutations of those who held to *tajsīm* (anthropomorphism), yet despite this he is a man who makes mistakes and is also correct. So that which he is correct in - and that is the majority - is to benefited from and Allāh's Mercy should be sought for him due to it, and that which he is incorrect in should not be blindly followed. Indeed he is excused for his mistakes because he is one of the *Imāms* of his time and it has been testified that he fulfilled the conditions of *ijtihād*...

From the astonishing qualities of this man was that he was the severest of people against the People of Innovation, the *Rawāfiḍah*, the *Ḥulūliyyah* and the *Ittiḥādiyyah*. His works on this are many and famous and his *fatāwā* on them cannot be counted, so how the eyes of these innovators must have found joy when they heard those who declared him to be a *kāfir*! And how delighted they must have been when they saw those who did not declare him to be a *kāfir* in turn being labeled *kāfir*! It is obligatory upon the one who has donned the robe of knowledge and possesses intelligence that he consider the words of a man based upon his well-known books or from the tongues of those who are trusted to accurately convey his words. Then he should isolate from all of this what is rejected and warn against it with the intention of giving sincere advice and to praise him for his excellent qualities and for what he was correct in, as is the way of the scholars.

If there were no virtues of *Shaykh* Taqī ad-Dīn except

> for his famous student *Shaykh* Shams ad-Dīn ibn al-Qayyim al-Jawziyyah, writer of many works, from which both his opponents and supporters benefited, then this would be a sufficient indication of his [ibn Taymiyyah's] great position. And how could it be otherwise when the Shāfiʿī *Imāms* and others, not to speak of the Ḥanbalīs, of his time testified to his prominence in the [Islāmic] sciences...[15]

4. Ibn Kathīr said,

> The least he would do when he heard something was to memorise it and then busy himself with learning it. He was intelligent and had much committed to memory, he became an *Imām* in *tafsīr* and everything linked to it and knowledgeable in *fiqh*. Indeed it was said that he was more knowledgeable of the *fiqh* of the *madhhabs* than the followers of those very same *madhhabs* in his time and other than his time. He was a scholar in *Uṣūl* and the branches of the religion, in grammar, the language and other textual and intellectual sciences.... no scholar of a science would speak to him except that he thought that that science was the specialty of ibn Taymiyyah. As for ḥadīth then he was the carrier of its flag, a *Ḥāfiẓ*, able to distinguish the weak from the strong, fully acquainted with the narrators....[16]

He also said,

> He was, may Allāh have mercy upon him, from the greatest of scholars but also from those who err and are cor-

[15] From Ibn Ḥajr's endorsement of *Radd al-Wāfir* contained at the end of the book.

[16] Ibn Kathīr, [14/118-119].

rect. However his errors with respect to his correct rulings were like a drop in a huge ocean and they are forgiven him as is authentically reported by Bukhārī,

> *When a ruler makes a ruling, and he is correct then he has two rewards, and if he has erred then he has one reward.*

5. *Al-Ḥāfiẓ* al-Mizzī said,

   I have not seen the likes of him and his own eye had not seen the likes of himself. I have not seen one who was more knowledgeable than he of the Book and the Sunnah of His Messenger, nor one who followed them more closely.[17]

6. *Al-Ḥāfiẓ* ʿAbdur-Raḥmān ibn Rajab al-Ḥanbalī said,

   He is the *Imām*, the legal Jurist, the *Mujtahid*, the Scholar of Ḥadīth, the *Ḥāfiẓ*, the Explainer of the Qurʾān, the Ascetic, Taqī ad-Dīn Abū al-ʿAbbās *Shaykh al-Islām*, the most knowledgeable of the knowledgeable. It is not possible to exaggerate his renown when he is mentioned and his fame does not require us to write a lengthy tract on him. He, may Allāh have mercy upon him, was unique in his time with respect to understanding the Qurʾān and knowledge of the realities of faith....[18]

---

[17] Bahjatul Baiṭār, *Ḥayāt Shaykh al-Islām ibn Taymiyyah* [p. 21].

[18] ibn Rajab, [2/387-392].

His Sayings

Shaykh al-Islām was famous for stating profound statements, below is a selection of some of them.

- Every punishment from Him is pure justice and every blessing from Him is pure grace.[19]

- Whoever desires everlasting bliss, let him adhere firmly to the threshold of servitude[20]

- The Lord loves to be loved.[21]

- Guidance is not attained except with knowledge and correct direction is not attained except with patience.[22]

- In this world there is a paradise, whoever does not enter it will not enter the Paradise of the Hereafter.[23]

- The one who is [truly] imprisoned is the one whose heart is imprisoned from Allāh and the captivated one is the one whose desires have enslaved him.[24]

---

[19] *Majmū' Fatāwā* [10/85]

[20] ibn al-Qayyim, *Madārij* [1/531]

[21] *Majmū' Fatāwā* [1/54]

[22] *Majmū' Fatāwā* [10/40]

[23] ibn al-Qayyim, *al-Wābil* [p. 69]

[24] Ibn al-Qayyim, *al-Wābil* [p. 69].

- This whole religion revolves around knowing the truth and acting by it, and action must be accompanied by patience.[25]

- Worship is founded upon the Legal Law and following it, not upon ones base desires and innovation.[26]

- If you do not taste the sweetness of an action in your heart, suspect it, for the Lord, Exalted is He, is the Appreciative.[27]

- The more the servant loves his Master, the less will he love other objects and they will decrease in number. The less the servant loves his Master, the more will he love other objects and they will increase in number.[28]

- Perpetually is the servant either the recipient of a blessing from Allāh, in which case he is need of gratitude; or he is the perpetrator of a sin, in which case he is in need of repentance; he is always moving from one blessing to another and is always in need of repentance.[29]

- Sins cause harm and repentance removes the cause.[30]

- Bearing witness to *tawḥīd* opens the door of good and repent-

[25] *Majmūʿ Fatāwā* [10/38]

[26] *Majmūʿ Fatāwā* [1/80]

[27] ibn al-Qayyim, *al-Madārij* [2/68]

[28] *Majmūʿ Fatāwā* [1/94]

[29] *Majmūʿ Fatāwā* [10/88]

[30] *Majmūʿ Fatāwā* [10/255]

ance from sins closes the door of evil.[31]

- The *Jihād* against the soul is the foundation for the *Jihād* against the disbelievers and hypocrites.[32]

- A man will never fear something besides Allāh unless it be due to a disease in his heart.[33]

- Trials and tribulation are like feeling the heat and cold, when one knows that they cannot be avoided, he will not feel anger at their onset, nor will he be distressed or disheartened.[34]

- The perfection of *tawḥīd* is found when there remains nothing in the heart except Allāh, the servant is left loving those He loves and what He loves, hating those He hates and what He hates, showing allegiance to those He has allegiance to, showing enmity to those He shows enmity towards, ordering what He orders and prohibiting what He prohibits.[35]

- In this world, man finds in the remembrance of Allāh, praising Him and worshipping Him, a delight that is incomparable to anything else.[36]

---

[31] *Majmū' Fatāwā* [10/256]

[32] ibn al-Qayyim, *ar-Rawḍah* [p. 478]

[33] al-Bazzār [p. 74]

[34] ibn al-Qayyim, *al-Madārij* [3/289]

[35] ibn al-Qayyim, *al-Madārij* [3/485]

[36] *Minhāj as-Sunnah* [5/389]

- The objective of asceticism is to leave all that harms the servants Hereafter and the objective of worship is to do all that will benefit his Hereafter.[37]

- Sins are like chains and locks preventing their perpetrator from roaming the vast garden of *tawḥīd* and reaping the fruits of righteous actions.[38]

- What can my enemies do to me? I have in my breast both my heaven and my garden. If I travel they are with me, never leaving me. Imprisonment for me is a chance to be alone with my Lord. To be killed is martyrdom and to be exiled from my land is a spiritual journey.[39]

His Death

Ibn Taymiyyah died while imprisoned on the twentieth of *Dhū-l-Qa'dah* of the year 728H, after ultimately being banned from reading or writing. He fell sick for the few days preceding his death.

His funeral was attended by a huge congregation despite the many lies and slanders being spread about him by certain innovators of his time. Al-Bazzār says,

> Once the people had heard of his death, not a single person in Damascus who was able to attend the prayer and wanted to remained except that he appeared and was present for it. As a result, the markets in Damascus were closed and all transactions of livelihood were

[37] *Majmū' Fatāwā* [14/458]

[38] *Majmū' Fatāwā* [14/49]

[39] ibn al-Qayyim, *Wābil* [p. 69]

> stopped...Governors, heads, scholars, jurists all came out. They say that none of the majority of the people failed to turn up - according to my knowledge - except three individuals; they were well known for their enmity for ibn Taymiyyah and thus, hid away from the people out of fear for their lives.[40]

Ibn Kathīr said,

> There were so many people in front of his funeral, behind it, to its right and to its left. None but Allāh could enumerate them, and then someone shouted, 'this is how the funerals of the *Imāms* of the *Sunnah* are to be!' At that the people started to cry... when the call to prayer for *Ẓuhr* was proclaimed they prayed after it straight away against the usual norm. Once they finished prayer, the deputy *khaṭīb* came out - as the main *khaṭīb* was absent and in Egypt - and he led the prayer over ibn Taymiyyah... then the people poured out from everywhere and all the doors of the *Masjid*... and they assembled at *al-Khayl* market. [41]

His Works

Ibn Taymiyyah was a prolific writer and authored many works spanning a broad range of topics. The sum of his writings were thought to consist of hundreds of volumes and even though a large number of them have been lost, many are still available and in print. A number of his works have also been translated and below is a list of these works followed by some of his works in Arabic. [42]

---

[40] al-Bazzār [pp. 82-83].

[41] Ibn Kathīr [14/138].

[42] None of the lists detailed below are meant to be exhaustive.

The books of, or about, ibn Taymiyyah available in the English language:

1. *Ibn Taymiyyah on Public and Private Law in Islam or Public Policy in Islamic Jurisprudence* [tr. Omar A. Farrukh, Khayats, 1966]
2. *A Seventh Century Sunni Creed: The Aqida al-Wastiya of ibn Taymiya* [tr. Merlin Swartz, the Hague: Mouton, 1973]
3. *Public Duties in Islam* [tr. Muhtar Holland, The Islamic Foundation, 1402/1982]
4. *Ibn Taymiyyah's Essay on the Jinn* [tr. Abu Ameenah Bilal Philips, 1409/1989]
5. *The Concise Legacy* [tr. Farhat Abbaas, Jam'iyyah Ihyaa Minhaaj as-Sunnah, 1415/1994]
6. *Introduction to the Principles of Tafseer* [tr. Muhammad Abdul Haqq Ansari, al-Hidaayah, 1414/1993]
7. *The Friends of Allāh and the Friends of Shayṭān* [trans. Abu Rumaysah, Dār as-Sunnah, 1421H/2000.
8. *Ibn Taymiyyah Against the Greek Logicians* [tr. Wal B. Hallaq, Oxford University Press, 1993]
9. *A Textbook on Orthodox Sunni Creed, the Creed of al-Wāsitiyyah - being a translation of al-'Aqīdah al-Wāsitiyyah* [trans. Abu Rumaysah, Dār as-Sunnah, 1430/2009].
10. *Fundamentals of Enjoining Good & Forbidding Evil* [tr. Abu Khalil & Muhammad al-Jibali, al-Qur'an & Sunnah Society of North America, 1997]
11. *Mukhatasar Iqtidaa as-Siraat al-Mustaqeem* [Dar-us-Salam Publications, 1416/1996]
12. *The Book of Eemaan* [compiled from the works of ibn Taymiyyah by Dr. Muhammad Nasim Yasim, al-Firdous Ltd., 1997]
13. *Diseases of the Hearts and their Cures* [tr. Abu Rumaysah, Dār as-Sunnah,1431/2010]
14. *Ibn Taymiyyah's Letters from Prison* [tr. Abu Ammar, Message

of Islam, 1419/1998]

15. *The Waasitah Between Allaah & The Creation* [tr. Abu Iyaad Amjad Rafiq, Invitation to Islaam, 1998]
16. *Al-Ubudiyyah* [tr. Nasir ud-Deen Khattaab,]; also translated as *Ibn Taymiyyah's Essay on Servitude* [tr. Abu Safwan Fareed ibn Haibatan, al-Hidaayah, 1420/1999]
17. *Kitab al-Iman: Book of Faith* [tr. Salman Hasan al-Ani, Iman Publishing House, 1999]
18. *Ibn Taimiya's Struggle Against Popular Religion: with an annotated translation of his Kitab Iqtida as-Sirat al-Mustaqim Mukhalafat Ashab al-Jahim* [Muhammad Umar Memon, the Hague: Mouton, 1976]
19. *Ibn Taymiyyah and his Projects of Reform* [Serajul Haque, Islamic Foundation of Bangladesh, 1982]
20. *Ibn Taymiyyah's Ethics* [Victor E. Makari, Scholars Press, 1983]
21. *A Muslim Theologian's Response to Christianity: Ibn Taymiyyah's al-Jawab as-Sahih* [ed. Thomas F. Michel, Caravan Books, 1985]
22. *Economic Concepts of Ibn Taymiyyah* [Abdul Azim Islahi, The Islamic Foundation, 1408/1988]
23. *The Political Thought of ibn Taymiyyah* [prof. Qamaruddin Khan, Adam Publishers & Distributers, 1992]
24. *Ibn Taymiyyah & The Islamization of Knowledge* [Taha Jabir al-Alwani, IIIT, 1994]
25. *The Relief from Distress* - An explanation to the *du'ā* of Yūnus[trans. Abu Rumaysah, Dār us-Sunnah, 1425/2005].

The available Arabic works of ibn Taymiyyah are many, from amongst them:

1. *Majmū' Fatāwā ibn Taymiyyah* [compiled by 'Abdur-Raḥmān ibn Qāsim and his son, Muḥammad in thirty-seven volumes] containing many monographs and treatise that he wrote.
2. *Fatāwā al-Kubrā*, in five volumes

3. *Fatāwā al-Miṣriyyah*
4. *Al-Jawāb as-Ṣaḥīḥ li man Baddala Dīn al-Masīḥ*, in six volumes
5. *Minhāj as-Sunnah an-Nabawiyyah*, in six volumes
6. *Darr Ta'āruḍ al-'Aql wa-n-Naql*, in twelve volumes
7. *As-Ṣārim al-Maslūl 'alā Shātim ar-Rasūl*, in three volumes
8. *Naqd at-Ta'sīs*
9. *Iqtiḍā as-Ṣirāṭ al-Mustaqīm li Mukhālafah Aṣḥāb al-Jaḥīm*, in two volumes
10. *Al-Istiqāmah*
11. *Naqd Marātib al-Ijmā'*
12. *ar-Radd 'alā al-Manṭiqiyyīn*
13. *ar-Radd 'alā al-Akhnā'ī*
14. *ar-Radd 'alā al-Bakrī*
15. *an-Nubuwwāt*
16. *Qā'idah 'Adhīmah fī-l-Farq bayn 'Ibādah Ahl al-Islām wa-l-Īmān wa 'Ibādah Ahl ash-Shirk wa-n-Nifāq*
17. *Al-Qawā'id an-Nūrāniyyah al-Fiqhiyyah*
18. *Tafsīr ibn Taymiyyah*, compiled by 'Abdu-r-Raḥmān 'Umayrī, in seven volumes.

INTRODUCTION TO PROPHET YŪNUS

Allāh's peace and blessings be upon him

وَإِنَّ يُونُسَ لَمِنَ ٱلْمُرْسَلِينَ ﴿١٣٩﴾

«Yūnus too was one of the Messengers...»

[*as-Ṣāffāt* (37): 139]

﴿ إِنَّآ أَوْحَيْنَآ إِلَيْكَ كَمَآ أَوْحَيْنَآ إِلَىٰ نُوحٍ وَٱلنَّبِيِّـۧنَ مِنۢ بَعْدِهِۦ ۚ
وَأَوْحَيْنَآ إِلَىٰٓ إِبْرَٰهِيمَ وَإِسْمَٰعِيلَ وَإِسْحَٰقَ وَيَعْقُوبَ
وَٱلْأَسْبَاطِ وَعِيسَىٰ وَأَيُّوبَ وَيُونُسَ وَهَٰرُونَ وَسُلَيْمَٰنَ ۚ
وَءَاتَيْنَا دَاوُۥدَ زَبُورًا ﴿١٦٣﴾

«We have revealed to you as We revealed to Nūḥ and the Prophets who came after him. We revealed to Ibrāhīm and Ismā'īl and Isḥāq and Ya'qūb and the Tribes, and 'Īsā and Ayyūb and Yūnus and Hārūn and Sulaymān. And We gave Dāwūd the Zabūr»

[*an-Nisā'* (4): 163]

وَإِسْمَٰعِيلَ وَٱلْيَسَعَ وَيُونُسَ وَلُوطًا ۚ وَكُلًّا فَضَّلْنَا عَلَى
ٱلْعَٰلَمِينَ ﴿٨٦﴾

«..and Ismā'īl, al-Yasā', Yūnus and Lūṭ. All of them We

favoured over all beings»

[*al-Anʿām* (6): 86]

فَٱجْتَبَٰهُ رَبُّهُۥ فَجَعَلَهُۥ مِنَ ٱلصَّٰلِحِينَ ﴿٥٠﴾

«His Lord chose him and made him one of the righteous»

[*al-Qalam* (68): 50]

Born in Ninevah, Mosul[1], Yūnus bin Matta was one of two Prophets who was named after his mother, the other being ʿĪsā. He was sent to his people as a Messenger to call them to the worship of Allāh alone, to call them to abandon their sinful ways. He spent thirty three years of his life in pursuit of this mission and in all of this time, only a handful of people believed; finally, in despair, Yūnus supplicated to his Lord that His punishment descend upon his nation. He was commanded to preach to his people for a further forty days, when three days remained he proclaimed amongst his people that punishment would afflict them in three days and fled,

لَّآ إِلَٰهَ إِلَّآ أَنتَ سُبْحَٰنَكَ إِنِّي كُنتُ مِنَ ٱلظَّٰلِمِينَ ﴿٨٧﴾

«...and *Dhū-n-Nūn* when he left in anger and thought We would not punish him»

[*al-Anbiyā'* (21): 87]

His people gathered together and agreed amongst themselves that Yūnus was a person who was not known to lie, and when they saw that he had indeed fled, they became certain of the imminent punishment and repented, so Allāh forgave them and showed them mercy,

---

[1] Capital of ancient Assyria, on the Tigris: its ruins can be seen opposite modern Mosul in northern Iraq.

فَلَوْلَا كَانَتْ قَرْيَةٌ ءَامَنَتْ فَنَفَعَهَآ إِيمَـٰنُهَآ إِلَّا قَوْمَ يُونُسَ لَمَّآ
ءَامَنُوا۟ كَشَفْنَا عَنْهُمْ عَذَابَ ٱلْخِزْىِ فِى ٱلْحَيَوٰةِ ٱلدُّنْيَا وَمَتَّعْنَـٰهُمْ
إِلَىٰ حِينٍ ﴿٩٨﴾

«How is it that there has never been a city who believed, whose belief brought them benefit, except the people of Yūnus? When they believed, We removed from them the punishment of disgrace in the life of this world and We let them have enjoyment for a time»

[*Yūnus (*10): 98]

In the meantime, Yūnus awaited news of what had happened to his people, and finally a traveler passed by him informing him that his people had become believers and the punishment had averted them. Fearing disgrace and being called a liar he determined not to return, and embarked upon a heavily laden ship destined for Tarshish, but it was not very long before they were overcome with bad weather. The travelers agreed that they must lighten their load by throwing some passengers overboard, they drew lots and the name of Yūnus came up, they were however reluctant to throw him overboard, seeing him to be a pious man and repeated the drawing of lots three times. His name came up each time.

إِذْ أَبَقَ إِلَى ٱلْفُلْكِ ٱلْمَشْحُونِ ﴿١٤٠﴾ فَسَاهَمَ فَكَانَ
مِنَ ٱلْمُدْحَضِينَ ﴿١٤١﴾

«When he ran away to the fully laden ship and cast lots and lost»

[*as-Ṣāffāt* (37): 140-141]

Upon being thrown into the sea, he was swallowed by a huge whale and by the decree of Allāh allowed to live in its belly, it is reported that at this time he supplicated saying, 'my Lord! I have been granted a place to pray where no one else has worshipped you before!'

فَٱلْتَقَمَهُ ٱلْحُوتُ وَهُوَ مُلِيمٌ ﴿١٤٢﴾

«...then the fish devoured him and he was to blame»
[*as-Ṣāffāt* (37): 142]

He remained in the belly of the whale, glorifying Allāh,

فَلَوْلَآ أَنَّهُۥ
كَانَ مِنَ ٱلْمُسَبِّحِينَ ﴿١٤٣﴾ لَلَبِثَ فِى بَطْنِهِۦٓ إِلَىٰ يَوْمِ يُبْعَثُونَ ﴿١٤٤﴾

«...had it not been that he was a man who glorified Allāh, he would have remained inside its belly until the Day that they were resurrected»
[*as-Ṣāffāt* (37): 143-144]

Realising that he had done something unbefitting in abandoning his people and fleeing before being granted permission by his Lord, and that this was the cause of his trial,

فَنَادَىٰ فِى ٱلظُّلُمَٰتِ أَن لَّآ إِلَٰهَ إِلَّآ أَنتَ سُبْحَٰنَكَ إِنِّى
كُنتُ مِنَ ٱلظَّٰلِمِينَ ﴿٨٧﴾ فَٱسْتَجَبْنَا لَهُۥ وَنَجَّيْنَٰهُ
مِنَ ٱلْغَمِّ ۚ وَكَذَٰلِكَ نُۨجِى ٱلْمُؤْمِنِينَ ﴿٨٨﴾

«He called out in the pitch darkness, "There is none worthy of worship save You! Glory be to You, far removed are You from any imperfection; I have been among the wrongdoers." We responded to him and rescued him from his grief, that is how We rescue the believers»
[*al-Anbiyā'* (21): 87-88]

at-Ṭabarī records on the authority of ibn Wahb that this supplication appeared beneath the Throne and the Angels said that they heard a very weak voice coming from a strange land. Allāh said, "Do you not know who that is? He is Our servant, Yūnus." The Angels said, 'Your servant Yūnus, from whom there has always ascended to You an accepted prayer and an accepted deed?' Allāh replied, "Yes" and commanded the whale to throw him out on the open shore.

﴿ فَنَبَذْنَٰهُ بِٱلْعَرَآءِ وَهُوَ سَقِيمٌ ﴿١٤٥﴾ وَأَنۢبَتْنَا عَلَيْهِ شَجَرَةً مِّن يَقْطِينٍ ﴿١٤٦﴾

«So We cast him up onto the beach and he was sick and We caused a gourd tree to grow over him...»

[*as-Ṣāffāt* (37): 145-146]

After having regained health and strength, Yūnus returned to his people to inform them that Allāh had indeed forgiven them and his people welcomed him with open arms,

﴿ وَأَرْسَلْنَٰهُ إِلَىٰ مِاْئَةِ أَلْفٍ أَوْ يَزِيدُونَ ﴿١٤٧﴾ فَـَٔامَنُوا۟ فَمَتَّعْنَٰهُمْ إِلَىٰ حِينٍ ﴿١٤٨﴾

«...We sent him to a hundred thousand or more. They believed and so We gave them enjoyment for a time»

[*as-Ṣāffāt* (37): 147-148]

The Prophet (ﷺ) said,

> The invocation of my brother Dhū-n-Nūn, "None has the right to be worshipped save You; glory be to You, far removed are You from any imperfection; I have been amongst the wrong-doers," none who is experiencing difficulty employs it except that Allāh would relieve him of his difficulty.

This book, authored by ibn Taymiyyah, may Allāh have mercy on him, explains in detail the meaning of the supplication of Yūnus and the meaning of this ḥadīth.[2]

Methodology of Translation

The author, may Allāh have mercy upon him, is famous for frequently diverting from the main topic of discussion and digressing to other issues. This often breaks the flow of the main topic and makes it difficult for the average reader to follow the discussion, hence the translator has opted to remove the lengthier digressions and place them in appendices, indicating each time where he has done so in the footnotes. The notes to the aḥādīth are based loosely around those given by Fawāz Zumarlī and the translator has also endeavored to present the verdicts of our early scholars to those of them found outside of the Two Ṣaḥīḥs; in addition the translator has added comments by the author, ibn Taymiyyah, from his other works to points that were only briefly touched upon or required further explanation.

And Allāh knows best

Abū Rumaysah
7th Ramaḍān, 1423H
12th November 2002

[2] References to the story: ibn Kathīr, *Qaṣaṣ al-Anbiyā'*, *Tafsīr*; at-Ṭabarī, *Tafsīr*; ibn Athīr, *al-Kāmil fi-t-Tārīkh*.

THE RELIEF FROM DISTRESS

An explanation to the *duʿā* of Yūnus

Shaykh al-Islām ibn Taymiyyah (d. 728H)

Shaykh al-Islām ibn Taymiyyah, may Allāh sanctify his soul, was asked about the saying of the Prophet (ﷺ) said,

> The invocation of my brother Dhū-n-Nūn, "None has the right to be worshipped save You; glory be to You, far removed are You from any imperfection; I have been amongst the wrong-doers," none who is experiencing difficulty employs it except that Allāh would relieve him of his difficulty.

i. What is the meaning of this supplication?

ii. Are their any unstated conditions that have to be met when one articulates it?

iii. What is the connection between belief in the heart and the meaning of this supplication such that it leads to the removal of difficulty?

iv. Why did he explicitly confess, 'I have been amongst the wrongdoers' when it is known that *tawḥīd* in itself leads to the removal of difficulty.

v. Is it sufficient to acknowledge ones sin alone, or must this be accompanied by repentance and the firm resolve not to repeat that sin in the future?

vi. Why is it that difficulty and harm is removed only when a person relinquishes any hope, reliance, and dependency upon the creation?

vii. How can the heart relinquish the characteristic of putting hope in the creation and depending upon them, and instead put its hope in Allāh, Exalted is He, and turn to Him in its entirety?

viii. What are the methods that would aid the heart in doing this?

He replied:

CHAPTER ONE

'What is the meaning of this supplication?'

ALL PRAISE AND THANKS are due to Allāh, the Lord of the worlds.

[1.1 The meaning of *du'ā*]

In the Qur'ān, the word supplication (*du'ā*) and invocation (*da'wah*) is used in two senses:

a. *Du'ā al-'Ibādah*: supplication through worship
b. *Du'ā al-Mas'alah*: the supplication of request[1]

Allāh, Exalted is He, says

[1] The first type of *du'ā* can be understood when one understands that every act of worship is done with the unstated plea that Allāh accept that action of worship and the desire to draw closer to him; and hence attain His pleasure. Hence every action of worship is a type of request to Allāh. The second type of *du'ā* is whereby one explicitly asks his Lord of something such as 'O Allāh! Grant me good in this world and the Hereafter.' The second type includes the first type and the first type necessitates the second type.

Refer to Abu Ammar Yasir Qadhi, *Du'ā, the weapon of the believer* [al-Hidaayah publishing, 2001]

فَلَا تَدْعُ مَعَ ٱللَّهِ إِلَٰهًا ءَاخَرَ فَتَكُونَ مِنَ ٱلْمُعَذَّبِينَ ﴿٢١٣﴾

«So do not supplicate to any other god along with Allāh or you will be among those who will be punished»

[*ash-Shu'arā'* (26): 213]

وَمَن يَدْعُ مَعَ ٱللَّهِ إِلَٰهًا ءَاخَرَ لَا بُرْهَٰنَ لَهُۥ بِهِۦ
فَإِنَّمَا حِسَابُهُۥ عِندَ رَبِّهِۦٓ ۚ إِنَّهُۥ لَا يُفْلِحُ ٱلْكَٰفِرُونَ ﴿١١٧﴾

«Whoever supplicates to another god along with Allāh, has no grounds for doing so at all and his reckoning is with his Lord. Indeed the disbelievers will never be successful»

[*al-Mu'minūn* (23): 117]

وَلَا تَدْعُ مَعَ ٱللَّهِ إِلَٰهًا ءَاخَرَ ۘ لَآ إِلَٰهَ إِلَّا
هُوَ ۚ كُلُّ شَىْءٍ هَالِكٌ إِلَّا وَجْهَهُۥ ۚ لَهُ ٱلْحُكْمُ وَإِلَيْهِ تُرْجَعُونَ ﴿٨٨﴾

«Do not supplicate to another god along with Allāh; there is none worthy of worship save Him...»

[*al-Qaṣaṣ* (28): 88]

وَأَنَّهُۥ لَمَّا قَامَ عَبْدُ ٱللَّهِ يَدْعُوهُ كَادُوا۟ يَكُونُونَ عَلَيْهِ لِبَدًا ﴿١٩﴾

«When the servant of Allāh stood, calling to Him, they almost swarmed all over him»

[*al-Jinn* (72): 19]

إِن يَدْعُونَ مِن دُونِهِۦٓ إِلَّآ إِنَٰثًا وَإِن يَدْعُونَ
إِلَّا شَيْطَٰنًا مَّرِيدًا ﴿١١٧﴾

«What they supplicate to apart from Him are female idols, what they supplicate to is an arrogant Shayṭān whom Allāh has cursed»

[*an-Nisā'* (4): 117]

لَهُۥ دَعۡوَةُ ٱلۡحَقِّۚ وَٱلَّذِينَ يَدۡعُونَ مِن دُونِهِۦ لَا يَسۡتَجِيبُونَ لَهُم بِشَيۡءٍ إِلَّا
كَبَٰسِطِ كَفَّيۡهِ إِلَى ٱلۡمَآءِ لِيَبۡلُغَ فَاهُ وَمَا هُوَ بِبَٰلِغِهِۦۚ

«The invocation of truth is made to Him alone. Those they supplicate to apart from Him do not respond to them at all. It is like one stretching out his cupped hands towards water to convey it to his mouth: it will never get there»

[*ar-Ra'd* (13): 14]

وَٱلَّذِينَ لَا يَدۡعُونَ مَعَ ٱللَّهِ إِلَٰهًا ءَاخَرَ وَلَا يَقۡتُلُونَ ٱلنَّفۡسَ
ٱلَّتِي حَرَّمَ ٱللَّهُ إِلَّا بِٱلۡحَقِّ وَلَا يَزۡنُونَۚ

«...those who do not supplicate to another god along with Allāh and do not kill anyone Allāh has made inviolate, except with right to do so, and do not fornicate...»

[*al-Furqān* (25): 68]

قُلۡ مَا يَعۡبَؤُاْ بِكُمۡ رَبِّي لَوۡلَا دُعَآؤُكُمۡۖ

«Say: what has my Lord to do with you if you do not supplicate [to Him]?...»

[*al-Furqān* (25): 77]

[In explanation to this] it is said, 'Were it not for your supplication to Him,' or, 'Were it not for His calling you.' This is because the verbal noun (*maṣdar*) is sometimes adjoined to the subject and other times to the object. However, here, its being adjoined to the subject is more likely as it necessary that the sentence have a subject. Hence the meaning of this verse would be, '...were it not for the fact that you supplicate to Him, worship Him and ask of Him.' [Then the verse proceeds,]

فَقَدْ كَذَّبْتُمْ فَسَوْفَ يَكُونُ لِزَامًا ﴿٧٧﴾

«...but you have denied the truth, so punishment is bound to come»

[*al-Furqān* (25): 77]

meaning a punishment that must be meted out to the deniers.[2]

Linguistically, the essential meaning of the word *ṣalāh* is *du'ā* because it comprises the meaning of the latter; both worship and request.

The words of Allāh, Exalted is He,

ٱدْعُونِىٓ أَسْتَجِبْ لَكُمْ

«Supplicate to Me and I will answer you»

[*Ghāfir* (40): 60]

have been explained in two ways:

a. Worship Me and enact my orders, I will respond to you [by accepting it]. It is in this sense that Allāh, Exalted is He, says,

وَيَسْتَجِيبُ ٱلَّذِينَ ءَامَنُوا۟ وَعَمِلُوا۟ ٱلصَّٰلِحَٰتِ

«He responds to those who have faith and do righteous actions»

---

[2] Refer to the exegesis of this verse in *al-Baḥr al-Muḥīṭ* [6/517-518]; *ibn Kathīr* [3/331]; *al-Muḥarrar al-Wajīz* [4/223]; *Zād al-Masīr* [6/112-113]; *Rūḥ al-Ma'ānī* [10/54-55]; and *at-Ṭabarī* [9/426-428]

[*ash-Shūrā* (42): 26]

This meaning of response is well known in the language, the poet said,

A supplicant supplicated, 'You who responds to the call!'
But there was none to respond to him at that time

b. Ask of Me and I will give you. The Two Ṣaḥīḥs record that the Prophet (ﷺ) said,

> Every night, when their remains the last third of the night, our Lord descends to the celestial heaven and says: Who is supplicating to Me that I may respond to him, who is asking of Me that I may grant him, who is seeking forgiveness that I may forgive him?[3]

Here the word *duʿā* has been mentioned followed by mention of asking and seeking forgiveness, even though the one seeking forgiveness is asking and the one asking is supplicating. However [the sequence is such] that the one asking to repress evil from himself has been mentioned after the one asking for the procurement of good, and both of these have been mentioned after mention of the supplicant who could be asking for both the aforementioned matters or others. This then is an example of mentioning the specific after having mentioned the general. Allāh, Exalted is He, says,

وَإِذَا سَأَلَكَ
عِبَادِي عَنِّي فَإِنِّي قَرِيبٌ أُجِيبُ دَعْوَةَ الدَّاعِ إِذَا دَعَانِ
فَلْيَسْتَجِيبُوا لِي وَلْيُؤْمِنُوا بِي لَعَلَّهُمْ يَرْشُدُونَ ﴿١٨٦﴾

«If My servants ask you about Me, I am near. I answer the

[3] Bukhārī [#1145, 6321, 7494] and Muslim [#758].

invocation of the caller when he invokes Me...»

[*al-Baqarah* (2): 186]

[1.2 The condition of the supplicant]

Every person who is asking is in a state that combines hope and fear, hence he is worshipping the asked. Every worshipper is also in a state that combines hope and fear, hoping for the mercy of the one asked and fearing his punishment. Hence every worshipper is one who asks, and every one who asks is a worshipper, therefore each term, when mentioned alone, includes the meaning of the other.[4] However, when they are both mentioned together then 'the

---

[4] The type of asking being discussed here is supplication to Allāh, the supplication of request. Allāh, Exalted is He says,

وَسْـَٔلُوا۟ ٱللَّهَ مِن فَضْلِهِۦٓ

«Ask Allāh for His bounty»

[*an-Nisā'* (4): 32]

And the Prophet (ﷺ) said, "When you ask, ask only of Allāh and when you seek help, seek help only from Allāh"; recorded by at-Tirmidhī. Ibn Rajab, *Jāmi'* [1/ 481] says, 'Know that asking of Allāh and not the creation is what is necessary. This is because to ask is to display humbleness and submissiveness before the one being asked as well as dependence upon him; it also contains an implicit acknowledgment that the one being asked has the ability to remove this harm, grant the object of desire, and promote benefit. It is not allowable to show humility, submissiveness and need except to Allāh alone because these matters exemplify the reality of worship. Aḥmad used to supplicate, "O Allāh! Just as You have prevented my face to prostrating to other than You, also prevent it from asking other than You." None is able to remove harm or promote the good save Him as He says,

وَإِن يَمْسَسْكَ ٱللَّهُ بِضُرٍّ فَلَا كَاشِفَ لَهُۥٓ إِلَّا هُوَ ۖ وَإِن يُرِدْكَ بِخَيْرٍ فَلَا رَآدَّ لِفَضْلِهِۦ ۚ يُصِيبُ بِهِۦ مَن يَشَآءُ مِنْ عِبَادِهِۦ ۚ

=

one asking' takes on the specific meaning of one who is seeking the procurement of good and the repression of evil by employing phrases denoting request; 'the one worshipping' takes on the specific meaning of one who desires the same, but does so through enacting the orders of Allāh and not by employing phrases denoting request.[5]

The point of discussion here[6] is that the words supplication and invocation carry both meanings [of worship and request]. Allāh, Exalted is He, says,

وَءَاخِرُ دَعْوَىٰهُمْ أَنِ ٱلْحَمْدُ لِلَّهِ رَبِّ ٱلْعَٰلَمِينَ ﴿١٠﴾

> «...Their final invocation is, 'All praise and thanks are due to Allāh, Lord of the Worlds!'»
>
> [*Yūnus* (10): 10]

In the ḥadīth it is mentioned,

> The most superior form of *dhikr* is [the statement], *'Lā*

=

> «If Allāh afflicts you with harm, no one can remove it except Him. If He desires good for you, no one can avert His favour»
>
> [*Yūnus* (10): 107]'

As for asking of human beings, in general this is not preferable unless needed, and to ask them for something that is outside of normal human capability constitutes *shirk*. However, even if someone were to ask another human in a permissible way, he still must have the belief that his request will only be satisfied if Allāh allows it. This issue is discussed further by the author in Chapter Five.

[5] The author, may Allāh have mercy upon him, here digresses to discuss the meanings of hope and fear as understood by the *Ṣūfīs* and *Ahlu-l-Kalām*, this discussion has been relegated to Appendix One.

[6] This is phrase commonly used by the author, may Allāh have mercy upon him, to show that he is returning to the point of discussion after having digressed.

ilāha illAllāh'[7] and the most superior supplication is *'al-ḥamdulillāh'* [8]

Recorded by ibn Mājah and ibn Abī ad-Dunyā.[9]

[1.3 The supplication of Yūnus]

The Prophet (ﷺ) said in the ḥadīth recorded by at-Tirmidhī and others,

> The invocation of my brother Dhū-n-Nūn, "None has the right to be worshipped save You; glory be to You, far removed are You from any imperfection; I have been amongst the wrong-doers," none who is experiencing difficulty employs it except that Allāh would relieve him of his difficulty.

He (ﷺ) called it an invocation because it includes both types of supplication.

(لَا إِلٰهَ إِلَّا أَنْتَ), *"none has the right to be worshipped save You"* comprises an acknowledgement of *Tawḥīd al-Ilāhiyyah*[10] which in turn includes one of the two types of supplication. This is because the *Ilāh* is the one who deserves supplication, both the supplication of worship and

[7] Meaning: none has the right to be worshipped save Allāh

[8] Meaning: all praise and thanks are for Allāh

[9] at-Tirmidhī [#3383], ibn Mājah [#3800] and ibn Abī ad-Dunyā, *ash-Shukr* [#102]. It was declared ṣaḥīḥ by ibn Ḥibbān, *as-Ṣaḥīḥ* [#846]; al-Ḥākim [#1834, 1852] with adh-Dhahabī agreeing and ḥasan by at-Tirmidhī, al-Baghawī, *Sharḥ as-Sunnah* [#1269] and al-Albānī, *as-Ṣaḥīḥah* [#1497]

[10] i.e. singling Allāh out alone for worship.

the supplication of request. He is Allāh, there is none worthy or worship save Him.

(إِنِّي كُنتُ مِنَ الظَّالِمِينَ), *"I have been amongst the wrongdoers"* comprises an acknowledgement of his sin which in turn includes the request for forgiveness. This is because the one seeking something, asking for it, either does so by stating phrases that denote this [clearly] or he does so by stating phrases that contain some information [that alludes to this], information about ones own state or the state of the one being asked or the state of both. Nūḥ, upon him be peace, said,

قَالَ رَبِّ إِنِّيٓ أَعُوذُ بِكَ أَنۡ أَسۡـَٔلَكَ مَا لَيۡسَ لِي بِهِۦ عِلۡمٞۖ وَإِلَّا تَغۡفِرۡ لِي وَتَرۡحَمۡنِيٓ أَكُن مِّنَ ٱلۡخَٰسِرِينَ ٤٧

«My Lord, I take refuge with You from asking You for anything about which I have no knowledge. If You do not forgive me and bestow mercy on me, I will be among the lost»

[*Hūd* (11): 47]

This is not a phrase which denotes an explicit request but rather contains information about Allāh that if He does not forgive him and show mercy to him, he would be of the losers. But this information alludes to the request for forgiveness. Likewise Ādam, upon him be peace, said,

قَالَا رَبَّنَا ظَلَمۡنَآ أَنفُسَنَا وَإِن لَّمۡ تَغۡفِرۡ لَنَا وَتَرۡحَمۡنَا لَنَكُونَنَّ مِنَ ٱلۡخَٰسِرِينَ ٢٣

«Our Lord! We have wronged ourselves. If You do not forgive us and bestow mercy on us, we will be among the lost»

[*al-A'rāf* (7): 23]

and Mūsā upon him be peace said,

رَبِّ إِنِّي لِمَآ أَنزَلْتَ إِلَيَّ مِنْ خَيْرٍ فَقِيرٌ ﴿٢٤﴾

«My Lord, I am truly in need of any good You have in store for me»

[*al-Qaṣaṣ* (28): 24]

This is a description of his condition, that he is needy of all that Allāh has given him of the good and alludes to asking Allāh to send good down to him.

At-Tirmidhī and others record that the Prophet (ﷺ) said,

> Whoever is diverted by the recitation of the Qur'ān from performing my *dhikr* and asking of Me, I would grant him the best of what I grant those asking.

At-Tirmidhī said that it was a ḥasan ḥadīth.[11] It was also reported on the authority of Mālik bin al-Ḥuwayrith[12] with the wording,

> Whoever is diverted by making *dhikr* of Me from asking of Me, I would grant him the best of what I grant those asking.

I think al-Bayhaqī recorded it with this wording from the Prophet

---

[11] at-Tirmidhī [#2926] and ad-Dārimī, *Faḍā'il al-Qur'ān* [#3356] on the authority of Abū Sa'īd al-Khudrī with a ḍa'īf jiddan isnād; refer to al-Albānī, *ad-Ḍa'īfah* [#1335].

Aḥādīth with similar meaning have been reported on the authority of 'Umar in al-Bayhaqī, *Shu'ab al-Īmān* [#573] and as-Suyūṭī, *al-Lālī* [2/288] said that al-Ḥāfiẓ ibn Ḥajr declared it ḥasan; Jābir in al-Bayhaqī [#574]; Hudhayfah in Abū Nu'āym [7/313]; and Mālik bin al-Ḥārithah in al-Bayhaqī [#575].

[12] Mālik bin al-Ḥārith as-Sulamī, refer to ibn Ḥajr, *Tahdhīb at-Tahdhīb* [10/12-13].

(ﷺ).[13]

Sufyān bin 'Uyaynah was asked about his (ﷺ) saying,

> The most superior supplication on the Day of 'Arafah is,
>
> «لَا إِلَهَ إِلَّا اللهُ وَحْدَهُ لَا شَرِيكَ لَهُ، لَهُ الْمُلْكُ وَلَهُ الْحَمْدُ، وَهُوَ عَلَى كُلِّ شَيْءٍ قَدِيرٌ»
>
> 'None has the right to be worshipped save Allāh, the One Who has no partner, to Him belongs the dominion, to Him belongs all praise and He is Omnipotent over all things.[14]

and [in explanation] he mentioned the previous ḥadīth and the lines of poetry recited by Abū-s-Salt in praise of ibn Jud'ān,

Should I mention my need or should your
Gifts suffice me, for sure giving gifts is part of your disposition
If a person was to praise you one day
The one who he is praising would suffice him

and proceeded to say, 'This is a created objected addressing another created object[15], what then of the Creator, Exalted is He?'[16]

---

[13] Refer to fn. 11

[14] at-Tirmidhī [#3585] and al-Maḥāmali, *ad-Du'ā* [#64] and it has witnesses being reported on the authority of Ṭalḥah in Mālik, *al-Muwaṭṭa* [#246]; 'Alī in at-Ṭabarānī, *ad-Du'ā,* [#874]; and ibn 'Umar in at-Ṭabarānī [#875].
It was declared ḥasan by at-Tirmidhī and al-Albānī [#1503]

[15] In another narration mentioned by al-Ḥāfiẓ ibn 'Abdu-l-Barr, *at-Tamhīd* [2/680], 'This is an object of creation saying of another that it is sufficient to praise him [to get what he desires] rather than directly ask him, what then of the Creator, Blessed and Exalted is He?'
=

In a similar vein, Mūsā, upon him be peace, supplicated, 'O Allāh! To You belongs all praise and to You does one complain, You are the One Who helps, through you does one seek succour and upon you does one place his reliance.' This is information [about Allāh] that alludes to a request.

In a similar vein, Ayyūb, upon him be peace, said,

وَأَيُّوبَ إِذْ
نَادَىٰ رَبَّهُۥٓ أَنِّي مَسَّنِيَ ٱلضُّرُّ وَأَنتَ أَرْحَمُ ٱلرَّٰحِمِينَ ﴿٨٣﴾

«...Great harm has afflicted me and You are the Most Merciful of the merciful»

[*al-Anbiyā'* (21): 83]

So he described himself and his Lord with a description that alludes to asking for His mercy so that his difficulty be removed.

This method is employed by way of displaying good manners in asking and in supplicating. Therefore if one says to another whom he respects and from whom he desires something, 'I am hungry, I am sick' he is displaying good manners in asking. This, even though if one were to say, 'Feed me, give me medicine', he is being resolute in his asking, the first method manifests ones state and informs another of this by way of humbleness and displaying need which in

=

[16] Al-Bayhaqī [#575] and al-Khaṭṭābi, *Sha'n ad-Du'ā* [#142].

Al-Ḥāfiẓ ibn 'Abdu-l-Barr [2/678] said, 'This ḥadīth shows us that the day of 'Arafah is better than other days, it shows us the excellence of this day and it proves that some days are better than others, but which these are can only be known through the Legal Law and not through reason or analogy. Days which are better as proven by the Legal Law are: Jumu'ah, 'Āshūrā', 'Arafah, Monday and Thursday. This ḥadīth also proves that supplication on the day of 'Arafah is predominately answered and it also proves that the best *dhikr* is *"Lā ilāha illAllāh"*.'

turn alludes to the request, whereas this method portrays a resolute desire and a straightforward request.

This latter method, the method of direct request, if it arises from one who is able to attain the object of desire from the one asked, it is said using the form of a command. The reason for this is either to express the need of the one asking or due to the benefit it contains. If it arises from one who is totally needy, being directed to one who is completely self-sufficient, then it is to be considered a simple request said by way of humility, displaying ones need and manifesting ones state.

Hence asking via describing ones state and need is better from the perspective of knowledge and description of ones state; asking directly is clearer with regards expressing ones intent and objective. This is why the generality of supplications are of the second type, the supplicant brings to mind what he desires and asks for it. So he asks immediately after his objective has come to mind without his pausing to mention or depict the condition of the one asking and the One being asked. If, however, this person were to mention his condition and the condition of the One being asked coupled with a direct request, this would be the better form of supplication.

When Abū Bakr asked the Prophet (ﷺ) to teach him a supplication which he could employ in the prayer, he replied,

«اللَّهُمَّ إِنِّي ظَلَمْتُ نَفْسِي ظُلْمًا كَثِيرًا، وَلَا يَغْفِرُ الذُّنُوبَ إِلَّا أَنْتَ،
فَاغْفِرْ لِي مَغْفِرَةً مِنْ عِنْدِكَ وَارْحَمْنِي إِنَّكَ أَنْتَ الْغَفُورُ الرَّحِيمُ»

> Say: O Allāh! I have oppressed my soul greatly and frequently and there is none to forgive sins save You, so forgive me with a forgiveness from Yourself and have

mercy on me, You are the All-Forgiving, Most Merciful.[17]

This supplication comprises the servant' mentioning his own state which in turn points to his need for forgiveness, it contains a description of the Lord stating that none is able to fulfill this goal save Him, it also contains an explicit request for forgiveness and it describes the Lord as being the All-Forgiving and Most Merciful which in turn are the qualities which must exist for the request to be fulfilled. Therefore this supplication and its likes are from the best of ways of asking.

Many supplications contain some of these aspects such as the saying of Mūsā (*alayhis-salām*),

وَمَا
مَن تَشَآءُ أَنتَ وَلِيُّنَا فَٱغْفِرْ لَنَا وَٱرْحَمْنَا وَأَنتَ خَيْرُ ٱلْغَٰفِرِينَ ﴿١٥٥﴾

«...You are our Protector so forgive us and bestow mercy on us»

[*al-A'rāf* (7): 155]

This supplication comprises a direct request along with a description of the Master that would lead to the need being fulfilled. He also said,

قَالَ رَبِّ إِنِّى ظَلَمْتُ نَفْسِى فَٱغْفِرْ لِى فَغَفَرَ لَهُۥٓ إِنَّهُۥ هُوَ
ٱلْغَفُورُ ٱلرَّحِيمُ ﴿١٦﴾

«My Lord! I have wronged myself. Forgive me...»

[*al-Qaṣaṣ* (28): 16]

This supplication contains a description of oneself as well as a direct request. He also said,

[17] Bukhārī [#834, 6326, 8387, 8388] and Muslim [#2707].

رَبِّ إِنِّي لِمَآ أَنزَلْتَ إِلَيَّ مِنْ خَيْرٍ فَقِيرٌ ﴿٢٤﴾

«My Lord, I am truly in need of any good You have in store for me»

[*al-Qaṣaṣ* (28): 24]

This supplication contains a description of oneself which in turn points to a request.

[1.4 The condition of Yūnus]

Now the question arises as to why it befitted the Companion of the Whale and others in similarly dire circumstances to supplicate by describing their states rather than asking directly? The response is that the situation calls for an acknowledgement that the evil that has afflicted one is because of his sin. Therefore the source of this evil is sin, the immediate objective is to repress the harm, to remove the difficulty, whereas the desire to ask for forgiveness comes secondary to this. However, he did not directly ask for the harm to be removed because he had the overwhelming feeling within himself that he had committed a sin, oppressed himself, and that he himself was the cause of this harm. Therefore it befitted his situation that he mention that which would remove the cause of harm, i.e. the acknowledgement of his sin. The soul, by its nature, seeks after its immediate need, in this case the removal of the immediate harm it faces before the removal of any harm it fears may occur in the future.

The immediate objective in this situation is the desire to see the harm removed followed by forgiveness, this was what was foremost in his mind, and the best way to acquire this was to efface the cause and hence he stated that which would accomplish his objective.

[1.5 Allāh does not wrong anyone]

This becomes clear when one understands the meaning of (سُبْحَانَكَ), *"glory be to You; far removed are You from any imperfection"* for this statement comprises exaltation of the Lord as well as absolving Him of all deficiency. The situation that Yūnus found himself in demanded that Allāh be absolved of oppression and that He be absolved of punishing without cause, therefore he said, 'You are Holy, absolved of oppressing me or punishing me without cause, rather I am the oppressor who has oppressed himself.' Allāh, Exalted is He, says,

وَمَا ظَلَمْنَٰهُمْ وَلَٰكِن كَانُوٓا۟ أَنفُسَهُمْ يَظْلِمُونَ ﴿١١٨﴾

«We did not wrong them; rather they wronged themselves»

[*an-Naḥl* (16): 118]

وَمَا ظَلَمْنَٰهُمْ وَلَٰكِن ظَلَمُوٓا۟ أَنفُسَهُمْ

«We did not wrong them; rather wronged themselves»

[*Hūd* (11): 101]

وَمَا ظَلَمْنَٰهُمْ وَلَٰكِن كَانُوا۟ هُمُ ٱلظَّٰلِمِينَ ﴿٧٦﴾

«We have not wronged them; it was they who were the wrongdoers»

[*az-Zukhruf* (43): 76]

رَبَّنَا ظَلَمْنَآ أَنفُسَنَا

«Our Lord! We have wronged ourselves»

[*al-A'rāf* (7): 23]

Similarly the Prophet (ﷺ) said in the ṣaḥīḥ ḥadīth reported by Muslim concerning the opening supplication in prayer,

اللَّهُمَّ أَنْتَ الْمَلِكُ لَا إِلَهَ إِلَّا أَنْتَ.
أَنْتَ رَبِّي وَأَنَا عَبْدُكَ، ظَلَمْتُ نَفْسِي وَاعْتَرَفْتُ بِذَنْبِي فَاغْفِرْ لِي
ذُنُوبِي جَمِيعًا إِنَّهُ لَا يَغْفِرُ الذُّنُوبَ إِلَّا أَنْتَ.

> O Allāh! You are the King, there is none worthy of worship besides You; You are my Lord and I am Your servant, I have wronged my soul and I acknowledge my sin, so forgive me all my sins for indeed none forgives sins save You.[18]

Bukhārī records the ḥadīth,

> The master of asking for forgiveness [is the supplication],

«اللَّهُمَّ أَنْتَ رَبِّي لَا إِلَهَ إِلَّا أَنْتَ، خَلَقْتَنِي وَأَنَا عَبْدُكَ،
وَأَنَا عَلَى عَهْدِكَ وَوَعْدِكَ مَا اسْتَطَعْتُ، أَعُوذُ بِكَ مِنْ شَرِّ
مَا صَنَعْتُ، أَبُوءُ لَكَ بِنِعْمَتِكَ عَلَيَّ، وَأَبُوءُ بِذَنْبِي فَاغْفِرْ لِي
فَإِنَّهُ لَا يَغْفِرُ الذُّنُوبَ إِلَّا أَنْتَ»

> 'O Allāh! You are my Lord, there is none worthy of worship save You. You created me and I am Your servant, I am trying to fulfill Your agreement and promise to the best of my ability. I take refuge with You from the evil I have wrought, I acknowledge Your favours to me and I confess my sin, so forgive me for none forgives sins save You.'

Whoever says this supplication with certainty when he

[18] Muslim [#771] and Abū Dāwūd [#760].

awakes in the morning and dies during that day, he will enter Paradise. Whoever says this supplication with certainty when he lies down to sleep in the evening and dies during that night, he will enter Paradise.' [19]

Hence it is upon the servant to acknowledge the justice of Allāh and His benevolence; He does not oppress man in the slightest and does not punish anyone except for a sin that he committed. He is always bestowing His grace upon man, therefore every punishment from him arises from pure justice, and every favour from him arises from His benevolence.

[1.6 The meaning of *Lā ilāha illAllāh* and *SubḥānAllāh*]

So the saying of Yūnus,(لَا إِلَٰهَ إِلَّا أَنتَ), *"there is none worthy of worship save You"* affirms that Allāh alone is singled out with regards to *ilāhiyyah. Ilāhiyyah* includes within it the affirmation of the perfection of Allāh's knowledge, power, mercy, and wisdom just as it comprises the affirmation of His benevolence. This is because the word *Ilāh* means the one who deserves to be worshipped, the *ma'lūh*. The fact that He deserves to be worshipped is because of His attributes that necessitate that He be loved with an absolute and complete love and that he be submitted to completely. The reality of worship is absolute and complete love combined with total submission and humility before Him.[20]

[19] Bukhārī [#6306] and an-Nasā'ī [8/279].

[20] The author, *Majmū' Fatāwā* [1/23] says, 'Allāh created the creation to worship Him, worship gathers together within its scope knowledge of Him, turning to Him in penitence, loving Him, and being sincere to Him. Through performing his *dhikr* do hearts find tranquillity and through seeing Him in the Hereafter will the eyes feel bliss. There is nothing that will be more beloved to the servants than =

His saying, (سُبْحَانَكَ), *"glory be to You; far removed are You from any imperfection"* comprises exaltation of Him combined with absolving Him of oppression and all other deficiencies. A mursal ḥadīth concerning this had been reported on the authority of Mūsā bin Ṭalḥa that the Prophet (ﷺ) said concerning a person stating, *'SubḥānAllāh'*,

It is absolving Allāh of all evil.[21]

Mere negation of something is not to be considered a praise until and unless it contains the affirmation [of its opposite], therefore the negation of evil and deficiency from Allāh necessitates the affirmation of His benevolence and perfection, and to Allāh belong the best and most beautiful Names.

=

seeing Him on that Day and there is nothing that is granted them in this life greater than faith.

Mans need of Him in worshipping Him is greater than his need of Him in His creating, nourishing and sustaining him, because worship is his object and source of fulfilment. There is no correction, no success, no felicity, no delight without worship and whoever turns away from the *dhikr* of his Lord,

فَإِنَّ لَهُۥ مَعِيشَةً ضَنكًا وَنَحْشُرُهُۥ يَوْمَ ٱلْقِيَـٰمَةِ أَعْمَىٰ

«...his life will be a dark and narrow one and on the Day of Rising We will gather him blind»

[*Ṭā Hā* (20): 124]

This is why Allāh will not forgive *shirk* but will forgive anything less than that to whoever He wills and this is why the statement, "None has the right to be worshipped save Allāh" is from the best of good deeds.'

[21] At-Ṭabarānī [#1753, 1754] and al-Bayhaqī, *Asmā' was-Ṣifāt* [1/76], its narrators are trustworthy and precise but it is mursal.

It is also reported from Ṭalḥah by al-Bayhaqī [1/76] with a ḍa'īf jiddan sanad and at-Ṭabarānī [#1752] via another route with a ḍa'īf sanad; see adh-Dhahabī, *at-Talkhīṣ* [#1848] and al-Haythamī, *Majma'* [10/94]

The same applies to the generality of what is mentioned in the Qur'ān of negating evil and deficiency from Allāh, each negation also affirms His benevolence and perfection. Allāh, Exalted is He, says,

ٱللَّهُ لَآ إِلَٰهَ إِلَّا هُوَ
ٱلْحَىُّ ٱلْقَيُّومُ ۚ لَا تَأْخُذُهُۥ سِنَةٌ وَلَا نَوْمٌ ۚ

> «Allāh, there is none worthy of worship save Him, the Living, the Self-Sustaining. He is not subject to drowsiness or sleep...»
>
> [*al-Baqarah* (2): 255]

So the negation of weariness and sleep from Him affirms the perfection of His life,

وَمَا مَسَّنَا مِن لُّغُوبٍ ﴿٣٨﴾

> «...and We were not affected by fatigue»
>
> [*Qāf* (50): 38]

This verse affirms the perfection of His power and ability. In a similar fashion saying *'SubḥānAllāh'* comprises absolving Him of all evil and oppression, this negation in turn comprises exaltation of Him. This is because the oppressor only ever oppresses because of his need to oppress or because of his ignorance, Allāh is in no need of anything and He knows everything. He stands in no need of anything whereas the whole creation stands in dire need of Him, this statement then implies complete exaltation.

[1.7 *Tahlīl* and *tasbīḥ* in the supplication]

Moreover this supplication combines *tahlīl*[22] with *tasbīḥ*[23]. The *tahlīl* is found in the statement, "None has the right to be worshipped save You" and the *tasbīḥ* is to be found in the statement, 'Glory be to You; far removed are You from any imperfection,' it is established in the Ṣaḥīḥ that the Prophet (ﷺ) said,

> The best and most noble statements after the Qur'ān are, and they are from the Qur'ān:
>
> «سُبْحَانَ اللهِ، وَالْحَمْدُ للهِ، وَلَا إِلَـهَ إِلَّا اللهُ، وَاللهُ أَكْبَرُ»
>
> *SubḥānAllāh, al-Ḥamdulillāh, Lā ilāha illAllāh* and *Allāhu Akbar*.[24]

Taḥmīd[25] goes hand-in-hand with *tasbīḥ* and follows on from it, *takbīr*[26] goes hand-in-hand with *tahlīl* and follows on from it. It is established in the Ṣaḥīḥ that the Prophet (ﷺ) was asked, 'Which speech is best and most noble' to which he replied,

> That which Allāh chose for his Angels:

---

[22] *Tahlīl*: the saying of (لا إله إلا الله) *'Lā ilāha illAllāh'* (none has the right to be worshipped save Allāh)

[23] *Tasbīḥ*: the saying of (سبحان الله) *'SubḥānAllāh'* (glory be to Allāh, far removed is He from any imperfection)

[24] Bukhārī [chpt. 19] and ibn Mājah [# 3811].

[25] *Taḥmīd*: the saying of (الحمد لله) *'Alḥamdulillāh'* (all praise is due for Allāh)

[26] *Takbīr*: the saying of (الله أكبر) *'Allāhu Akbar'* (Allāh is the greatest)

«سُبْحَانَ اللهِ وَبِحَمْدِهِ»

SubḥānAllāhi wa biḤamdihī.[27]

The Two Ṣaḥīḥs record that the Prophet (ﷺ) said,

> There are two statements that are light upon the tongue, heavy in the Scales, and beloved to the All-Merciful:
>
> «سُبْحَانَ اللهِ وَبِحَمْدِهِ سُبْحَانَ اللهِ الْعَظِيمِ»
>
> *SubḥānAllāhi wa biḤamdihī* and *SubḥānAllāhi-l-ʿAẓīm.*[28]

Allāh, Exalted is He says,

فَسَبِّحْ بِحَمْدِ رَبِّكَ

«...then glorify your Lord's praise...»

[*an-Naṣr* (110): 3]

And the Angels said,

وَنَحْنُ نُسَبِّحُ بِحَمْدِكَ

«...when we glorify You with praise...»

[*al-Baqarah* (2): 30]

So these two statements, one has been mentioned conjoined with *taḥmīd* and the other has been mentioned conjoined with *taʿẓīm*[29], we have mentioned that *tasbīḥ* comprises the negation of all evil and defects from Allāh and in turn includes the affirmation of all beau-

---

[27] Muslim [#2731] and at-Tirmidhī [#3593].

[28] Bukhārī [#6406, 6682] and Muslim [#2964].

[29] *Taʿẓīm*: the exaltation and magnification of Allāh

tiful qualities and perfection. *Taḥmīd* has been mentioned in the same context as *ta'ẓīm*[30] in just the same way that *jalāl* (majesty) is mentioned alongside *ikrām* (honour and reverence)[31], not every thing that is exalted is necessarily beloved and praised and neither is everything that is beloved necessarily praised and exalted. It has already been mentioned that worship is founded upon complete love, exemplified by praise, in the phrase *SubḥānAllāhi wa biḤamdihī,* and complete humility, exemplified by exaltation in the phrase *SubḥānAllāhi-l-'Aẓīm.*; hence in worship one experiences love of Allāh and praise of His beautiful qualities, just as one experiences humbleness before Him arising from His grandeur and magnificence. Moreover it comprises magnification and reverence, for Allāh is the One who is deservedly described with possessing *al-jalāl* and *al-ikrām* and is deservedly magnified and revered.

Some people think that *al-Jalāl* is from His negatory (*ṣalbī*) Attributes[32] whereas *al-Ikrām* is from the affirmatory (*thubūtī*) Attributes[33], this being mentioned by ar-Rāzī and others. The correct position is that they are both affirmatory, the affirmation of perfection necessarily implies the negation of all defects, however these two Attributes mention two types of affirmation, His worthiness of being loved and His worthiness of being exalted. Allāh, Exalted is

---

[30] i.e. in the ḥadīth, both *taḥmid* and *ta'ẓīm* have been mentioned after the *tasbīḥ*.

[31] i.e in His Name, *Dhū-l-Jalāl wa-l-Ikrām* (the One possessing majesty and honour)

[32] i.e. all that Allāh has negated from Himself in His Book or upon the tongue of His Messenger (ﷺ); these are obligatory to negate along with affirming their opposite in its state of perfection. So for example one must negate oppression and wrongdoing along with affirming perfect justice for Him.

[33] i.e. those Attributes that Allāh has affirmed for Himself in His Book or upon the tongue of His Messenger (ﷺ); these it is obligatory to affirm. Refer to the author's, *Tadmūriyyah* [pp. 57+]

He, says

إِنَّ ٱللَّهَ هُوَ ٱلْغَنِيُّ ٱلْحَمِيدُ ﴿٢٦﴾

«Allāh is Rich Beyond Need, the Praiseworthy»
[*Luqmān* (31): 26]

Sulaymān, upon whom be peace, said,

فَإِنَّ رَبِّي غَنِيٌّ كَرِيمٌ ﴿٤٠﴾

«...my Lord is Rich Beyond Need, Generous»
[*an-Naml* (27): 40]

Similary Allāh says,

لَهُ ٱلْمُلْكُ وَلَهُ ٱلْحَمْدُ

«Sovereignty and praise belongs to Him»
[*at-Taghābun* (64): 1]

Many people who possess sovereignty and richness are not praised, rather censured; this is because praise includes mentioning the good qualities of someone which are beloved, therefore it is to mention the good qualities of someone out of love of him. Many of those who are praised and loved to some extent are found to have some sort of inability and weakness which negates exaltation, self-dependency, richness and true dominion. The first type of person is feared and not loved, the second type is loved and praised yet not feared, perfection lies in the combination of both as is mentioned in a narration, 'The believer is nourished with sweetness and awe.' In the description of the Prophet (ﷺ) it is mentioned,

Whoever unexpectedly saw him would stand in awe of

him and whoever got to know him, loved him.[34]

In many contexts *tasbīḥ* has been mentioned alongside *taḥmīd* and *tahlīl* alongside *takbīr* just as one finds in the phrases of the *adhān*.[35] Moreover each term in these two categories includes the meaning of the other when mentioned alone; *tasbīḥ* and *taḥmīd* both include the meaning of *ta'ẓīm* and affirm all that is deserving of being praised, this in turn necessitates godliness for godliness includes the object being beloved and that none deserves complete love but it. Praise is to inform about the praised through mentioning those qualities that are beloved, and perfect praise is given to godly Attributes. This is why the phrase, 'all praise is due to Allāh' has been made the commencement of an address, indeed any matter of importance that is not begun with it is deprived of all good.

So the phrase, (سُبْحَانَكَ), *"glory be to You; far removed are You from any imperfection"*, affirms the *ta'ẓīm* of Allāh as has preceded, this is why He said,

فَسَبِّحْ بِٱسْمِ رَبِّكَ ٱلْعَظِيمِ ﴿٧٤﴾

«So glorify the name of your Lord, the Magnificent!»
[*al-Wāqi'ah* (56): 74]

The Prophet (ﷺ) said,

Say this in your *rukū'*

[34] at-Tirmidhī [#3638] and in *ash-Shamā'il* [#460] with a ḍa'īf sanad but it has other routes that raise it to the level of ḥasan.

[35] *Adhān*: the call to prayer

Recorded by the authors of the Sunan.[36] He (ﷺ) also said,

> As for the *rukū'*, magnify the Lord therein, as for the *sujūd*, exert yourself in supplicating therein.

Recorded by Muslim.[37]

So he appointed *ta'ẓīm* for the *rukū'* and *tasbīḥ* comprises this meaning.

Hence his (ﷺ) statement, *"SubḥānAllāhi wa biḤamdihī"* affirms His being absolved of all defects, His exaltation and magnification, His godliness, and His praise. As for his saying, *"Lā ilāha illAllāhu wAllāhu Akbar"*, the phrase *"Lā ilāha illAllāh"* affirms His praise, for all of it is included in His godliness, and the phrase *"Allāhu Akbar"* serves to exalt and magnify Him because grandeur (*kibriyā'*) comprises *ta'ẓīm*; however grandeur is the more complete way of exalting and magnifying Him and this is why the legislated words in the prayer and *adhān* employ the phrase, *"Allāhu Akbar"* and not *"Allāhu A'ẓam"*.

It is established in the Ṣaḥīḥ that the Prophet (ﷺ) said,

> Grandeur is my upper garment and Majesty is my lower garment, whoever contends with me in any of them, I will punish him.[38]

It is known that the upper garment is better than the lower, hence

---

[36] Abū Dāwūd [#869] and ibn Mājah [#887] on the authority of 'Uqbah bin 'Āmir with a ḍa'īf sanad as pointed out by adh-Dhahabī [#818] and it was ruled to be ḍa'īf by al-Albānī, *al-Irwā'* [#334].

[37] Muslim [#479] and Abū Dāwūd [#876].

[38] Muslim [#2620] and Abū Dāwūd [#4090].

grandeur is more encompassing than *ta'ẓīm* and this is why it was used.

So His saying,(سُبْحَانَكَ),*"glory be to You; far removed are You from any imperfection"*, explicitly negates any evil or defect from Allāh and at the same time contains *ta'ẓīm* of Him.

So both these phrases carry the meaning of the other when mentioned alone and take on their specific meanings when mentioned together. The same applies to every Name of Allāh for it necessarily includes the meaning of other Names because it points to the *dhāt*[39] of Allāh and the *dhāt* necessitates the meaning of other Names, this by *luzūm*.[40] At the same time each Name points to the *dhāt* and to its own specific meaning by *muṭābaqah*,[41] and it points to one of these two by *taḍammun*.[42]

---

[39] *Dhāt*: Person or Essence

[40] *Luzūm*: necessary implication. For example the Name Creator also proves that Allāh has the Attributes of knowledge and power by necessary implication.

[41] *Muṭābaqah*: correlation. For example the Name Creator points to the *dhāt* of Allāh and proves that He has the correlating Attribute of creation.

[42] *Taḍammun*: inclusion. For example the Name Creator proves that Allāh has the Attribute of creation which is included within it.

[1.8 Summary of the meaning of the supplication]

The saying of the supplicant, (لَا إِلَٰهَ إِلَّا أَنتَ سُبْحَانَكَ), *"there is none worthy of worship save You; glory be to You; far removed are You from any imperfection"*, includes within it the meaning of the four phrases that are the best and most superior words after the Qur'ān. These four phrases in turn encompass the meanings of the beautiful Names of Allāh and His lofty Attributes, hence they contain perfect praise.

His saying, (إِنِّي كُنتُ مِنَ الظَّالِمِينَ), *"I have been amongst the wrong doers"* comprises an acknowledgement of the reality of his situation. It is not possible for any of the servants to ever be free of wrongdoing or to declare himself free of it, especially when intimately conversing with his Lord. It is established in the Ṣiḥāḥ that the Prophet (ﷺ) said,

> It is not desirable that a servant say, 'I am better than Yūnus bin Matta'

He (ﷺ) also said,

> Whoever says, 'I am better than Yūnus bin Matta' has lied.[43]

Whoever thinks he is better than Yūnus, thinking that he has no need to acknowledge his sins, is a liar. This is why the leaders of the creation would never think themselves better than Yūnus in this respect, instead they would acknowledge just as was done by their father Ādam and the seal of the Prophets, Muḥammad (ﷺ).

---

[43] Bukhārī [#3415, 3416, 4604, 4631, 4805] and Muslim [#2376].

CHAPTER TWO

'Why does this supplication remove harm?'

[2.1 Reliance, hope and fear is to be placed in Allāh alone]

THE ANSWER IS THAT NONE save Allāh can remove harm,

وَإِن يَمْسَسْكَ ٱللَّهُ بِضُرٍّ فَلَا كَاشِفَ لَهُۥٓ إِلَّا هُوَ ۖ وَإِن يَمْسَسْكَ بِخَيْرٍ فَهُوَ عَلَىٰ كُلِّ شَىْءٍ قَدِيرٌ ﴿١٧﴾

«If Allāh touches you with harm, none can remove it but Him. If He touches you with good, He has power over all things»

[*al-An'ām* (6): 17]

Sins are a cause for the onset of harm and asking for forgiveness removes its causes,

وَمَا كَانَ ٱللَّهُ لِيُعَذِّبَهُمْ وَأَنتَ فِيهِمْ ۚ وَمَا كَانَ ٱللَّهُ مُعَذِّبَهُمْ وَهُمْ يَسْتَغْفِرُونَ ﴿٣٣﴾

«Allāh would never punish them while you were among them. Allāh would not punish them as long as they sought forgiveness»

[*al-Anfāl* (8): 33]

So He, Exalted is He, informed us that He would not punish the penitent. It is mentioned in a *ḥadīth*,

> Whoever frequently asks for forgiveness, Allāh would appoint for him relief from every worry, a way out from every difficulty and provision coming from unimagined sources.[1]

Allāh, Exalted is He, says,

وَمَا أَصَٰبَكُم مِّن مُّصِيبَةٍ فَبِمَا كَسَبَتْ أَيْدِيكُمْ وَيَعْفُوا۟ عَن كَثِيرٍ ﴿٣٠﴾

«Any disaster that strikes you is through what your own hands have earned and He pardons much»

[*ash-Shūrā* (42): 30]

His saying, (إِنِّي كُنتُ مِنَ الظَّالِمِينَ) *'I have been amongst the wrong-doers'* is an acknowledgment of his sin and also a request for forgiveness because this acknowledgment implicitly includes this request within it.

[1] Abū Dāwūd [#1518], ibn Mājah [#3819] and Aḥmad [#2234] on the authority of ibn ʿAbbās.

The isnād is ḍaʿīf as ruled by adh-Dhahabī [#7677], ibn Ḥibbān as per al-ʿIrāqi, *al-Mughnī* [#1027], al-Manāwī, *Fayḍ al-Qadīr* [#8508], and al-Albānī, *ad-Ḍaʿīfah* [#705].

His saying, (لَا إِلَٰهَ إِلَّا أَنْتَ) *'none has the right to be worshipped save You'* affirms *Tawḥīd al-Ilāhiyyah*. Good can only be procured by the will of Allāh, everything He wills, is, and everything He does not will, is not. The obstacle to this good on the part of the servant is his sins, anything else that is outside the ability of the servant occurs by the decree of Allāh. This even though the actions of the servant occur by the decree of Allāh, Exalted is He, Allāh has appointed the observance of the legislated and the leaving of the prohibited to be the means to felicity and success.

Therefore the testification to *tawḥīd* opens the door to good and asking for forgiveness closes the door to evil.

This is why it is desirable to only attach ones hope to Allāh[2] and not to fear oppression and wrong-doing from Him for Allāh does not oppress the servant in the slightest, instead it is they who oppress themselves. He should, however, fear that Allāh recompense him for his sins and this is why 'Alī (*raḍiyAllāhu 'anhu*) said, 'The servant should not put his hope in any save his Lord and not fear anything save his sins.' The Prophet (ﷺ) entered upon a sick person and asked,

'In what state does this sickness find you?' he replied, 'I

[2] al-Ḥalīmī, *al-Minhāj fī Shu'ab al-Īmān*, said, 'Hope takes on a number of forms: 1) hoping to attain what is desired 2) hoping to keep it after it has been attained 3) hoping to keep at bay all that is disliked and that it not occur 4) hoping to see the end of anything that is disliked that has already occurred. When the feeling of hope becomes deeply ingrained in a person, it leads to a state of submissiveness and humility in the same way that this state is achieved when fear takes firm root in the heart. This is because hope and fear go hand in hand, the one who is in a state of fear hopes for the opposite of what he fears - He supplicates to Allāh and asks of Him; likewise the one in state of hope fears losing what he desires and hence takes refuge with Allāh from this and asks of Him. Hence there is no one who is in a state of fear except that he too is in a state of hope and vice-versa.'

> hope in Allāh and fear my sins.' He (ﷺ) said, 'These two never come together in the heart of a servant on such occasions except that Allāh grants him what he hopes and saves him from what he fears.' [3]

Hence hope should be placed in Allāh and not any object of creation, not the ability or strength of a person or his actions. To put hope in other than Allāh is a form of *shirk*, this applies even though Allāh has set up means and causes (*asbāb*) that lead to the procurement of good, but these means cannot exist independently, rather their must exist something that supports and aids them to achieve the goal, just as any obstacle hindering this achievement must be absent; hence it cannot be achieved and it cannot endure except by the will of Allāh, Exalted is He.[4]

---

[3] At-Tirmidhī [#983], ibn Mājah [#4261] and an-Nasā'ī, *'Amal al-Yawm wal-Layla* [#1062] on the authority of Anas.

Similar aḥādīth are recorded on the authority of 'Umar by al-Bayhaqī [#1003] and Sa'īd bin al-Musayyab by at-Ṭabarānī.

At-Tirmidhī said that it was gharīb (and in one text ḥasan gharīb), al-Mundhirī said it was ḥasan as per *Tuḥfatu-l-Aḥwadhī* [4/58] as did al-Albānī, *Ṣaḥīḥ at-Tirmidhī* [#785].

[4] Ibn al-Qayyim, while discussing the aḥādīth concerning taking medicine, says, 'These aḥādīth prove that causes and their effects exist and that to take to them does not negate *tawakkul*, just as it is not negated when someone takes food and drink to remove hunger and thirst. Indeed the reality of *tawḥīd* is not attained and completed except by taking to those means that Allāh has appointed in order to attain their effects, to deny their existence is to impair ones *tawakkul* and to impute the order and wisdom of Allāh with deficiency. To abandon these means is a deficiency that negates *tawakkul* whose reality is that the heart place its reliance upon Allāh, Exalted is He, in attaining worldly and religious benefit and repressing worldly and religious harm. In order to complete this reliance one must take to the causes otherwise one is denying wisdom and the Legal Law, so the servant must not think that what is in reality deficiency is *tawakkul* and what is in reality *tawakkul* is deficiency.' - 'Abdur-Raḥmān Āli ash-Shaykh, *Fatḥ al-Majīd* [p. 60]

This is why it is said that to place ones reliance and hope in the means is to commit *shirk*, to deny the existence of the means is a sign of stupidity, and to turn away from them altogether is to impute the Divine Law with deficiency.[5] This is why Allāh, Exalted is He, says,

فَإِذَا فَرَغْتَ فَٱنصَبْ ﴿٧﴾ وَإِلَىٰ رَبِّكَ فَٱرْغَب ﴿٨﴾

«So when you have finished, work on, and to your Lord direct your longing and attention!»

[*ash-Sharḥ* (94): 7-8]

Thereby ordering us to place our fervent desire in Him alone. He also says,

وَعَلَى ٱللَّهِ فَتَوَكَّلُوٓا۟ إِن كُنتُم مُّؤْمِنِينَ ﴿٢٣﴾

«Put your trust in Allāh if you are believers»

[*al-Mā'idah* (5): 23]

The heart does not place its reliance except in one from whom it hopes for something. Therefore whoever places hope in his strength, ability, actions, friend, relative, teacher etc., not considering Allāh, has placed a form of reliance upon that cause. Whoever places his hope in an object of creation will ultimately be disappointed for he is committing *shirk*,

[5] For everything lawful that one may wish to acquire, Allāh has appointed a means to attaining it as has preceded, for example marriage as a means to having children. If one marries and places his reliance upon marital relations and not upon the One who grants children, he has committed *shirk*; to deny that such means exist is to deny what is ingrained in our nature; and to deny that the act has any benefit at all is to accuse the Legal Law which has put the institution of marriage in place. The same applies to supplication, which is the reason why the author has brought up this principle.

حُنَفَآءَ لِلَّهِ غَيۡرَ مُشۡرِكِينَ بِهِۦۚ وَمَن يُشۡرِكۡ بِٱللَّهِ فَكَأَنَّمَا خَرَّ مِنَ
ٱلسَّمَآءِ فَتَخۡطَفُهُ ٱلطَّيۡرُ أَوۡ تَهۡوِي بِهِ ٱلرِّيحُ فِي مَكَانٖ سَحِيقٖ

«...As for anyone who associates others with Allāh, it is as though he had fallen from the sky and the birds had seized him and carried him away, or the wind had dropped him in a distant place»

[*al-Ḥajj* (22): 31]

Similarly the polytheist fears objects of creation and places his hope in them and therefore lives in a state of dread as Allāh, Exalted is He, says,

سَنُلۡقِي
فِي قُلُوبِ ٱلَّذِينَ كَفَرُواْ ٱلرُّعۡبَ بِمَآ أَشۡرَكُواْ بِٱللَّهِ
مَا لَمۡ يُنَزِّلۡ بِهِۦ سُلۡطَٰنٗا

«We will cast terror into the hearts of the disbelievers because they have associated others with Allāh for which He has not sent down any authority»

[*Āli ʿImrān* (3): 151]

To be free of *shirk* is to be in safety as Allāh, Exalted is He, says,

ٱلَّذِينَ ءَامَنُواْ وَلَمۡ يَلۡبِسُوٓاْ إِيمَٰنَهُم بِظُلۡمٍ أُوْلَٰٓئِكَ لَهُمُ ٱلۡأَمۡنُ
وَهُم مُّهۡتَدُونَ ٨٢

«Those who have faith and do not mix up their faith with any wrong-doing, they are the ones who are safe; it is they who are guided»

[*al-Anʿām* (6): 82]

The Prophet (ﷺ) explained wrong-doing in this verse to mean *shirk*, it is recorded in the Ṣaḥīḥ on the authority of ibn Masʿūd,

> When this verse was revealed it bore down heavily on the Companions of the Prophet (ﷺ) and they said, 'Who amongst us has not committed wrong?' The Prophet (ﷺ) said, "This refers to *shirk*, have you not heard the saying of the righteous servant,
>
> إِنَّ ٱلشِّرْكَ لَظُلْمٌ عَظِيمٌ ﴿١٣﴾
>
> «Associating others with Allāh is a terrible wrong»
> [*Luqmān* (31): 13]" [6]

Allāh, Exalted is He, says,

وَمِنَ
ٱلنَّاسِ مَن يَتَّخِذُ مِن دُونِ ٱللَّهِ أَندَادًا يُحِبُّونَهُمْ كَحُبِّ ٱللَّهِ ۖ
وَٱلَّذِينَ ءَامَنُوٓا۟ أَشَدُّ حُبًّا لِّلَّهِ ۗ وَلَوْ يَرَى ٱلَّذِينَ ظَلَمُوٓا۟ إِذْ يَرَوْنَ
ٱلْعَذَابَ أَنَّ ٱلْقُوَّةَ لِلَّهِ جَمِيعًا وَأَنَّ ٱللَّهَ شَدِيدُ ٱلْعَذَابِ ﴿١٦٥﴾
إِذْ تَبَرَّأَ ٱلَّذِينَ ٱتُّبِعُوا۟ مِنَ ٱلَّذِينَ ٱتَّبَعُوا۟ وَرَأَوُا۟ ٱلْعَذَابَ
وَتَقَطَّعَتْ بِهِمُ ٱلْأَسْبَابُ ﴿١٦٦﴾ وَقَالَ ٱلَّذِينَ ٱتَّبَعُوا۟ لَوْ أَنَّ
لَنَا كَرَّةً فَنَتَبَرَّأَ مِنْهُمْ كَمَا تَبَرَّءُوا۟ مِنَّا ۗ كَذَٰلِكَ يُرِيهِمُ ٱللَّهُ
أَعْمَٰلَهُمْ حَسَرَٰتٍ عَلَيْهِمْ ۖ وَمَا هُم بِخَٰرِجِينَ مِنَ ٱلنَّارِ ﴿١٦٧﴾

> «Some people set up equals with Allāh, loving them as they should love Allāh. But those who have faith have greater love for Allāh. If only you could see those who do wrong at the time when they see the punishment, and that truly all strength belongs to Allāh, and that Allāh is

[6] Bukhārī [#32, 3360, 3428, 3429, 4629, 4776, 6918] and Muslim [#124]

severe in punishment. When those who were followed disown those who followed them, and they see the punishment, and the connection between them is severed; those who followed will say, 'If only we could have another chance, we would disown them as they have disowned us.' In this way Allāh will show them their actions as a cause of anguish and remorse for them. They will never leave the Fire»

[*al-Baqarah* (2): 165-167]

قُلِ ٱدْعُوا۟ ٱلَّذِينَ زَعَمْتُم مِّن دُونِهِۦ فَلَا
يَمْلِكُونَ كَشْفَ ٱلضُّرِّ عَنكُمْ وَلَا تَحْوِيلًا ﴿٥٦﴾ أُو۟لَٰٓئِكَ ٱلَّذِينَ
يَدْعُونَ يَبْتَغُونَ إِلَىٰ رَبِّهِمُ ٱلْوَسِيلَةَ أَيُّهُمْ أَقْرَبُ وَيَرْجُونَ
رَحْمَتَهُۥ وَيَخَافُونَ عَذَابَهُۥٓ ۚ إِنَّ عَذَابَ رَبِّكَ كَانَ مَحْذُورًا ﴿٥٧﴾

«Say: 'Call on those you make claims for apart from Him. They possess no power to remove any harm from you or to change anything.' Those they call on are themselves seeking the means by which they might approach their Lord - [striving as to] which of them would be closest to Him - and are hoping for His mercy and fearing His punishment. The punishment of your Lord is truly something to be feared»

[*al-Isrā'* (17): 56-57]

This is why Allāh has mentioned the causes and ordered us not to depend upon them and instead to place our hope in Him alone.[7]

---

[7] The author, *Majmū' Fatāwā* [10/185-187], says, 'Whoever depends upon an object of creation to help him, or provide for him, or guide him, his heart will submit to it and servitude will be engendered in it in proportion to the level of submission. This applies even if the person is a leader asking of his subjects who he controls, for the intelligent one looks to the realities not to what is superficially

=

He, Exalted is He, says when the Angels descended to reinforce the armies of the believers,

﴿وَمَا جَعَلَهُ ٱللَّهُ إِلَّا بُشْرَىٰ لَكُمْ وَلِتَطْمَئِنَّ قُلُوبُكُم بِهِۦ ۗ وَمَا ٱلنَّصْرُ إِلَّا مِنْ عِندِ ٱللَّهِ ٱلْعَزِيزِ ٱلْحَكِيمِ ﴿١٢٦﴾﴾

«Allāh only did this for it to be good news for you and so that your hearts might be at rest by it; help comes from no one but Allāh, the Almighty, the All-Wise»

[*Āli 'Imrān* (3): 126]

﴿إِن يَنصُرْكُمُ ٱللَّهُ فَلَا غَالِبَ لَكُمْ ۖ وَإِن يَخْذُلْكُمْ فَمَن ذَا ٱلَّذِى يَنصُرُكُم مِّنۢ بَعْدِهِۦ ۗ وَعَلَى ٱللَّهِ فَلْيَتَوَكَّلِ ٱلْمُؤْمِنُونَ ﴿١٦٠﴾﴾

«If Allāh helps you, no one can vanquish you. If He forsakes you, who can help you after that? So let the believers put their trust in Allāh»

[*Āli 'Imrān* (3): 160]

=

apparent. When a man's heart gives in to a woman, even if she be permissible for him, it becomes enslaved to her and whatever she commands, it will readily do, even though outwardly he is her master. The enslavement of the heart is more serious than the enslavement of the body and the servitude of the heart is greater than the servitude of the body... True freedom is the freedom of the heart and true servitude is the servitude of the heart just as true richness is the richness of the soul... when the heart tastes the relish of worshipping Allāh, being sincere to Him, it will know that there is nothing sweeter or more delightful than this. Man will only leave one object of love for another if he finds that other more beloved to him or fears something distasteful happening. Therefore undesirable love can be removed by directing attention to desirable love or by fearing harm.'

[2.2 Avarice and Begging]

We have previously mentioned that supplication is of two types, worship and request; both these types can only be directed to Allāh. Whoever sets up another god alongside Allāh is blameworthy; the one who is hoping in something is asking for it and seeking after it, this is why it is not allowed to place ones hope except in Allāh nor to ask other than Him, and this is why the Prophet (ﷺ) said,

> What you have been given of this wealth without being avaricious or asking for it, take it; if not then do not let your soul crave it.[8]

The Two Ṣaḥīḥs record the ḥadīth of Abū Saʿīd al-Khudrī who said,

> We were afflicted by severe poverty and so I came to the Messenger of Allāh (ﷺ) to ask of him only to find him addressing the people, saying, 'People! Whatever good I have, I will never withhold it from you. He who suffices with what he has, Allāh would grant him sufficiency (*istighnā'*); he who refrains from begging, Allāh would save him from want (*istiʿfāf*); and he who is patient and steadfast, Allāh would grant him the accord to be patient for none has been given a gift that is better and greater than patience.'[9]

Istighnā' means that the heart not place its hope in anything or crave it.

[8] Bukhārī [#1473, 7163, 7164] and Muslim [#1045]

[9] Bukhārī [#1469, 6470] and Muslim [#1053]

Isti'fāf means that no one ask of another and this is why when Aḥmad bin Ḥanbal was asked about absolute reliance he replied, 'Severing off all craving for creation,'[10] meaning that there not be in your heart the idea that any object of creation gave you what came to you. It was then asked of him, 'What is the proof for this?' to which he replied, 'The statement of al-Khalīl when Jibrīl asked him if he needed anything from him, 'From you, no!'''[11]

This shows us that the servant in his pursuit of that which would benefit him and in his avoidance of all that which would harm him can only turn his heart towards Allāh, and this is why the one in straitened circumstances says, 'There is none worthy of worship save You.' It is reported in the Two Ṣaḥīḥs on the authority of ibn 'Abbās that the Prophet (ﷺ) used to say in difficult occasions,

«لَا إِلَـٰهَ إِلَّا اللهُ الْعَظِيمُ الْحَلِيمُ، لَا إِلَـٰهَ إِلَّا اللهُ رَبُّ الْعَرْشِ الْعَظِيمِ،
لَا إِلَـٰهَ إِلَّا اللهُ رَبُّ السَّمٰوَاتِ وَرَبُّ الأَرْضِ وَرَبُّ الْعَرْشِ الْكَرِيمِ»

> There is none worthy of worship save Allāh, the Exalted, the Forebearing. There is none worthy of worship except Allāh, the Lord of the Great Throne. There is none

[10] al-Bayhaqī [2/99] records that 'Alī bin Aḥmad was asked about *tawakkul* to which he replied, 'That you relinquish yourself from depending on your strength and ability, or the strength and ability of those like you.' Muḥammad bin Sulaymān said, '*Tawakkul* is that your heart never think that there is anyone who can bring you benefit or harm save Him; that you accept calmly everything that happens to you without aversion.'

[11] i.e. at the point of his being hurled into the fire. Al-Bayhaqī [#1293] records from Abū Ya'qūb who said, 'The true reality of *tawakkul* was realized by Ibrāhīm the Khalīl of the All-Merciful, in that state in which he said to Jibrīl, "From you, no" because his soul was totally absorbed of Allāh and hence he no longer saw anything else besides Him, he was in a state of utter awe from Allāh, for the sake of Allāh. This is from the signs of *Tawḥīd* and Allāh manifesting His power for His Prophet, upon whom be peace.'

> worthy of worship except Allāh, the Lord of the heavens and the earth, the Lord of the Noble Throne.[12]

These statements are a living testimony to *Tawḥīd*, they actualise the servant worshipping his Lord and they show that he only puts his hope in Him, therefore these statements are said by way delivering information that itself comprises a request.

[2.3 Sincerity in testifying to *Tawḥīd*]

People may say the testification that none has the right to be worshipped save Allāh upon their tongues, but when it is said sincerely, coming from the heart - it takes on board a completely different reality. It is in accordance to ones actualisation of *Tawḥīd* that one completes his servitude of Allāh,

أَرَءَيْتَ
مَنِ ٱتَّخَذَ إِلَٰهَهُۥ هَوَىٰهُ أَفَأَنتَ تَكُونُ عَلَيْهِ وَكِيلًا ﴿٤٣﴾
أَمْ تَحْسَبُ أَنَّ أَكْثَرَهُمْ يَسْمَعُونَ أَوْ يَعْقِلُونَ ۚ إِنْ هُمْ إِلَّا
كَٱلْأَنْعَٰمِ ۖ بَلْ هُمْ أَضَلُّ سَبِيلًا ﴿٤٤﴾

> «Have you seen him who has taken his whims and desires to be his god? Will you then be his guardian? Do you suppose that most of them hear or understand? They are like cattle, indeed they are even more astray!»
>
> [*al-Furqān* (25): 43-44]

This describes the state of the polytheists, those who worshipped whatever seemed fair to them, thereby taking gods besides Allāh, loving them as they should love Allāh. This is why al-Khalīl said,

---

[12] Bukhārī [#6345, 6346, 7426, 7431] and Muslim [#2730]

لَآ أُحِبُّ ٱلْءَافِلِينَ ﴿٧٦﴾

«I do not love what sets»

[*al-An'ām* (6): 76]

The nation of Ibrāhīm never rejected the existence of a Creator, but they used to worship whatever seemed fair to them, whatever they thought would bring them benefit such as the sun, the moon, and the stars. Ibrāhīm explained that those things that set, disappear from their worshippers and can be covered by clouds; they are unable to see their worshippers, hear their words or know anything about their conditions; they are unable to bring benefit or harm to them - so why should they be worshipped?

The more the servant increases in sincerity in his saying of, 'None has the right to be worshipped save Allāh' the weaker becomes servitude to his base desires and the more sins is he able to avoid. Allāh, Exalted is He, says,

كَذَٰلِكَ لِنَصْرِفَ عَنْهُ ٱلسُّوٓءَ
وَٱلْفَحْشَآءَ ۚ إِنَّهُۥ مِنْ عِبَادِنَا ٱلْمُخْلَصِينَ ﴿٢٤﴾

«That happened so We might avert from him all evil and lust. He was Our chosen servant»

[*Yūsuf* (12): 24]

So the reason given for his being turned away from evil and indecent acts was that he was from the chosen servants of Allāh and it is about such servants that Allāh, Exalted is He says,

إِنَّ عِبَادِى لَيْسَ لَكَ عَلَيْهِمْ سُلْطَٰنٌ ۚ

«But as for My servants, you will have no authority over them»

[*al-Isrā'* (17): 65]

Satan said,

قَالَ فَبِعِزَّتِكَ لَأُغْوِيَنَّهُمْ أَجْمَعِينَ ﴿٨٢﴾ إِلَّا عِبَادَكَ مِنْهُمُ الْمُخْلَصِينَ ﴿٨٣﴾

«By Your might, I will mislead all of them except for Your chosen servants among them»

[*Ṣād* (38): 82-83]

It is established in the Ṣaḥīḥ that the Prophet (ﷺ) said,

> Whoever says, 'None has the right to be worshipped save Allāh' sincerely from his heart, Allāh would make the Fire prohibited for him.[13]

Sincerity negates the cause that makes one enter the Fire. Therefore whoever enters the Fire, from amongst those who did say this statement, entered it because they never actualised that level of sincerity which would have made the Fire forbidden them. Instead there would be found in his heart some form of *shirk* that made him deserve entry into the Fire. *Shirk* is more hidden than the walk of an ant across a rock. It is for this reason that the servant is ordered to say in every prayer,

إِيَّاكَ نَعْبُدُ وَإِيَّاكَ نَسْتَعِينُ ﴿٥﴾

«You alone we worship and You alone we ask for help»

[*al-Fātiḥah* (1): 5]

Satan enjoins the person to commit *shirk* and the soul inclines towards obeying him, so the soul is always turning to other than Allāh, either out of fear of it or in hope of it. Therefore the servant

[13] Aḥmad [5/236] and ibn Ḥibbān [#200] with a ṣaḥīḥ isnād.

is always in need of purifying his *Tawḥīd* of Allāh. Ibn Abī ʿĀṣim and others record that the Prophet (ﷺ) said,

> Satan says, 'I destroy people through sins and they destroy me through saying 'None has the right to be worshipped save Allāh' and seeking forgiveness. When I realised this I incited their base desires such that they sin and do not seek forgiveness, thinking instead that they were doing good.'[14]

The person who obeys his desires rather than revelation falls under the category of those who take their desires as gods besides Allāh and ends up committing a form of *shirk* that prevents him from seeking forgiveness. In contrast, whoever actualises *tawḥīd* and seeks forgiveness will have evil removed from him and this is why Dhū-n-Nūn said, 'None has the right to be worshipped save You; glory be to You, far removed are You from any imperfection; I have been amongst the wrong-doers.'

[2.4 The wisdom in mentioning *Tawḥīd* alongside forgiveness]

It is for this reason that *tawḥīd* is mentioned alongside asking for forgiveness in many places,

فَٱعْلَمْ أَنَّهُۥ لَآ إِلَٰهَ إِلَّا ٱللَّهُ وَٱسْتَغْفِرْ لِذَنۢبِكَ
وَلِلْمُؤْمِنِينَ وَٱلْمُؤْمِنَٰتِ ۗ وَٱللَّهُ يَعْلَمُ مُتَقَلَّبَكُمْ وَمَثْوَىٰكُمْ ﴿١٩﴾

«Know that there is none worthy of worship save Allāh

---

[14] Abū Yaʿlā [#136] and ibn Abī ʿĀṣim [#7].
It was ruled to be ḍaʿīf by as-Suyūṭī and al-Haythamī as per al-Manāwī [#5586] and al-Albānī ruled it to be mawḍūʿ.

and ask forgiveness for your wrongdoing...»

[*Muḥammad* (47): 19]

أَلَّا تَعْبُدُوٓا۟ إِلَّا ٱللَّهَ ۚ إِنَّنِى لَكُم مِّنْهُ نَذِيرٌ وَبَشِيرٌ ﴿٢﴾ وَأَنِ ٱسْتَغْفِرُوا۟
رَبَّكُمْ ثُمَّ تُوبُوٓا۟ إِلَيْهِ

«Do not worship anyone but Allāh! I am a warner and a bringer of good news to you from Him. Ask you Lord for forgiveness and then turn in repentance to Him»

[*Hūd* (11): 2-3]

وَإِلَىٰ عَادٍ
أَخَاهُمْ هُودًا ۚ قَالَ يَٰقَوْمِ ٱعْبُدُوا۟ ٱللَّهَ مَا لَكُم مِّنْ إِلَٰهٍ
غَيْرُهُۥٓ ۖ إِنْ أَنتُمْ إِلَّا مُفْتَرُونَ ﴿٥٠﴾ يَٰقَوْمِ لَآ أَسْـَٔلُكُمْ عَلَيْهِ
أَجْرًا ۖ إِنْ أَجْرِىَ إِلَّا عَلَى ٱلَّذِى فَطَرَنِىٓ ۚ أَفَلَا تَعْقِلُونَ ﴿٥١﴾
وَيَٰقَوْمِ ٱسْتَغْفِرُوا۟ رَبَّكُمْ ثُمَّ تُوبُوٓا۟ إِلَيْهِ

«And to 'Ād we sent their brother Hūd. He said, 'My people! Worship Allāh, there is none worthy of worship save Him; you are merely inventors of falsehood. My people! I do not ask you for any wage for it, my wage is the responsibility of Him who brought me into being, will you not use your intellect? My people! Ask forgiveness of your Lord and then to turn to Him in repentance'»

[*Hūd* (11): 50-52]

فَٱسْتَقِيمُوٓا۟ إِلَيْهِ وَٱسْتَغْفِرُوهُ

«So take a straight course to Him and ask His forgiveness»

[*Fuṣṣilat* (41): 6]

The Prophet (ﷺ) advised us to say at the end of the gathering,

«سُبْحَانَكَ اللَّهُمَّ وَبِحَمْدِكَ، أَشْهَدُ أَنْ لَا إِلَهَ إِلَّا أَنْتَ، أَسْتَغْفِرُكَ وَأَتُوبُ إِلَيْكَ».

"Glory be to You, far removed are You from any imperfection; all praise is due to You. I bear witness that none has the right to be worshipped save You, I ask Your forgiveness and turn to You."

If the gathering was one of mercy, this supplication would be like a seal to it; if the gathering was one in which idle speech was indulged in, this supplication would serve as expiation for it.[15]

It is also reported that he (ﷺ) used to say upon completing ablution,

«أَشْهَدُ أَنْ لَا إِلَهَ إِلَّا اللهُ وَحْدَهُ لَا شَرِيكَ لَهُ، وَأَشْهَدُ أَنَّ مُحَمَّدًا عَبْدُهُ وَرَسُولُهُ..».

I bear witness that none has the right to be worshipped save Allāh, who has no partner, and I bear witness that Muḥammad is His servant and Messenger.

«اللَّهُمَّ اجْعَلْنِي مِنَ التَّوَّابِينَ وَاجْعَلْنِي مِنَ الْمُتَطَهِّرِينَ».

O Allāh! Make me amongst the penitent and make me amongst those who purify themselves.[16]

This supplication comprises *tawḥīd* and seeking forgiveness and it

[15] The referencing for this follows.

[16] Muslim [#234] and Abū Dāwūd [#169, 170]

commences with the two testifications that form the foundation of this religion - that we not worship any save Allāh and we do not obey any save His Messenger.

It is also reported that he (ﷺ) would say,

«سُبْحَانَكَ اللَّهُمَّ وَبِحَمْدِكَ، أَشْهَدُ أَنْ لَا إِلَهَ إِلَّا أَنْتَ، أَسْتَغْفِرُكَ وَأَتُوبُ إِلَيْكَ».

> Glory be to You, far removed are You from any imperfection; all praise is due to You. I bear witness that none has the right to be worshipped save You, I ask Your forgiveness and turn to You.[17]

This is the supplication that serves as expiation for a gathering and has been legislated to be said at the end of a gathering and upon the completion of ablution. Similarly the Prophet (ﷺ) would say at the end of his prayer,

«اللَّهُمَّ اغْفِرْ لِي مَا قَدَّمْتُ، وَمَا أَخَّرْتُ، وَمَا أَسْرَرْتُ، وَمَا أَعْلَنْتُ، وَمَا أَسْرَفْتُ، وَمَا أَنْتَ أَعْلَمُ بِهِ مِنِّي. أَنْتَ الْمُقَدِّمُ، وَأَنْتَ الْمُؤَخِّرُ لَا إِلَهَ إِلَّا أَنْتَ».

[17] at-Tirmidhī [#3433] and Aḥmad [#8818, 10415] on the authority of Abū Hurayrah.

Similar aḥādīth are reported on the authority of Sā'ib by Aḥmad [#15729]; 'Abdullāh bin 'Amr and Abū Barza by Abū Dāwūd [#4858, 4859]; 'Ā'ishah and Jubayr by an-Nasā'ī [3/71-72]; Anas by al-Bazzār [#3123]; Rāfi' by an-Nasā'ī, *'Amal* [#427]; ibn Mas'ūd by at-Ṭabarānī [#4445]; and Zubayr by at-Ṭabarānī, *as-Ṣaghīr* [#970].

It was declared ṣaḥīḥ by ibn Ḥibbān [#594], al-Ḥākim [#1969-1971], adh-Dhahabī, and al-Albānī, *Ṣaḥīḥ at-Targhīb* [#1516].

> O Allāh! Forgive me for my previous and later [sins], what I have done in secret and in open, for that of which You know better than I, You are the One who brings forward and leaves behind. There is none worthy of worship save You.[18]

Here he (ﷺ) commenced with supplication and ended with the testification of *tawḥīd*, this because it is legislated to supplicate at the end of the prayer, so he ended with the testification [rather than started with it]. In other cases [such as the previous one], this was not the intent in which case commencing with *tawḥīd* is the better course.

The type of supplication which comprises praise is better than that type of supplication that comprises request and asking, however in some specific circumstances it could be that the latter is better than the former due to some external factor. Similarly prayer is better than recitation, recitation is better than remembrance (*dhikr*), and remembrance is better than the supplication of request, yet despite this there could be circumstances, times or places, in which the latter are better than former. The beginning of this religion, its end, its outer, and its inner is all *tawḥīd*, and making ones religion sincerely for the sake of Allāh alone is the actualisation of 'None has the right to be worshipped save Allāh'.

[18] Muslim [#771] and Abū Dāwūd [#760, 761]

[2.5 The correct understanding of *Tawḥīd*]

The Muslims, even though all of them testify to it, differ greatly in their actualisation of it. Some think that *tawḥīd* is merely to believe that Allāh is the creator of everything and its Lord[19] and hence end up not differentiating between that aspect of *tawḥīd* which even the polytheists affirmed and the *tawḥīd* which the Messengers called to, the *tawḥīd* of singling out Allāh alone for worship;[20] they do not combine between *tawḥīd* of belief and *tawḥīd* of deed.

The polytheists never said that the creation was created by two gods, nor that there was a god alongside Allāh who created any aspect of it, instead they would say as Allāh informed us about them,

وَلَئِن سَأَلْتَهُم مَّنْ خَلَقَ السَّمَٰوَٰتِ وَالْأَرْضَ لَيَقُولُنَّ اللَّهُ

«If you asked them, 'Who created the heavens and the earth?' They would say, 'Allāh'»

[*Luqmān* (31): 25]

وَمَا يُؤْمِنُ أَكْثَرُهُم بِاللَّهِ إِلَّا وَهُم مُّشْرِكُونَ ﴿١٠٦﴾

«Most of them do not have faith in Allāh without associating others with Him»

[*Yūsuf* (12): 106]

---

[19] i.e. they only affirm *Tawḥīd ar-Rubūbiyyah.*

[20] i.e. *Tawḥīd al-Ilāhiyyah* or *Tawḥīd al-'Ibādah*

قُل لِّمَنِ ٱلْأَرْضُ وَمَن فِيهَآ إِن
كُنتُمْ تَعْلَمُونَ ﴿٨٤﴾ سَيَقُولُونَ لِلَّهِ ۚ قُلْ أَفَلَا تَذَكَّرُونَ
﴿٨٥﴾ قُلْ مَن رَّبُّ ٱلسَّمَٰوَٰتِ ٱلسَّبْعِ وَرَبُّ ٱلْعَرْشِ ٱلْعَظِيمِ
﴿٨٦﴾ سَيَقُولُونَ لِلَّهِ ۚ قُلْ أَفَلَا تَتَّقُونَ ﴿٨٧﴾ قُلْ مَنۢ بِيَدِهِۦ
مَلَكُوتُ كُلِّ شَىْءٍ وَهُوَ يُجِيرُ وَلَا يُجَارُ عَلَيْهِ إِن
كُنتُمْ تَعْلَمُونَ ﴿٨٨﴾ سَيَقُولُونَ لِلَّهِ ۚ قُلْ فَأَنَّىٰ تُسْحَرُونَ ﴿٨٩﴾

«Say, 'To whom does the earth belong and everyone in it, if you have any knowledge?' They will say, 'To Allāh.' Say, 'Will you not then take heed?' Say, 'Who is the Lord of the seven heavens and the Lord of the Mighty Throne?' They will say, 'Allāh.' Say, 'Will you not then fear Him?' Say, 'In whose hand is the dominion over everything, He who gives protection and from whom no protection can be given, if you have any knowledge?' They will say, 'Allāh's.' Say, 'So how have you been bewitched?'»

[*al-Mu'minūn* (23): 84-89]

Yet despite their belief that Allāh alone was the creator, they set up gods alongside Him, deities they appointed as intercessors between them and Him saying, 'We only worship them that they may draw us closer to Allāh' and they would love them as they should have loved Allāh. Committing *shirk* in ones love, worship, supplication, and request[21] is something separate from committing *shirk* in belief and affirmation [of the existence of Allāh], as He, Exalted is He, says,

[21] i.e. *shirk* in deeds

وَمِنَ النَّاسِ مَن يَتَّخِذُ مِن دُونِ ٱللَّهِ أَندَادًا يُحِبُّونَهُمْ كَحُبِّ ٱللَّهِ ۖ وَٱلَّذِينَ ءَامَنُوٓا۟ أَشَدُّ حُبًّا لِّلَّهِ ۗ

«Some people set up equals with Allāh, loving them as they should love Allāh. But those who have faith have greater love for Allāh»

[*al-Baqarah* (2): 165]

So whoever loves any object of creation as he should love Allāh, has committed *shirk* and has taken partners besides Allāh, loving them as he should love Allāh, even if he believes that Allāh is the sole creator. This is the reason why Allāh and His Messenger (ﷺ) differentiated between one who loves an object of creation for the sake of Allāh and one who loves an object of creation alongside Allāh. The first person appoints Allāh alone as his object of worship and absolute love and loves no other alongside Him; but when he comes to know that Allāh loves His Prophets and righteous servants, he too loves them for this reason; similarly when he comes to know that Allāh loves the performance of the legislated and the abandonment of the prohibited, he too loves this. Therefore his love for these matters is an offshoot of his love for Allāh, arising by virtue of it and therefore part of his love for Allāh.[22] This is totally the opposite to the one who sets up partners besides Allāh, placing

[22] The author, *Majmū' Fatāwā* [10/48-49] says, 'Loving Allāh and His Messenger is from the greatest obligations of faith and the greatest of its foundations, indeed it is the source of every action of faith and religion just as belief is the source of every statement of faith and religion. Every single motion arises as a result of love, be it praiseworthy or blameworthy. Therefore all actions of faith and religion arise only as a result of praiseworthy love, the foundation of which is the love of Allāh, Exalted is He. Allāh does not accept any action that is not done seeking His face and therefore any action that arises as a result of blameworthy love is not righteous in the Sight of Allāh.'

his hope and fear in them[23], or obeys them without knowing that obeying them is to obey Allāh, or takes them as intercessors without knowing that Allāh has granted permission for this. Allāh, Exalted is He, says,

وَيَعْبُدُونَ مِن دُونِ ٱللَّهِ
مَا لَا يَضُرُّهُمْ وَلَا يَنفَعُهُمْ وَيَقُولُونَ هَٰٓؤُلَآءِ شُفَعَٰٓؤُنَا
عِندَ ٱللَّهِ

«They worship, instead of Allāh, what can neither harm them nor help them, saying, 'These are our intercessors with Allāh'»

[*Yūnus* (10): 18]

ٱتَّخَذُوٓا أَحْبَارَهُمْ
وَرُهْبَٰنَهُمْ أَرْبَابًا مِّن دُونِ ٱللَّهِ وَٱلْمَسِيحَ ٱبْنَ
مَرْيَمَ وَمَآ أُمِرُوٓا إِلَّا لِيَعْبُدُوٓا إِلَٰهًا وَٰحِدًا ۖ
لَّآ إِلَٰهَ إِلَّا هُوَ ۚ سُبْحَٰنَهُۥ عَمَّا يُشْرِكُونَ ﴿٣١﴾

«They have taken their rabbis and monks as lords besides Allāh, and also the Messiah, son of Mary. Yet they were commanded to worship only one God; there is none worthy of worship save Him! Glory be to Him above anything they associate with Him!»

[*at-Tawbah* (9): 31]

---

[23] The author, *Majmū' Fatāwā* [10/61] says, 'Now if love is the foundation of every religious action, hope and fear then arise as a consequence of it and furthermore lead to it. Every person who hopes in something does so because he loves it, every person who fears something runs from the object of fear in order to attain something beloved.'

'Adī bin Ḥātim said to Prophet (ﷺ), 'But they never worshipped them' to which he replied,

> They made the lawful unlawful for them and they obeyed them. That was their worship of them.[24]

Allāh, Exalted is He, says,

أَمْ لَهُمْ شُرَكَٰٓؤُا۟ شَرَعُوا۟ لَهُم مِّنَ ٱلدِّينِ مَا لَمْ يَأْذَنۢ بِهِ ٱللَّهُ

> «Or do they have partners who have laid down a religion for them for which Allāh has not given any authority?»
> [*ash-Shūrā* (42): 21]

---

[24] at-Tirmidhī [#3095] and at-Ṭabarānī, *al-Kabīr* [#218, 219].

At-Tirmidhī said that it was gharīb and it was declared ḥasan by al-Albānī, *Ṣaḥīḥ at-Tirmidhī* [#2471].

The author said in explanation to this ḥadīth, 'These people are of two types: *The First*: Those who know that their leaders have altered the religion and they follow them in their alteration, therefore they believe in the lawfulness of what Allāh has made unlawful and the unlawfulness of what Allāh has made lawful, following thereby these leaders of theirs while knowing that they are opposing the religion of the Messengers. This is disbelief and Allāh and His Messenger have declared it to be *shirk*...*The Second*: They still have the belief in the lawfulness of what Allāh made lawful and the unlawfulness of what Allāh made unlawful, but they followed them in disobeying Allāh, in the same way that the Muslim may commit a sin while knowing it to be so. These people have the same ruling as the sinners and the Prophet (ﷺ) said, 'Obedience is only in the good''' - Āli ash-Shaykh [p. 91]

وَيَوْمَ يَعَضُّ ٱلظَّالِمُ عَلَىٰ يَدَيْهِ يَقُولُ
يَٰلَيْتَنِى ٱتَّخَذْتُ مَعَ ٱلرَّسُولِ سَبِيلًا ﴿٢٧﴾ يَٰوَيْلَتَىٰ لَيْتَنِى لَمْ أَتَّخِذْ
فُلَانًا خَلِيلًا ﴿٢٨﴾ لَّقَدْ أَضَلَّنِى عَنِ ٱلذِّكْرِ بَعْدَ إِذْ جَآءَنِى ۗ
وَكَانَ ٱلشَّيْطَٰنُ لِلْإِنسَٰنِ خَذُولًا ﴿٢٩﴾

«The Day when a wrongdoer will bite his hands and say, 'Alas for me! If only I had gone the way of the Messenger! Alas for me! If only I had not taken so-and-so for a friend! He led me astray from the Reminder after it came to me.' Satan always leaves man in the lurch!»

[*al-Furqān* (25): 27-29]

[2.6 The obligation to obey the Prophet (ﷺ)]

It is obligatory to obey the Messenger, because to obey him is to obey Allāh - therefore the lawful is what he made lawful, the unlawful is what he made unlawful and the religion is only that which he legislated. Those besides the Messenger, the scholars and leaders, are only to be obeyed if obeying them entails obedience to Allāh. This is the condition in which they are to be obeyed and in such a circumstance, obeying them falls under obeying Allāh and His Messenger (ﷺ),

يَٰٓأَيُّهَا ٱلَّذِينَ ءَامَنُوٓا۟ أَطِيعُوا۟ ٱللَّهَ وَأَطِيعُوا۟ ٱلرَّسُولَ وَأُو۟لِى
ٱلْأَمْرِ مِنكُمْ ۖ

«You who have faith! Obey Allāh and obey the Messenger and those in command among you»

[*an-Nisā'* (4): 59]

In this verse, Allāh did not say, 'Obey Allāh and obey His Messenger and obey those in authority over you' rather He made obedience to those in authority to fall under obedience to His Messenger and for this reason did not say, 'obey those in authority over you' by repeating the word 'obey'. This is because whoever obeys the Messenger has obeyed Allāh, hence whenever the Messenger of Allāh commands us with something it is not for us to ascertain whether Allāh has commanded it or not. This is not the case with those of authority for they could command to that which is disobedience to Allāh, so it is not necessarily the case that obedience to them is always obedience to Allāh; indeed when they command something it must first be ascertained whether Allāh has ordered this or not - be the one commanding a scholar or a ruler. Included in this is *taqlīd* of scholars and obeying military commanders etc, only through this method is the religion established in its entirety,

وَقَٰتِلُوهُمْ حَتَّىٰ
لَا تَكُونَ فِتْنَةٌ وَيَكُونَ ٱلدِّينُ كُلُّهُۥ لِلَّهِ

«Fight them until there is no more trial and the religion is wholly for Allāh»

[*al-Anfāl* (8): 39]

When he (ﷺ) was asked about a person who fought to show his courage, or fought for nationalism, or fought to show off, he replied,

> Whoever fights so that the word of Allāh be made supreme, he is the one who has fought in the way of Allāh.[25]

Moreover many people love a Khalīfah, or a scholar, or a leader to such an extremity that they end up setting him up as a partner along with Allāh, this even if they claim that they love Allāh [only]. Like-

[25] Bukhārī [#123, 2810, 3126, 7458] and Muslim [#1904]

wise whoever appoints anyone besides the Messenger who must be obeyed in everything he commands and prohibits, even if this contradict the legislation of Allāh and His Messenger, has set up a partner alongside Allāh. Such a person might even do what the Christians did with Christ: supplicate to him and seek succour from him. He would love those who love this partner and hate those who hate him, obligate his obedience in everything and hence put him in the place of Allāh and His Messenger. This is that type of *shirk* that is talked about in His saying,

وَمِنَ النَّاسِ مَن يَتَّخِذُ مِن دُونِ اللَّهِ أَندَادًا يُحِبُّونَهُمْ كَحُبِّ اللَّهِ وَالَّذِينَ آمَنُوا أَشَدُّ حُبًّا لِّلَّهِ

«Some people set up equals with Allāh, loving them as they should love Allāh. But those who have faith have greater love for Allāh»

[*al-Baqarah* (2): 165]

[2.7 The explanation of *Īmān*]

Therefore *tawḥīd* and *shirk* takes place in the statements of the heart and its actions and this is why Junaid said, '*Tawḥīd* is the statement of the heart and *tawakkul* is the action of the heart.' He meant by *tawḥīd* here the foundational belief[26] because he mentioned it

[26] The author, *Majmū' Fatāwā* [7/186-187] says, 'The foundation of faith is that faith which takes root in the heart, this faith must have two components: the belief of the heart accompanied with its acknowledgement and cognisance; the first element is referred to as the statement of the heart (*qawl al-qalb*). Al-Junaid said, "*Tawḥīd* is the statement of the heart and reliance (*tawakkul*) is the action of the heart (*'amal al-qalb*)." Therefore it is necessary that there exist the statement of the heart and its actions, then ensuing from this, the statement of the body and its actions. The action of the heart must exist such as loving Allāh and His Messenger, fearing Allāh, loving what Allāh and His Messenger love and hating what they hate, making ones actions sincere for Him and having *tawakkul* in Him. =

alongside *tawakkul*, however when it is mentioned by itself it encompasses the statements of the heart and its actions and *tawakkul* is from the perfection of *tawḥīd*. The same applies to the word *Īmān*, when it is mentioned alone it encompasses outward and inward actions and it is said, '*Īmān* is statement and action' i.e. the statement of the heart and tongue and the action of the heart and limbs, it is in this respect that the Prophet (ﷺ) said,

> Faith comprises sixty odd branches, the highest of which is the saying, 'None has the right to be worshipped save Allāh', the lowest of which is to remove something harmful from the path, and modesty is a branch of faith.[27]

and it is in this respect that Allāh, Exalted is He, says,

إِنَّمَا ٱلْمُؤْمِنُونَ ٱلَّذِينَ ءَامَنُوا۟ بِٱللَّهِ وَرَسُولِهِۦ ثُمَّ لَمْ يَرْتَابُوا۟
وَجَٰهَدُوا۟ بِأَمْوَٰلِهِمْ وَأَنفُسِهِمْ فِى سَبِيلِ ٱللَّهِ ۚ أُو۟لَٰٓئِكَ هُمُ
ٱلصَّٰدِقُونَ ﴿١٥﴾

=

The heart is the foundation, when it contains cognisance and firm intent this must show on the body necessarily, it is not possible that this not happen. This is why the Prophet (ﷺ) said in the ṣaḥīḥ ḥadīth, 'In the body there is a piece of flesh, if it is sound, the body is sound, but if it is corrupt, the whole body will be corrupt, indeed it is the heart.' Abū Hurayrah said, 'The heart is the king and the limbs are its soldiers, if the king is good, the soldiers will be good but if the king is vile, so too will be his soldiers.' ... So if the heart is correct by virtue of its having faith in terms of knowledge and action of heart, this must mean that the body will also be correct in its speech and action upon the dictates of that faith. This is why the *Imāms* of the *Ahlu-l-Ḥadīth* said that faith was speech and action. Inward and outward speech and inward and outward action, the outer must follow the inner and this is why some of the Companions said regarding one who prayed lazily, 'If his heart were submissive, so too would his limbs be. ' Refer also to *Majmū' Fatāwā* [7/644-646] for an important discussion concerning this.

[27] Bukhārī [#9] and Muslim [#35]

«The believers are only those who have had faith in Allāh and His Messenger and then have had no doubt and have done *Jihād* with their wealth and themselves in the Way of Allāh. They are the ones who are true to their word»

[*al-Ḥujurāt* (49): 15]

إِنَّمَا ٱلْمُؤْمِنُونَ ٱلَّذِينَ إِذَا ذُكِرَ ٱللَّهُ وَجِلَتْ
قُلُوبُهُمْ وَإِذَا تُلِيَتْ عَلَيْهِمْ ءَايَٰتُهُۥ زَادَتْهُمْ إِيمَٰنًا وَعَلَىٰ رَبِّهِمْ
يَتَوَكَّلُونَ ﴿٢﴾ ٱلَّذِينَ يُقِيمُونَ ٱلصَّلَوٰةَ وَمِمَّا رَزَقْنَٰهُمْ
يُنفِقُونَ ﴿٣﴾ أُوْلَٰٓئِكَ هُمُ ٱلْمُؤْمِنُونَ حَقًّا

«The believers are those who hearts tremble when Allāh is mentioned, whose faith increases when His verses are recited to them, and who put their trust in their Lord; those who establish the prayer and give of what We have provided for them. They are the believers in truth»

[*al-Anfāl* (8): 2-4]

إِنَّمَا ٱلْمُؤْمِنُونَ ٱلَّذِينَ ءَامَنُواْ بِٱللَّهِ وَرَسُولِهِۦ وَإِذَا كَانُواْ مَعَهُۥ
عَلَىٰٓ أَمْرٍ جَامِعٍ لَّمْ يَذْهَبُواْ حَتَّىٰ يَسْتَـْٔذِنُوهُ

«The believers are those who have faith in Allāh and His Messenger and who, when they are with him on a matter of common concern, do not leave until they have asked him for permission»

[*an-Nūr* (24): 62]

Absolute faith (*al-Īmān al-Muṭlaq*) includes within it Islām[28] as is recorded in the Two Ṣaḥīḥs from the Prophet (ﷺ) that he said to the

[28] i.e. the outward actions required by Islām.

delegation of ʿAbd al-Qais,

> I enjoin you to have *Īmān* in Allāh, do you know what *Īmān* in Allāh is? The testification that none has the right to be worshipped save Allāh and that Muḥammad is the Messenger of Allāh, the establishment of the prayer, the giving of zakāt, and the giving of one fifth of the war booty.[29]

It is for this reason that some of the *Salaf* said, 'Every *mu'min* is a Muslim but not every Muslim is a *mu'min*.'[30]

However if the word *Īmān* is mentioned alongside words such as action (*ʿamal*) or Islām, then the two take on specific meanings such as in His saying,

إِنَّ ٱلَّذِينَ ءَامَنُوا۟ وَعَمِلُوا۟ ٱلصَّٰلِحَٰتِ

«Those who have faith and work righteous deeds»
[*al-Kahf* (18): 107]

such usage is frequently seen in the Qur'ān. This usage can also be seen in the authentic ḥadīth wherein Jibrīl asked the Prophet (ﷺ) about Islām, *Īmān* and *Iḥsān* to which he replied,

> 'Islām is to testify that none has the right to be worshipped save Allāh and that Muḥammad is the Messenger of Allāh, to establish the prayer, the give the *zakāt*, to fast the month of Ramaḍān and to perform the pilgrimage to the House.' He then asked, 'What is *Īmān*?' He replied, 'That you believe in Allāh, His Angels, His Books, His Messengers, the resurrection after death, and that you believe in the

[29] Bukhārī [#53. 87, 523, 1398, 3095, 6176, 7266, 7556] and Muslim [#17]

[30] ibn Mandah, *al-Īmān* [1/120] and al-Aṣbahāni, *al-Ḥujjah* [1/410]

> Divine Decree - the good of it and the bad of it.' He asked, 'What is *iḥsān*?' He replied, 'That you worship Allāh as if you are seeing Him, and even though you cannot see him then indeed He sees you.'[31]

So this text differentiates the meaning of *Īmān* and Islām due to their being mentioned together, whereas the previous text included the meaning of Islām within *Īmān* due to the latter being mentioned alone.

The same applies to word action (*'amal*) for the word Islām mentioned previously falls under the meaning of action. Outward actions are the necessary outcome of the *Īmān* that takes root in the heart. Hence if *Īmān* takes root in the heart, it must manifest itself on the limbs by way of necessity and the *Īmān* in the heart must comprise the belief of the heart and its submission. Were the heart to believe that Muḥammad is the Messenger of Allāh, yet hate him and disdain obeying him, it has not achieved *Īmān*. The word *Īmān*, part of its meaning is belief but it is not synonymous with it, one does not say to one who believes in something that he is a *mu'min* in that something. If one were to say, 'I believe that one is half of two and that heaven is above us and the earth below us' and other such matters that everyone knows and sees, it is not said of this person that he is a *mu'min* in these matters. Rather it is only employed when one informs of unseen affairs such as in the saying of the brothers of Yūsuf,

وَمَآ أَنتَ بِمُؤْمِنٍ لَّنَا وَلَوْ كُنَّا صَٰدِقِينَ ﴿١٧﴾

«...but you are never going to believe us now...»
[*Yūsuf* (12): 17]

[31] Muslim [#8] and Abū Dāwūd [#4695-4697]

for they were informing [Ya'qūb] of matters that were hidden from him.[32]

The point of discussion here is that the word *Īmān* is used in some narrations and is derived from the word *amn*[33] just as the word *iqrār* is derived from *qarra.*[34] Therefore the *mu'min* is one who has safety and security and the *muqirr* is one who has settled and accepted something, this necessarily requires the heart to act by the dictates of its belief. So if one knows that Muḥammad is the Messenger of Allāh, yet does not add to this love, respect, and honour of him and instead hates him and disdains to follow him, such a person cannot be said to be a *mu'min* in him, rather he is a *kāfir* in him.

It is for this reason that Iblīs, Pharaoh, and the People of the Book, those who knew him as they knew their own sons, are disbelievers. Iblīs did not deny the narrative or the one informing, instead he disdained to obey the command of his Lord,

وَجَحَدُوا بِهَا وَاسْتَيْقَنَتْهَا أَنفُسُهُمْ ظُلْمًا وَعُلُوًّا فَانظُرْ كَيْفَ
كَانَ عَاقِبَةُ الْمُفْسِدِينَ ﴿١٤﴾

«...and they repudiated them wrongly and haughtily, in spite of their own certainty about them»

[*an-Naml* (27): 14]

Mūsā said to Pharaoh,

[32] Here the author digresses to explain the different usages of the word *Īmān* as found in the Qur'ān. This discussion has been relegated to Appendix 2.

[33] Meaning: safety and security

[34] Meaning: to establish, settle, dwell, abide

قَالَ لَقَدْ عَلِمْتَ مَآ أَنزَلَ هَٰٓؤُلَآءِ إِلَّا رَبُّ ٱلسَّمَٰوَٰتِ وَٱلْأَرْضِ بَصَآئِرَ

«You know that no one sent these down but the Lord of the heavens and earth to be clear proofs»

[*al-Isrā'* (17): 102]

Allāh, Exalted is He, says,

ٱلَّذِينَ ءَاتَيْنَٰهُمُ ٱلْكِتَٰبَ يَعْرِفُونَهُۥ كَمَا يَعْرِفُونَ أَبْنَآءَهُمْ

«Those We have given the Book recognise him as they recognise their own sons»

[*al-Baqarah* (2): 146]

Therefore the mere fact that the heart may know the truth is of no benefit if this knowledge is not accompanied by its necessary dictates such as the heart loving this truth and following it. Indeed the most severely punished people on the Day of Judgment would be those who did not act according to their knowledge, the Prophet (ﷺ) used to say,

اللّٰهُمَّ! إِنِّي أَعُوذُ بِكَ مِنْ عِلْمٍ لَا يَنْفَعُ، وَ نَفْسٍ لَا تَشْبَعُ، وَ دُعَاءٍ لَا يُسْمَعُ، وَ قَلْبٍ لَا يَخْشَعُ،

O Allāh! I take refuge with You from knowledge that does not benefit, from a soul that is never satisfied, from a supplication that is not heard and from a heart that does not fear Allāh.[35]

The Jahmiyyah held that the mere knowledge of the heart and its belief constitutes *Īmān*, and that whenever a divine text pointed to the lack of *Īmān* of a person, this proved that person did not have

[35] Muslim [#2722] and at-Tirmidhī [#3572]

the knowledge and belief in the heart. This is from the profoundest ignorance of both the Divine Law and the dictates of the intellect; the reality of this stance leads to regarding both the believer and disbeliever to be on par.[36] It was for this reason that Wakīʿ bin al-Jarrāḥ, Aḥmad bin Ḥanbal and other Imāms ruled the Jahmiyyah to be disbelievers.[37] It is well known that a person could know the truth, yet hate it because of some other reason, hence not everyone who disdains to accept the truth is ignorant of it. Therefore *Īmān* must consist of belief and its actions and this is the meaning of the *Salaf* when they said, '*Īmān* is speech and action.'[38]

Moreover, were the heart to truly actualise belief and complete

---

[36] Refer to the author's, *al-Īmān* [pp. 72-92] for a further exposition on this issue and likewise al-Aṣfahānī [1/405]

[37] al-Aṣfahānī [1/405] and al-Lālikāʾī, *Usūl Iʿtiqād* [5/885-889]

[38] al-Lālikāʾī [4/832, 4/848-850], al-Ājurrī, *ash-Sharīʿah* [p. 130] and the author's, *al-Īmān* [pp. 101-102]

The author, *Majmūʿ Fatāwā* [7/171] says, 'Those of the *Salaf* who said that *Īmān* was speech and action intended thereby the speech of the heart and tongue and action of the heart and limbs. [Those who added to this definition] belief did so because they thought or feared that people would understand that 'speech' [mentioned in the previous definition] refers only to speech of the tongues. Those who defined it as "Speech, action and intention" did so because they understood that 'speech' covers both belief [in the heart] and articulation of the tongue, but they feared that people may not understand that intention was also covered by 'action' and so they added this. Those who added "following the Sunnah' did so because no action is beloved to Allāh unless it is compliance to the Sunnah. None of these meant to include in this definition absolutely every speech and action, rather that speech and action which is legislated. Their purpose in giving these definitions was to refute the Murjiʿah who presumed that *Īmān* was belief and nothing else. Those who defined *Īmān* to have four components, such as ʿAbdullāh at-Tusturī, explained themselves by saying, "Speech, action, intention, and Sunnah: if *Īmān* is speech without action, this is disbelief; if it is speech and action without intention, this is hypocrisy; if it is speech, action and intention but without Sunnah, this is innovation."'

love - that love which leads to the desire to act by its dictates - this must necessarily lead to the performance of bodily actions. This is because a full desire to do something of ones own volition, accompanied with the ability to do so, must end up with the observance of that thing. The thing will only not happen if the ability is lacking or the desire is lacking. Therefore when the heart accepts and acknowledges that Muḥammad is the Messenger of Allāh, and loves him completely, this fact alone will prevent him from any hesitation in saying the testifications of faith, provided he has the ability to do so.

Abū Ṭālib knew full well that Muḥammad was the Messenger of Allāh, he also loved him - but his love of him did not arise as a result of his love of Allāh, rather due to relations - this is why when he was asked to articulate the testification of faith on his death bed, he did not accept them because he loved his religion more than he loved his cousin. Now, were he to have loved him because he was the Messenger of Allāh, for sure he would have said then. This was the love of him as exemplified by Abū Bakr about whom Allāh, Exalted is He, said,

وَسَيُجَنَّبُهَا
ٱلْأَتْقَى ﴿١٧﴾ ٱلَّذِى يُؤْتِى مَالَهُۥ يَتَزَكَّىٰ ﴿١٨﴾ وَمَا لِأَحَدٍ عِندَهُۥ مِن
نِّعْمَةٍ تُجْزَىٰٓ ﴿١٩﴾ إِلَّا ٱبْتِغَآءَ وَجْهِ رَبِّهِ ٱلْأَعْلَىٰ ﴿٢٠﴾ وَلَسَوْفَ يَرْضَىٰ ﴿٢١﴾

«Those who have most *taqwā* will be far removed from it: those who give their wealth to purify themselves - not to repay someone else for a favour done - desiring only the Face of their Lord Most High. They will certainly be satisfied»

[*al-Layl* (92): 17-21]

and this was the love him as was exemplified by the other believers such as 'Umar, 'Uthmān and 'Alī. Hence the love that Abū Ṭālib had for Muḥammad was a love that was a love alongside the love of Allāh and not a love that was for the sake of Allāh and this is why Allāh did not accept his deed of aiding and sheltering the Messenger of Allāh. Allāh only accepts that action which is done seeking His face.

This is why *Īmān* and *tawḥīd* must be accompanied by the actions of the heart in order to realise them, actions such as love and making the religion sincerely for Allāh. The religion cannot be religion when devoid of actions because religion is obedience and worship. Allāh has revealed two chapters entitled *ikhlāṣ* (sincerity),

قُلْ يَٰٓأَيُّهَا ٱلْكَٰفِرُونَ ﴿١﴾

«Say, 'O Disbelievers!...»

[*al-Kāfirūn* (109): 1]

قُلْ هُوَ ٱللَّهُ أَحَدٌ ﴿١﴾

«Say, 'He is Allāh the One'»

[*al-Ikhlāṣ* (112): 1]

One of them deals with making *tawḥīd* of Allāh in speech and belief, the other deals with making *tawḥīd* of Allāh in deed and desire. Concerning the first case He says,

قُلْ هُوَ ٱللَّهُ أَحَدٌ ﴿١﴾ ٱللَّهُ ٱلصَّمَدُ ﴿٢﴾ لَمْ يَلِدْ
وَلَمْ يُولَدْ ﴿٣﴾ وَلَمْ يَكُن لَّهُۥ كُفُوًا أَحَدٌۢ ﴿٤﴾

«Say, 'He is Allāh the One. Allāh, the Everlasting Sustainer of all. He has not given birth and was not born. Nothing is comparable to Him'»

[*al-Ikhlāṣ* (112): 1-4]

thereby ordering him to adhere to this *tawḥīd*, concerning the second case He says,

قُلْ يَٰٓأَيُّهَا ٱلْكَٰفِرُونَ ﴿١﴾ لَآ أَعْبُدُ مَا تَعْبُدُونَ ﴿٢﴾
وَلَآ أَنتُمْ عَٰبِدُونَ مَآ أَعْبُدُ ﴿٣﴾ وَلَآ أَنَا۠ عَابِدٌ مَّا عَبَدتُّمْ ﴿٤﴾
وَلَآ أَنتُمْ عَٰبِدُونَ مَآ أَعْبُدُ ﴿٥﴾ لَكُمْ دِينُكُمْ وَلِىَ دِينِ ﴿٦﴾

«Say, 'O disbelievers! I do not worship what you worship and you do not worship what I worship. Nor will I worship what you worship and nor will you worship what I worship. You have your religion and I have mine'»
[*al-Kāfirūn* (109): 1-6]

thereby ordering him to say that which would necessitate his absolvement of any worship for other than Allāh and his affirmation of sincere worship for Him alone.

[2.8 The foundation of worship]

The foundation of *'ibādah* (worship) is desire and intention, when the word is mentioned alone it also includes the meaning of *tawakkul* and the likes. When it is mentioned alongside *tawakkul*, *tawakkul* takes on part of its meaning just in the same way that we previously discussed about the word *Īmān*. Allāh, Exalted is He, says,

وَمَا خَلَقْتُ ٱلْجِنَّ وَٱلْإِنسَ إِلَّا لِيَعْبُدُونِ ﴿٥٦﴾

«I only created jinn and mankind to worship Me»
[*adh-Dhāriyāt* (51): 56]

يَٰٓأَيُّهَا ٱلنَّاسُ ٱعْبُدُوا۟ رَبَّكُمُ ٱلَّذِى خَلَقَكُمْ
وَٱلَّذِينَ مِن قَبْلِكُمْ لَعَلَّكُمْ تَتَّقُونَ ﴿٢١﴾

«O mankind! Worship your Lord who created you and those before you...»

[*al-Baqarah* (2): 21]

These verses and those like them include in their meaning the performance of all that is obligatory, amongst which is *tawakkul*, and the leaving of all that is prohibited. Allāh says in another place,

إِيَّاكَ نَعْبُدُ وَإِيَّاكَ نَسْتَعِينُ ۝٥

«You alone we worship and You alone we ask for help»

[*al-Fātiḥah* (1): 5]

فَٱعْبُدْهُ وَتَوَكَّلْ عَلَيْهِ

«So worship Him and put your trust in Him»

[*Hūd* (11): 123]

This methodology of usage of words occurs frequently in the Qur'ān, the meaning of a word will vary from a general meaning to a specific meaning depending on whether it is mentioned alone or alongside another.[39]

Therefore loving Allāh alone, putting ones reliance in Him alone, fearing Him alone etc, all fall under the meaning of the word *tawḥīd*. Allah, Exalted is He, says concerning love,

وَمِنَ
ٱلنَّاسِ مَن يَتَّخِذُ مِن دُونِ ٱللَّهِ أَندَادًا يُحِبُّونَهُمْ كَحُبِّ ٱللَّهِ
وَٱلَّذِينَ ءَامَنُوٓا۟ أَشَدُّ حُبًّا لِّلَّهِ

[39] Here the author digresses to give examples of various 'word-pairs' used in the Qur'ān. This discussion has been relegated to Appendix 3.

«Some people set up equals with Allāh, loving them as they should love Allāh. But those who have faith have greater love for Allāh»

[*al-Baqarah* (2): 165]

قُلْ إِن
كَانَ ءَابَآؤُكُمْ وَأَبْنَآؤُكُمْ وَإِخْوَٰنُكُمْ وَأَزْوَٰجُكُمْ وَعَشِيرَتُكُمْ
وَأَمْوَٰلٌ ٱقْتَرَفْتُمُوهَا وَتِجَٰرَةٌ تَخْشَوْنَ كَسَادَهَا وَمَسَٰكِنُ
تَرْضَوْنَهَآ أَحَبَّ إِلَيْكُم مِّنَ ٱللَّهِ وَرَسُولِهِۦ وَجِهَادٍ
فِى سَبِيلِهِۦ فَتَرَبَّصُوا۟ حَتَّىٰ يَأْتِىَ ٱللَّهُ بِأَمْرِهِۦ ۗ وَٱللَّهُ لَا يَهْدِى
ٱلْقَوْمَ ٱلْفَٰسِقِينَ ﴿٢٤﴾

«Say, 'If your fathers, or your sons, or your brothers, or your wives, or your tribe, or any wealth you have acquired, or any business you fear may slump, or any house which pleases you, are dearer to you that Allāh and His Messenger and doing *Jihād* in His Way, then wait until Allāh brings about His command...'»

[*at-Tawbah* (9): 24]

وَمَن
يُطِعِ ٱللَّهَ وَرَسُولَهُۥ وَيَخْشَ ٱللَّهَ وَيَتَّقْهِ فَأُو۟لَٰٓئِكَ هُمُ ٱلْفَآئِزُونَ

«All who obey Allāh and His Messenger and have awe of Allāh and *taqwā* of Him, they are the ones who are victorious»

[*an-Nūr* (24): 52]

thereby appointing obedience for Allāh and His Messenger but fear and *taqwā*[40] is for Allāh alone. Allāh, Exalted is He, says,

وَلَوْ أَنَّهُمْ رَضُوا۟ مَآ ءَاتَىٰهُمُ ٱللَّهُ
وَرَسُولُهُۥ وَقَالُوا۟ حَسْبُنَا ٱللَّهُ سَيُؤْتِينَا ٱللَّهُ مِن فَضْلِهِۦ
وَرَسُولُهُۥٓ إِنَّآ إِلَى ٱللَّهِ رَٰغِبُونَ ﴿٥٩﴾

«If only they had been pleased with what Allāh and His Messenger had given them and had said, 'Allāh is enough for us. Allāh will give us of His bounty as will His Messenger. It is in Allāh that we place our longing and attention'»

[*at-Tawbah* (9): 59]

فَإِذَا فَرَغْتَ فَٱنصَبْ ﴿٧﴾ وَإِلَىٰ رَبِّكَ فَٱرْغَب ﴿٨﴾

«So when you have finished, work on, and to your Lord direct your longing and attention!»

[*ash-Sharḥ* (94): 7-8]

thereby appointing desire, hope, and seeking reward for Allāh alone. These matters are explained more fully in other places.

The point of this discussion is to show that when a person says, 'None has the right to be worshipped save Allāh' he has singled Him out alone for worship and this includes belief in Allāh manifesting itself in speech and action. The polytheists believed that Allāh was

---

[40] The author, *Majmū' Fatāwā* [10/433] says, '*Taqwā* is that the person act in obedience to Allāh upon a light from Him and that he abandon disobedience to Him upon a light from Him, fearing the punishment of Allāh.'

He also says, *Majmū' Rasā'il* [1/256], '*Taqwā* in actions comes about by meeting two requirements, the first that the deed be sincerely for Allāh; meaning by this that one desire only the Face of Allāh and not associate anything else in the worship of his Lord, the second that the deed be something Allāh has commanded and loves, i.e. it be in conformity to the Legal Law and not in accordance to some other law that Allāh has not allowed to be followed.'

the Lord of everything, but they set up other gods alongside him, hence they did not single Him out alone in godship, i.e. they did not worship Him alone or ask of Him alone, as Allāh says,

إِيَّاكَ نَعْبُدُ وَإِيَّاكَ نَسْتَعِينُ ﴿٥﴾

«You alone we worship and You alone we ask for help»
[*al-Fātiḥah* (1): 5]

[2.9 Misdirected intentions]

A person could intend to ask Allāh alone and put his reliance in Him alone, yet in matters that Allāh does not love, rather detests and prohibits. Such a person may be sincere in his asking and relying but he is not sincere in his worship and obedience and this is the state of many of those who commit false practices amongst those who claim spiritual unveilings and carry out various machinations that contradict the command of Allāh and His Messenger. Many of these ask Allāh for help to do what they desire, but because these deeds do not conform to the order of Allāh and His Messenger they attain some temporal benefit but their end will be evil indeed! Allāh, Exalted is He, says,

وَإِذَا مَسَّكُمُ الضُّرُّ فِي الْبَحْرِ ضَلَّ مَن تَدْعُونَ إِلَّا إِيَّاهُ فَلَمَّا نَجَّاكُمْ
إِلَى الْبَرِّ أَعْرَضْتُمْ وَكَانَ الْإِنسَانُ كَفُورًا ﴿٦٧﴾

«When harm occurs to you at sea, those you call on vanish - except for Him alone! But when He delivers you to dry land, you turn away. Man truly is ungrateful»
[*al-Isrā'* (17): 67]

وَإِذَا مَسَّ
ٱلْإِنسَٰنَ ٱلضُّرُّ دَعَانَا لِجَنۢبِهِۦٓ أَوْ قَاعِدًا أَوْ قَآئِمًا فَلَمَّا كَشَفْنَا
عَنْهُ ضُرَّهُۥ مَرَّ كَأَن لَّمْ يَدْعُنَآ إِلَىٰ ضُرٍّ مَّسَّهُۥ

«When harm touches man, he calls on Us, lying on his side, or sitting down, or standing up. Then when We remove harm from him he carries on as if he had never called on Us when the harm first touched him»

[*Yūnus* (10): 12]

Another group of people desire the obedience of Allāh and His Messenger but they do not fully implement *tawakkul* and asking His help. These people will be rewarded for their good intentions and for their actions of obedience, however they will meet with disappointment in what they desired due to their failure to actualise *tawakkul* and asking His help. This is why these people are often tried with weakness or despair sometimes and self conceit on others; if his desire is not fulfilled it is because of his weakness and perhaps he falls into a state of despair, if his desire is fulfilled he thinks it to be because of his strength and ability and therefore falls into self conceit. He could even become so confident of himself that he thinks that his desire will definitely be met, yet face disappointment, Allāh says,

لَقَدْ نَصَرَكُمُ ٱللَّهُ فِى مَوَاطِنَ
كَثِيرَةٍ ۙ وَيَوْمَ حُنَيْنٍ ۙ إِذْ أَعْجَبَتْكُمْ كَثْرَتُكُمْ فَلَمْ
تُغْنِ عَنكُمْ شَيْـًٔا وَضَاقَتْ عَلَيْكُمُ ٱلْأَرْضُ
بِمَا رَحُبَتْ ثُمَّ وَلَّيْتُم مُّدْبِرِينَ ﴿٢٥﴾ ثُمَّ أَنزَلَ ٱللَّهُ سَكِينَتَهُۥ
عَلَىٰ رَسُولِهِۦ وَعَلَى ٱلْمُؤْمِنِينَ وَأَنزَلَ جُنُودًا لَّمْ تَرَوْهَا
وَعَذَّبَ ٱلَّذِينَ كَفَرُوا۟ ۚ وَذَٰلِكَ جَزَآءُ ٱلْكَٰفِرِينَ ﴿٢٦﴾
ثُمَّ يَتُوبُ ٱللَّهُ مِنۢ بَعْدِ ذَٰلِكَ عَلَىٰ مَن يَشَآءُ ۗ وَٱللَّهُ غَفُورٌ
رَّحِيمٌ ﴿٢٧﴾

«Allāh has helped you on many occasions, including the Day of Ḥunayn when your great number delighted you but did not help you in any way, and the earth seemed narrow to you for all its great breadth, and you turned your backs... Then after that Allāh will turn to anyone He wills. Allāh is Ever-Forgiving, Most Merciful»

[*at-Tawbah* (9): 25-27]

[2.10 Ostentation and conceit]

Many people fall into a combination of ostentation and self conceit. Ostentation falls under committing *shirk* by way of the creation and self conceit falls under committing *shirk* by way of ones own soul - this is the state of the arrogant. The ostentatious have not fully realised the verse,

إِيَّاكَ نَعْبُدُ

«You alone we worship...»

[*al-Fātiḥah* (1): 5]

and the self conceited have not fully realised the verse,

وَإِيَّاكَ نَسْتَعِينُ ۝٥

«...and You alone we ask for help»

[*al-Fātiḥah* (1): 5]

Hence whoever actualises the first part of the verse is saved from ostentation and whoever actualises the second part of the verse is saved from self conceit. The famous ḥadīth mentions,

> Three are the destructive traits: miserliness that is obeyed; lust that is followed; and a person being amazed with himself.[41]

Worse than both the previous two categories of people[42] are those who do not worship Allāh and neither ask His help, instead asking and worshipping another, these are polytheists, committing *shirk* in both affairs.[43] From amongst these are those who worship the devils and perform devilish feats. In order to perform these they do acts that the devils like such as lying, indecent sins, and supplicating with concocted supplications beloved to the devils. All of this has been explained in other places. These people could end up performing miracles which they think are from amongst the miracles performed by the *Awliyā'* whereas in reality they are akin to the states of magi-

---

[41] al-Bazzār [#80] on the authority of Anas and its isnād was declared ḍa'īf by al-'Irāqī [#61, 3348].

Similar aḥādīth are also reported on the authority of ibn 'Abbās, ibn Abī Awfā, Abū Hurayrah and ibn 'Umar as recorded by al-Haythamī [1/91] all with weak asānīd as stated by al-'Uqaylī and it was due to these that al-Mundhirī, *at-Targhīb* [1/162] and al-Albānī [#1802] declared the ḥadīth ḥasan.

[42] i.e those who place *tawakkul* in Allāh but ask for prohibited things and those who desire lawful things but do not place their *tawakkul* in Allāh alone.

[43] i.e. *shirk* by creation and *shirk* by ones own soul.

cians and fortune tellers. It is for this reason that it is necessary to differentiate the conditions that arise from faith, the conditions that arise from states of the soul, and the conditions that arise by way of the devils.

The fourth and last category of people are the adherents to *tawḥīd*, those who make their religions sincerely for Allāh and hence worship only Him and put their *tawakkul* in Him alone.

When a person in difficulty says, 'None has the right to be worshipped save You' it is possible that he only have in his mind one of the two categories of *tawḥīd*, but whoever meets with the favour of Allāh will bring to mind both categories. When a person is in difficulty his primary concern is to remove the harm and promote the good, so when he says, 'None has the right to be worshipped save You' his primary intention could only be that none removes harm save You and none bestows grace save You. Such a person has only fulfilled the dictates of *Tawḥīd ar-Rubūbiyyah* along with asking of Him and putting his *tawakkul* in Him, but *Tawḥīd al-Ilāhiyyah* could be absent - i.e. worshipping Him alone and worship of Him cannot come about except by obeying Him and His Messenger. Whoever brings this fact to mind as well when he is saying, 'None has the right to be worshipped save You' such a person is one who is truly worshipping Allāh and truly putting his *tawakkul* in Him, he is also implementing His saying,

فَٱعْبُدْهُ وَتَوَكَّلْ عَلَيْهِ

«So worship Him and put your trust in Him»
[*Hūd* (11): 123]

عَلَيْهِ تَوَكَّلْتُ وَإِلَيْهِ أُنِيبُ ﴿٨٨﴾

«'...I have my trust in Him and I turn to Him...'»

[*Hūd* (11): 88]

وَٱذۡكُرِ ٱسۡمَ رَبِّكَ وَتَبَتَّلۡ إِلَيۡهِ تَبۡتِيلٗا ٨
رَّبُّ ٱلۡمَشۡرِقِ وَٱلۡمَغۡرِبِ لَآ إِلَٰهَ إِلَّا هُوَ فَٱتَّخِذۡهُ وَكِيلٗا ٩

«Remember the Name of your Lord and devote yourself completely to Him. Lord of the East and West - there is none worthy of worship save Him - so take Him as your Guardian«»

[*al-Muzzammil* (73): 8-9]

Moreover if his object of desire is something prohibited, he is sinful, if his object of desire is something permissible, not desiring that this object aid him in someway in the worship of Allāh, he is neither sinful nor rewarded, if his aim is that this object aid him in the worship of Allāh, he is rewarded.

[2.11 The Messenger-Servant and Prophet-King]

This is what distinguishes the Messenger-Servant from the Prophet-King. Our Prophet, Muḥammad, was given the choice between being one or the other and chose to be a Messenger-Servant. The Messenger-Servant is one who only does that which he is commanded, hence everything he does is worship of Allāh;[44] He is a

[44] as opposed to the Prophet-King who is allowed to dispense with some affairs as he wills, Allāh says about such a Prophet-King, Solomon,

فَسَخَّرۡنَا لَهُ ٱلرِّيحَ تَجۡرِي بِأَمۡرِهِۦ رُخَآءً حَيۡثُ أَصَابَ ٣٦ وَٱلشَّيَٰطِينَ
كُلَّ بَنَّآءٖ وَغَوَّاصٖ ٣٧ وَءَاخَرِينَ مُقَرَّنِينَ فِي ٱلۡأَصۡفَادِ ٣٨ هَٰذَا
عَطَآؤُنَا فَٱمۡنُنۡ أَوۡ أَمۡسِكۡ بِغَيۡرِ حِسَابٖ ٣٩

=

pure servant, dispensing the order of the One who sent him as is established in Ṣaḥīḥ al-Bukhārī that he said,

> By Allāh, I do not grant anybody anything nor prevent anybody from anything. I am only a distributor, I place things where I am ordered.[45]

Meaning, 'I do not give except where I am ordered to give and I do not prevent except where I am ordered to prevent, I only obey Allāh in this' and he would apportion charity and war booty accordingly. This is the reason why, when property and wealth is mentioned adjoined to Allāh and His Messenger, the reference is to that which should be spent in the obedience of Allāh and His Messenger[46] and

---

=

> «...so We subjected to him the wind blowing gently by his command wherever he directed, and also the devils [of jinn] - every builder and diver and others bound together in shackles. [We said], 'This is Our gift, so grant or withhold without account»
>
> [*Ṣād* (38): 36-39],

'meaning give as you wish and withhold as you wish, either way you will not be judged. The Prophet-King does what Allāh has obligated upon him and leaves what Allāh has prohibited, and is free to act as he wills with regards the worldly authority and wealth granted him without incurring any sin. However the Servant-Messenger does not give to anyone or withhold from anyone, except by the order of his Lord...as such all his actions constitute worship of Allāh, Exalted is He' - *al-Furqān* [p. 92]

[45] A similar wording to this is recorded by Bukhārī [#3117] and Abū Dāwūd [#2929]

[46] The author, *al-Furqān* [p. 92] says, 'The most correct opinion of the scholars is that such property should be distributed in the way loved by Allāh and His Messenger as dictated by the *ijtihād* of the Muslim leader. This is the chosen opinion of Mālik and others from the *Salaf* and has also been mentioned in one report from Aḥmad. It is also said that this property should be distributed amongst the

=

it does not mean that this property actually belongs to the Messenger as thought by a group of the legal jurists. Allāh, Exalted is He, says,

قُلِ ٱلْأَنفَالُ لِلَّهِ وَٱلرَّسُولِ

«Say, 'Booty belongs to Allāh and the Messenger'»
[*al-Anfāl* (8): 1]

وَٱعْلَمُوٓا۟ أَنَّمَا غَنِمْتُم مِّن شَىْءٍ فَأَنَّ لِلَّهِ خُمُسَهُۥ وَلِلرَّسُولِ
وَلِذِى ٱلْقُرْبَىٰ وَٱلْيَتَـٰمَىٰ وَٱلْمَسَـٰكِينِ وَٱبْنِ ٱلسَّبِيلِ إِن
كُنتُمْ ءَامَنتُم بِٱللَّهِ وَمَآ أَنزَلْنَا عَلَىٰ عَبْدِنَا

«Know that when you take any booty a fifth of it belongs to Allāh and to the Messenger, and to close relatives, orphans, the very poor and the travellers, if you have faith in Allāh and in what We sent down to Our servant»
[*al-Anfāl* (8): 41]

=
five categories as is the opinion of ash-Shāfi'ī and Aḥmad in his famous opinion or that it should be distributed amongst the three categories as is the opinion of Abū Ḥanīfah, may Allāh have mercy on them.'

The five categories referred to are: Allāh and His Messenger, the close relatives of the Messenger who are Banī Hāshim and Banī Muṭṭalib, the orphans, the needy and the wayfarers as per *al-Anfāl* (8): 41. The three categories referred to are the orphans, the needy and the wayfarer.

وَمَآ أَفَآءَ ٱللَّهُ
عَلَىٰ رَسُولِهِۦ مِنۡهُمۡ فَمَآ أَوۡجَفۡتُمۡ عَلَيۡهِ مِنۡ خَيۡلٖ وَلَا رِكَابٖ
وَلَٰكِنَّ ٱللَّهَ يُسَلِّطُ رُسُلَهُۥ عَلَىٰ مَن يَشَآءُۚ وَٱللَّهُ عَلَىٰ كُلِّ شَيۡءٖ
قَدِيرٞ ٦ مَّآ أَفَآءَ ٱللَّهُ عَلَىٰ رَسُولِهِۦ مِنۡ أَهۡلِ ٱلۡقُرَىٰ فَلِلَّهِ وَلِلرَّسُولِ
وَلِذِي ٱلۡقُرۡبَىٰ وَٱلۡيَتَٰمَىٰ وَٱلۡمَسَٰكِينِ وَٱبۡنِ ٱلسَّبِيلِ كَيۡ لَا يَكُونَ
دُولَةَۢ بَيۡنَ ٱلۡأَغۡنِيَآءِ مِنكُمۡۚ وَمَآ ءَاتَىٰكُمُ ٱلرَّسُولُ فَخُذُوهُ وَمَا
نَهَىٰكُمۡ عَنۡهُ فَٱنتَهُواْۚ وَٱتَّقُواْ ٱللَّهَۖ إِنَّ ٱللَّهَ شَدِيدُ ٱلۡعِقَابِ ٧

«Whatever booty from them Allāh has given to His Messenger - and you spurred on neither horse nor camel in its acquisition, but Allāh gives power to His Messengers over anyone He wills, Allāh has power over all things - whatever booty Allāh gives to His Messenger from city dwellers belongs to Allāh and His Messenger, to the near relatives, and orphans, and the very poor and travellers, so that it does not become something that circulates amongst the rich among you...»

[*al-Ḥashr* (59): 6-7]

thereby mentioning the same for war booty as He did for the one-fifth allotment.[47]

---

[47] Here, the author digresses to discuss various fiqh issues to do with the war booty; this discussion is relegated to Appendix 4.

[2.12 *ar-Rubūbiyyah* and *al-Ilāhiyyah*]

The point of this discussion is to show the state of a servant, whose servitude is only for Allāh, who worships Him and asks Him for help and therefore lives His saying,

إِيَّاكَ نَعْبُدُ وَإِيَّاكَ نَسْتَعِينُ ﴿٥﴾

«You alone we worship and You alone we ask for help»

[*al-Fātiḥah* (1): 5]

who lives and actualises *Tawḥīd ar-Ilāhiyyah* and *Tawḥīd ar-Rubūbiyyah*. Now, even though *al-Ilāhiyyah* includes *ar-Rubūbiyyah* and *ar-Rubūbiyyah* necessitates *al-Ilāhiyyah*,[48] when mentioned together they take on their specific meanings, as in His sayings,

قُلْ أَعُوذُ بِرَبِّ ٱلنَّاسِ ﴿١﴾ مَلِكِ ٱلنَّاسِ ﴿٢﴾ إِلَٰهِ ٱلنَّاسِ ﴿٣﴾

«Say, 'I take refuge with the Lord of mankind, the King of mankind, the God of mankind...'»

[*an-Nās* (114): 1-3]

ٱلْحَمْدُ لِلَّهِ رَبِّ ٱلْعَٰلَمِينَ ﴿٢﴾

«All praise and thanks are due for Allāh the Lord of the worlds»

[*al-Fātiḥah* (1): 2]

[48] The belief that Allāh is the creator, nourisher, sustainer - the Lord - necessarily leads one to realise that He alone should be worshipped, hence *Rubūbiyyah* leads to *Ilāhiyyah*. The fact that one worships Alāh alone and nothing else is because he has come to believe that only Allāh is the creator, sustainer etc., hence *Ilāhiyyah* includes *Rubūbiyyah*.

thereby mentioning the name Allāh and Lord, for Allāh is the One who is worshipped and deserves to be worshipped and the Lord is the One who regulates the affairs of His servants and sustains them. This is why worship is linked to the name Allāh and asking linked to the name, Lord; this is because worship is the goal for which creation was created and hence *Ilāhiyyah* is the objective, *Rubūbiyyah* comprises within it the creation of the creation and hence deals with their point of commencement.[49] When the one praying says,

إِيَّاكَ نَعْبُدُ وَإِيَّاكَ نَسْتَعِينُ ﴿٥﴾

«You alone we worship and You alone we ask for help»
[*al-Fātiḥah* (1): 5]

he begins by mentioning the objective and then mentions the means to this which is the point of commencement - worship is the objective and asking for help is the means to attaining it. Because worship is linked to the name, Allāh, the legislated phrases of remembrance contain this Name, '*Allāhu Akbar, Allāhu Akbar*' for the call to prayer;

[49] As-Sa 'di, *Tafsīr* says, 'The Lord is the One Who nourishes and sustains the whole of the Creation, meaning everything besides Allāh, by the very fact of His creating them, His preparing for them all that they need and His favouring them with great blessings which if removed would also remove any possibility of the creation surviving. Therefore every blessing they possess is from Him, Exalted is He. His sustaining His creation is of two types: General and Specific. As for the general then it is His creating the Creation, granting them provisions and guiding them to that which would benefit them in order to have them survive in this world. As for the specific then it is His sustaining His friends with faith and making them conform to it, perfecting and completing it for them, repressing all that would make them turn away from it, bridling any hindering factors that may be set up between them and Him, and safe-guarding them from all evil. It is possible that the reason behind the fact that most of the supplications made by the Prophets employed the word 'Lord' was due to it carrying this meaning, for all of the things they desired through their supplications fell under His Specific Lordship.'

'I testify that none has the right to be worshipped save Allāh' for the testification to Islām; 'All pure and good works are for Allāh' in the *tashahhud*; and '*SubḥānAllāh, al-Ḥamdulillāh, Lā ilāha illAllāh, Allāhu Akbar.*'

As for request, frequently do we find that it is done with the name, Lord,

قَالَا رَبَّنَا ظَلَمْنَآ أَنفُسَنَا وَإِن لَّمْ تَغْفِرْ لَنَا وَتَرْحَمْنَا لَنَكُونَنَّ مِنَ الْخَٰسِرِينَ ﴿٢٣﴾

«'Our Lord! We have wronged ourselves. If You do not forgive us and have mercy on us, we will be among the lost'»

[*al-A'rāf* (7): 23]

قَالَ رَبِّ إِنِّيٓ أَعُوذُ بِكَ أَنْ أَسْـَٔلَكَ مَا لَيْسَ لِي بِهِۦ عِلْمٌ

«'My Lord! I take refuge with You from asking You for anything about which I have no knowledge...'»

[*Hūd* (11): 47]

قَالَ رَبِّ إِنِّي ظَلَمْتُ نَفْسِي فَٱغْفِرْ لِي

«'My Lord! I have wronged myself so forgive me'»

[*al-Qasas* (28): 16]

رَّبَّنَآ إِنِّيٓ أَسْكَنتُ مِن ذُرِّيَّتِي بِوَادٍ غَيْرِ ذِي زَرْعٍ عِندَ بَيْتِكَ ٱلْمُحَرَّمِ رَبَّنَا لِيُقِيمُوا۟ ٱلصَّلَوٰةَ

«'...Our Lord! I have settled my offspring by Your Sacred House in an uncultivated valley. Our Lord! Let them establish the prayer...'»

[*Ibrāhīm* (14): 37]

وَإِذْ يَرْفَعُ إِبْرَٰهِـۧمُ ٱلْقَوَاعِدَ مِنَ ٱلْبَيْتِ وَإِسْمَٰعِيلُ رَبَّنَا تَقَبَّلْ مِنَّآ ۖ إِنَّكَ أَنتَ ٱلسَّمِيعُ ٱلْعَلِيمُ ﴿١٢٧﴾

«'...Our Lord! Accept this from us! You are the All-Hearing, the All-Knowing...'»

[*al-Baqarah* (2): 127]

رَبَّنَآ ءَاتِنَا فِى ٱلدُّنْيَا حَسَنَةً وَفِى ٱلْـَٔاخِرَةِ حَسَنَةً وَقِنَا عَذَابَ ٱلنَّارِ ﴿٢٠١﴾

«'Our Lord! Give us good in this world and good in the Hereafter and safeguard us from the punishment of the Fire'»

[*al-Baqarah* (2): 201]

It is reported that Mālik said, 'I dislike that a person say while supplicating, "O My Master! O My Master! O Ḥannān! O Ḥannān!" Rather he should supplicate as the Prophets supplicated, "Our Lord! Our Lord!" ' Recorded by al-'Utbī, *al-'Utbiyyah.* Allāh, Exalted is He, says concerning those bestowed depth of understanding,

ٱلَّذِينَ يَذْكُرُونَ ٱللَّهَ قِيَـٰمًا وَقُعُودًا وَعَلَىٰ جُنُوبِهِمْ وَيَتَفَكَّرُونَ فِى خَلْقِ ٱلسَّمَـٰوَٰتِ وَٱلْأَرْضِ رَبَّنَا مَا خَلَقْتَ هَـٰذَا بَـٰطِلًا سُبْحَـٰنَكَ فَقِنَا عَذَابَ ٱلنَّارِ ﴿١٩١﴾

«...those who remember Allāh standing, sitting and lying on their sides, and reflect on the creation of the heavens and the earth: 'Our Lord! You have not created this for nothing. Glory be to You! Safeguard us from the punishment of the Fire...'»

[*Āli 'Imrān* (3): 191]

So when a servant wishes to ask, it is befitting that he ask employing the name, 'Lord', however were he to employ the name, 'Allāh' because this name includes within its boundaries the name, 'Lord', this is good. When a servant wishes to worship, the name 'Allāh' is more befitting to be used. When one begins by praising Allāh, he should mention the name, 'Allāh' and when he wishes to supplicate, he should mention the name, 'Lord'; this is why Yūnus said,

لَّآ إِلَٰهَ إِلَّآ أَنتَ سُبْحَٰنَكَ إِنِّي كُنتُ مِنَ ٱلظَّٰلِمِينَ ﴿٨٧﴾

«None has the right to be worshipped save You; glory be to You, far removed are You from any imperfection; I have been amongst the wrong-doers»

[*al-Anbiyā'* (21): 87]

while Ādam said,

قَالَا رَبَّنَا ظَلَمْنَآ أَنفُسَنَا وَإِن لَّمْ تَغْفِرْ لَنَا وَتَرْحَمْنَا لَنَكُونَنَّ مِنَ
ٱلْخَٰسِرِينَ ﴿٢٣﴾

«Our Lord! We have wronged ourselves. If You do not forgive us and have mercy on us, we will be among the lost»

[*al-A'rāf* (7): 23]

This is because Yūnus (*'alayhis salām*) left in a state of exasperation and Allāh, Exalted is He says,

فَٱصْبِرْ لِحُكْمِ رَبِّكَ وَلَا تَكُن كَصَاحِبِ ٱلْحُوتِ إِذْ نَادَىٰ وَهُوَ مَكْظُومٌ ﴿٤٨﴾

«So wait steadfastly for the judgment of your Lord and do not be like the Companion of the Fish»

[*al-Qalam* (68): 48]

فَٱلْتَقَمَهُ ٱلْحُوتُ وَهُوَ مُلِيمٌ ﴿١٤٢﴾

«Then the fish devoured him and he was to blame»
[*as-Ṣāffāt* (37): 142]

hence he committed that which he could be reprimanded for, therefore it was befitting for him to begin by praising his Lord and to acknowledge that none deserves to be worshipped save Him, implying that ones desires should not be submitted to for in doing so leads to the weakening of worshipping Allāh alone. It is reported that Yūnus (*ʿalayhis-salām*) felt remorse at the punishment being lifted from his people after he had threatened them with it, he feared that they would accuse him of lying and hence left them in a state of exasperation. It was because of this that he said,

لَّآ إِلَٰهَ إِلَّآ أَنتَ

«There is none worthy of worship save You...»
[*al-Anbiyāʾ* (21): 87]

these words absolve any besides Allāh of godship, be it by way of submitting to the desires of the soul or obeying an object of creation, this is why he went on to say,

سُبْحَٰنَكَ إِنِّي كُنتُ مِنَ ٱلظَّٰلِمِينَ ﴿٨٧﴾

«...glory be to You, far removed are You from any imperfection; I have been amongst the wrong-doers»
[*al-Anbiyāʾ* (21): 87]

the servant says these words on occasions when he assumes something to be other than what it is or desires something that is not good.

As for Ādam, he first confessed his sin by saying,

قَالَا رَبَّنَا ظَلَمْنَا أَنفُسَنَا وَإِن لَّمْ تَغْفِرْ لَنَا وَتَرْحَمْنَا لَنَكُونَنَّ مِنَ
الْخَاسِرِينَ ﴿٢٣﴾

«Our Lord! We have wronged ourselves. If You do not forgive us and have mercy on us, we will be among the lost»

[*al-A'rāf* (7): 23]

there was no one with Ādam who was competing with godship who would take from him the desire to do what Allāh ordered, rather he thought that Satan spoke the truth when he said,

وَقَاسَمَهُمَا إِنِّي لَكُمَا لَمِنَ النَّاصِحِينَ ﴿٢١﴾ فَدَلَّاهُمَا بِغُرُورٍ

«He swore to them, 'I am one of those who give good advice.' So he enticed them to do it by means of trickery»

[*al-A'rāf* (7): 21-22]

Satan deceived them and made out that he was a sincere advisor to them, therefore when they accepted this from him, it befitted their condition to say,

قَالَا رَبَّنَا ظَلَمْنَا أَنفُسَنَا وَإِن لَّمْ تَغْفِرْ لَنَا وَتَرْحَمْنَا لَنَكُونَنَّ مِنَ
الْخَاسِرِينَ ﴿٢٣﴾

«Our Lord! We have wronged ourselves. If You do not forgive us and have mercy on us, we will be among the lost»

[*al-A'rāf* (7): 23]

due to their negligence, not due to their submitting to their base desire or in pursuit of some temporal benefit that would contend with godship; these two were in need of having their knowledge and intent perfected; hence they confessed their need of their Lord besides whom none could fulfil their need.

So Dhū-n-Nūn confessed his negligence in fulfilling the duties of *Ilāhiyyah* by virtue of his leaving his people in a state of exasperation, in a state where he disliked the fact that his people were saved, hence desiring something that contended with his love of Allāh. When the servant says, 'None has the right to be worshipped save You' he is clearing his heart of worshipping his desires. It is reported,

> There is no god worshipped under the expanse of the heaven which is more severe in the sight of Allāh then desires that are submitted to.[50]

Therefore Yūnus (*'alayhis-salām*) perfected his *Ilāhiyyah* of Allāh and removed any intent to follow his desires, hence there was nothing left in his heart that would contend with the *Ilāhiyyah* of the Truth, indeed he was from amongst those who made the religion sincerely for Allāh, being one of the greatest chosen servants of Allāh.

It is possible that the likes of this situation occur to someone and after its passing, there remain in him some type of exasperation, anger to the decree, or some evil whispers concerning His wisdom and mercy. In this case the servant stands in need of absolving himself of two matters: corrupt intent and corrupt desires. He should know that wisdom and justice lies in what was decreed for him, not in what he thinks should have happened, hence his desires should

---

[50] At-Ṭabarānī [#7502] and ibn Abī 'Āṣim [#3] on the authority of Abū Umāmah. It is mawḍū' as ruled by ibn al-Jawzī and endorsed by adh-Dhahabī, *Tartīb al-Mawḍū'āt* [#956] and al-Albānī; al-Haythamī [1/188] said that its isnād contains a matrūk narrator.

be compliant to the order of Allāh such that he ends in a state that feels no opposition to His order,

فَلَا وَرَبِّكَ لَا يُؤْمِنُونَ
حَتَّىٰ يُحَكِّمُوكَ فِيمَا شَجَرَ بَيْنَهُمْ ثُمَّ لَا يَجِدُوا
فِيٓ أَنفُسِهِمْ حَرَجًا مِّمَّا قَضَيْتَ وَيُسَلِّمُوا تَسْلِيمًا ﴿٦٥﴾

«No, by your Lord, they are not believers until they make you their judge in the disputes that break out between them, and then find no resistance within themselves to what you decide and submit themselves completely»
[*an-Nisā'* (4): 65]

It is reported that the Prophet (ﷺ) said,

> By the One in whose hand is my soul, none of you believes until his very desire complies to what I have brought.

Reported by Abū Ḥātim in his Ṣaḥīḥ.[51]

In the Ṣaḥīḥ it is recorded that 'Umar said, 'O Messenger of Allāh! By Allāh you are more beloved to me than myself' to which he (ﷺ) said,

Now O 'Umar![52]

In the Ṣaḥīḥ it is recorded that he (ﷺ) said,

---

[51] Ibn Abī 'Āṣim [#15] and ad-Daylamī [#7960] with a ḍa'īf isnād as ruled by ibn Rajab, *Jāmi'* [#41].

[52] Bukhārī [#3694, 6264, 6632] and Abū Dāwūd [#2942]

> None of you believes until I am more beloved to him than his father, son and the whole of mankind.[53]

Allāh, Exalted is He, says,

قُلْ إِن
كَانَ ءَابَآؤُكُمْ وَأَبْنَآؤُكُمْ وَإِخْوَٰنُكُمْ وَأَزْوَٰجُكُمْ وَعَشِيرَتُكُمْ
وَأَمْوَٰلٌ ٱقْتَرَفْتُمُوهَا وَتِجَٰرَةٌ تَخْشَوْنَ كَسَادَهَا وَمَسَٰكِنُ
تَرْضَوْنَهَآ أَحَبَّ إِلَيْكُم مِّنَ ٱللَّهِ وَرَسُولِهِۦ وَجِهَادٍ
فِى سَبِيلِهِۦ فَتَرَبَّصُوا۟ حَتَّىٰ يَأْتِىَ ٱللَّهُ بِأَمْرِهِۦ ۗ وَٱللَّهُ لَا يَهْدِى
ٱلْقَوْمَ ٱلْفَٰسِقِينَ ﴿٢٤﴾

> «Say, 'If your fathers, or your sons, or your brothers, or your wives, or your tribe, or any wealth you have acquired, or any business you fear may slump, or any house which pleases you, are dearer to you that Allāh and His Messenger and doing *Jihād* in His Way, then wait until Allāh brings about His command...'»
>
> [*at-Tawbah* (9): 24]

So if *Īmān* is not attained except through the servant taking the Messenger (ﷺ) as judge and fully accepting his judgment, that his desire comply to what he has brought, that the Messenger and *Jihād* take precedence over the love he has for himself, his property and family, what then would one say with respect to Allāh?!

Therefore whoever sees a people who he thinks deserve to be punished, but Allāh forgives them and shows mercy to them, and he finds a dislike for this, this is due to one of two reasons: his desire

[53] Bukhārī [#15] and Muslim [#44]

opposes the order of Allāh or his presumption opposes the knowledge of Allāh and Allāh is All-Knowing, All-Wise. When you truly come to know that He is the All-Knowing, the All-Wise, all causes for dislike dissolve and disappear. As for those matters that He has ordered us to dislike such as disbelief, sin, and transgression; we are required to obey Him in this. But these matters are not like his lifting the punishment from a people for this is an action of His that we cannot dislike; instead we are required to like it. For a person to dislike such matters is to follow a desire that contends with *Ilāhiyyah*, in such a case the servant must complete his *tawḥīd* by saying, 'None has the right to be worshipped save You.' It is upon us to love what He loves, to be content with what He is pleased with, to order what He orders, and prohibit what He prohibits. So for example if He loves those who repent and those who purify themselves, it is upon us to love them as well.

[2.13 The Infallibility of Prophets]

This discussion is centred on the following principle: the Prophets (*'alayhim-salām*) are infallible when it comes to them conveying the message from Allāh, Exalted is He, by agreement of the Muslim nation. This is why it is obligatory to have *Imān* in everything they brought,

قُولُوٓاْ ءَامَنَّا بِٱللَّهِ وَمَآ
أُنزِلَ إِلَيۡنَا وَمَآ أُنزِلَ إِلَىٰٓ إِبۡرَٰهِـۧمَ وَإِسۡمَٰعِيلَ وَإِسۡحَٰقَ وَيَعۡقُوبَ
وَٱلۡأَسۡبَاطِ وَمَآ أُوتِيَ مُوسَىٰ وَعِيسَىٰ وَمَآ أُوتِيَ ٱلنَّبِيُّونَ
مِن رَّبِّهِمۡ لَا نُفَرِّقُ بَيۡنَ أَحَدٖ مِّنۡهُمۡ وَنَحۡنُ لَهُۥ مُسۡلِمُونَ ١٣٦
فَإِنۡ ءَامَنُواْ بِمِثۡلِ مَآ ءَامَنتُم بِهِۦ فَقَدِ ٱهۡتَدَواْۖ وَّإِن تَوَلَّوۡاْ فَإِنَّمَا
هُمۡ فِي شِقَاقٖۖ فَسَيَكۡفِيكَهُمُ ٱللَّهُۚ وَهُوَ ٱلسَّمِيعُ ٱلۡعَلِيمُ

«Say, 'We have faith in Allāh and what was sent down to us and what was sent down to Ibrāhīm, Ismā'īl, Ya'qūb and the Tribes, and what was given to Mūsā and 'Īsā, and what all the Prophets were given by their Lord. We do not differentiate between any of them and we are Muslims submitted to Him.' So if they believe as you believe, then they are guided, but if they turn away, they are entrenched in hostility. Allāh will be enough for you against them, He is the All-Hearing, the All-Knowing»

[*al-Baqarah* (2): 136-137]

وَلَٰكِنَّ
ٱلْبِرَّ مَنْ ءَامَنَ بِٱللَّهِ وَٱلْيَوْمِ ٱلْءَاخِرِ وَٱلْمَلَٰٓئِكَةِ وَٱلْكِتَٰبِ
وَٱلنَّبِيِّـۧنَ

«...rather, those with true devoutness are those who have faith in Allāh and the Last Day, the Angels, the Book and the Prophets...»

[*al-Baqarah* (2): 177]

ءَامَنَ ٱلرَّسُولُ بِمَآ أُنزِلَ
إِلَيْهِ مِن رَّبِّهِۦ وَٱلْمُؤْمِنُونَ ۚ كُلٌّ ءَامَنَ بِٱللَّهِ وَمَلَٰٓئِكَتِهِۦ وَكُتُبِهِۦ
وَرُسُلِهِۦ لَا نُفَرِّقُ بَيْنَ أَحَدٍ مِّن رُّسُلِهِۦ ۚ

«The Messenger has faith in what has been revealed to him from his Lord, and so do the believers. Each one has faith in Allāh, His Angels, His Books and His Messengers. We do not differentiate between any of His Messengers»

[*al-Baqarah* (2): 285]

Non-prophets are not infallible, even if they be the *Awliyā'* of Allāh;

it is for this reason that whoever curses the Prophets is killed by agreement of the Legal Jurists, but this is not the case with cursing others.

This infallibility of the Prophets is what allows the purpose of prophethood and messengership to be fulfilled. The Prophet is one who informs about Allāh and the Messenger is one whom Allāh has sent, hence every Messenger is a Prophet but not every Prophet is a Messenger and they are infallible in what they convey from Allāh.[54]

As for their infallibility in matters other than conveying the message, the people differ about this: is their infallibility in these matters established via the intellect or via the revelation? Could they commit major or minor sins, if so any or just some? Is it that they are infallible from endorsing sins but not from committing them? Are they infallible only in their conveyance of the revelation? Were they preserved from disbelief and sins before they were commissioned? All of these are discussed in detail in other places.

The opinion of the majority, in conformity to what is reported from the *Salaf*, is that they can never endorse sin.[55] They refuted the claims of those who stated that it was possible that they endorse sin. The evidences presented by those who propound [the absolute] infallibility of the Prophets, when considered carefully, only prove this opinion [held by the majority], and not theirs. Moreover, none of

---

[54] Here the author digresses to discuss some sub-issues related to infallibility; this discussion has been relegated to Appendix 5.

[55] The author, *Radd ʿalā al-Bakrī* [2/622] said, 'People have two opinions with regards the possibility of Prophets committing sins. The *Salaf* and the majority were of the opinion that this was possible but it was impossible for them to endorse sin. Many people were of the opinion that it was not possible for them to commit sin at all.'

the evidences presented by those who state that they could endorse sin actually go to prove their case.

Those who say that they were [absolutely] infallible depend upon the fact that it is legislated to follow them and this is not permissible unless their actions be free of sin. However, it is known that following them is only legislated in those matters they endorsed, not in matters they prohibited and later retracted, just as the command and prohibition is only to be obeyed when it is not abrogated; it is not permissible to consider the abrogated commands and prohibitions to be obligatory or prohibited let alone to make it obligatory to follow them. They also state that committing sins negates perfection, or the committing of sin is much more serious and vile when it arises from one who has been greatly blessed, or that sins lead to aversion of that person and other similar logical arguments. But all of this holds true only if sins are persisted in and not retracted, Allāh accepts sincere repentance and by virtue of it raises the ranks of the one who does it. Some of the *Salaf* said, 'Dāwūd (*'alayhis-salām*) was better after his repentance than he was before his sin,' others said, 'If repentance was not the most beloved thing to Him, he would not have tested the best of creation with sins.'

[2.14 Repentance]

The ḥadīth of repentance is established in the Ṣiḥāḥ,

> Allāh shows more joy at the repentance of His servant than a man who encamps at a dangerous place, with him is his riding beast carrying his food and drink. He rests his head and falls asleep for a short while and awakes to find his animal missing, [he searches for it] until he is very thirsty and hungry and decides to go back to his place where he once again falls asleep. When he awakes

the second time he finds his animal standing besides him.[56]

Allāh, Exalted is He, says,

إِنَّ ٱللَّهَ يُحِبُّ ٱلتَّوَّٰبِينَ وَيُحِبُّ ٱلْمُتَطَهِّرِينَ ﴿٢٢٢﴾

«Allāh loves those who turn in repentance and loves those who purify themselves»

[*al-Baqarah* (2): 222]

إِلَّا مَن تَابَ وَءَامَنَ وَعَمِلَ عَمَلًا صَٰلِحًا
فَأُوْلَٰٓئِكَ يُبَدِّلُ ٱللَّهُ سَيِّـَٔاتِهِمْ حَسَنَٰتٍ ۗ وَكَانَ ٱللَّهُ غَفُورًا
رَّحِيمًا ﴿٧٠﴾

«...except for those who turn in repentance and have faith and work righteous deeds, Allāh will transfer the wrong actions of such people into good - Allāh is Ever-Forgiving, Most Merciful»

[*al-Furqān* (25): 70]

There is a ḥadīth in the Ṣaḥīḥ which mentions that Allāh would present the minor sins of a person to him on the Day of Judgment and withhold the major sins, and he would admit to them, all the while fearing that his major sins were soon to be presented, upon which Allāh would say,

"I have forgiven you and altered every evil deed to a good deed." He will say, 'But my Lord! I have committed sins that I have not yet seen!'[57]

---

[56] Bukhārī [#6309] and Muslim [#2747]

[57] Muslim [#190] and at-Tirmidhī [#2596]

meaning that when he saw his bad deeds being altered, he then wished to see his major sins, which he was previously in fear of, so that they too could be altered to good deeds. It is known that his state after this alteration is much greater than the state he would have been in had he not committed the sins and had there been no alteration.

A group of the *Salaf*, amongst whom was Sa'īd bin Jubair, said, 'A servant could perform a good deed and enter Hell on account of it, and a servant could commit a sin and enter Paradise on account of it. The first performed the good deed and became boastful and exultant to such an extent that he entered Hell, the second committed the sin and remained in fear of it and persisted in asking for forgiveness until he entered Paradise.' Allāh, Exalted is He, says,

إِنَّا عَرَضْنَا ٱلْأَمَانَةَ عَلَى ٱلسَّمَٰوَٰتِ
وَٱلْأَرْضِ وَٱلْجِبَالِ فَأَبَيْنَ أَن يَحْمِلْنَهَا وَأَشْفَقْنَ مِنْهَا وَحَمَلَهَا
ٱلْإِنسَٰنُ ۖ إِنَّهُۥ كَانَ ظَلُومًا جَهُولًا ﴿٧٢﴾ لِّيُعَذِّبَ ٱللَّهُ ٱلْمُنَٰفِقِينَ
وَٱلْمُنَٰفِقَٰتِ وَٱلْمُشْرِكِينَ وَٱلْمُشْرِكَٰتِ وَيَتُوبَ ٱللَّهُ
عَلَى ٱلْمُؤْمِنِينَ وَٱلْمُؤْمِنَٰتِ ۗ وَكَانَ ٱللَّهُ غَفُورًا رَّحِيمًا ﴿٧٣﴾

«We offered the trust to the heavens and the earth and the mountains but they refused to take it on and shrank from it. But man took it on, he is indeed wrongdoing and ignorant. This was so that Allāh might punish the men and women of the hypocrites and the men and women of the polytheists, and turn towards the men and women of the believers. Allāh is Ever-Forgiving, Most Merciful»
[*al-Aḥzāb* (33): 72-73]

The objective of every person is to be amongst those believers, male and female, whom Allāh has forgiven.

This opinion[58] is proven by countless texts from the Book, the authentic Sunnah and the Books that were revealed before the Qur'ān. Those who reject this opinion interpret these texts with interpretations that resemble those of the Jahmiyyah[59], Qadariyyah[60] and Dahriyyah[61] to the texts concerning the Names and Attributes of Allāh, the texts concerning the decree, and the texts concerning the resurrection. They are of the same nature as the interpretations of the Qarāmiṭa[62], known by necessity to be false. They amount to distorting words from their correct context, it is even possible that some of those who do this, even though they intend to honour and exalt the Prophets, fall into denial or disbelief of them.

Moreover, the infallibility which is proven by the texts of the Legal Law, the intellect, and consensus, is their infallibility in conveying the message. This is of no benefit to them as they do not accept the meanings of what the Prophets conveyed, instead they distort the texts or they end up being like the illiterate who know nothing of the Book except their own assumptions.

---

[58] i.e. that Prophets can commit sins.

[59] An early sect that denied the Names and Attributes of Allāh, followers of Jahm bin Ṣafwān.

[60] An early sect that denied *qadr*, or divine decree, stating instead the man has a complete free will.

[61] A sect that denied the reality of the Resurrection, Judgment, Paradise, and Hell.

[62] A sect, branching off from the Shī'a, that based itself around esoteric exegesis of the Qur'ān and Aḥādīth, stating that texts commanding prayer and zakāt etc. were all merely metaphors.

Allāh, Exalted is He, frequently mentions the repentance of the Prophets and their asking forgiveness. Ādam and his wife said,

قَالَا رَبَّنَا ظَلَمْنَآ أَنفُسَنَا وَإِن لَّمْ تَغْفِرْ لَنَا وَتَرْحَمْنَا لَنَكُونَنَّ مِنَ ٱلْخَٰسِرِينَ ﴿٢٣﴾

«Our Lord! We have wronged ourselves. If You do not forgive us and have mercy on us, we will be among the lost»

[*al-A'rāf* (7): 23]

Nūḥ said,

قَالَ رَبِّ إِنِّىٓ أَعُوذُ بِكَ أَنْ أَسْـَٔلَكَ مَا لَيْسَ لِى بِهِۦ عِلْمٌ ۖ وَإِلَّا تَغْفِرْ لِى وَتَرْحَمْنِىٓ أَكُن مِّنَ ٱلْخَٰسِرِينَ ﴿٤٧﴾

«My Lord! I take refuge with You from asking You for anything about which I have no knowledge. If You do not forgive me and have mercy on me, I will be among the lost»

[*Hūd* (11): 47]

al-Khalīl said,

رَبَّنَا ٱغْفِرْ لِى وَلِوَٰلِدَىَّ وَلِلْمُؤْمِنِينَ يَوْمَ يَقُومُ ٱلْحِسَابُ ﴿٤١﴾

«Our Lord! Forgive me and my parents and the believers on the Day the Reckoning takes place»

[*Ibrāhīm* (14): 41]

وَٱلَّذِىٓ أَطْمَعُ أَن يَغْفِرَ لِى خَطِيٓـَٔتِى يَوْمَ ٱلدِّينِ

«...He who I sincerely hope will forgive my mistakes on the Day of Reckoning» [*ash-Shu'arā'* (26): 82]

Mūsā said,

أَنتَ وَلِيُّنَا فَٱغۡفِرۡ لَنَا وَٱرۡحَمۡنَاۖ وَأَنتَ خَيۡرُ ٱلۡغَٰفِرِينَ ﴿١٥٥﴾
وَٱكۡتُبۡ لَنَا فِي هَٰذِهِ ٱلدُّنۡيَا حَسَنَةٗ وَفِي ٱلۡأٓخِرَةِ إِنَّا
هُدۡنَآ إِلَيۡكَۚ

«...You are our protector so forgive us and have mercy on us. You are the Best of Forgivers. Prescribe for us good in this world and the Hereafter, we have truly turned to You»

[*al-A'rāf* (7): 155-156]

قَالَ رَبِّ إِنِّي ظَلَمۡتُ نَفۡسِي فَٱغۡفِرۡ لِي فَغَفَرَ لَهُۥٓۚ إِنَّهُۥ هُوَ
ٱلۡغَفُورُ ٱلرَّحِيمُ ﴿١٦﴾

«My Lord! I have wronged myself so forgive me...»

[*al-Qaṣaṣ* (28): 16]

فَلَمَّآ أَفَاقَ
قَالَ سُبۡحَٰنَكَ تُبۡتُ إِلَيۡكَ وَأَنَا۠ أَوَّلُ ٱلۡمُؤۡمِنِينَ ﴿١٤٣﴾

«When he regained consciousness he said, 'Glory be to You! I turn to you in repentance and I am the first of the believers'»

[*al-A'rāf* (7): 143]

Allāh, Exalted is He, informs us of Dāwūd that he,

فَٱسۡتَغۡفَرَ رَبَّهُۥ وَخَرَّۤ رَاكِعٗاۤ وَأَنَابَ

> «Begged forgiveness from his Lord and fell down prone, prostrating, and repented»
>
> [*Ṣād* (38): 24-25]

Sulaymān said,

قَالَ رَبِّ ٱغْفِرْ
لِى وَهَبْ لِى مُلْكًا لَّا يَنۢبَغِى لِأَحَدٍ مِّنۢ بَعْدِىٓ ۖ إِنَّكَ أَنتَ ٱلْوَهَّابُ ﴿٣٥﴾

> «My Lord! Forgive me and give me a kingdom the like of which will never be granted to anyone after me. Truly You are the Ever-Giving»
>
> [*Ṣād* (38): 35]

As for Yūsuf, the sincerely truthful, Allāh did not mention any sin of his, and this is why no mention is made of repentance from him, instead He said,

كَذَٰلِكَ لِنَصْرِفَ عَنْهُ ٱلسُّوٓءَ
وَٱلْفَحْشَآءَ ۚ إِنَّهُۥ مِنْ عِبَادِنَا ٱلْمُخْلَصِينَ ﴿٢٤﴾

> «That happened so We might avert from him all evil and lust. He was Our chosen servant»
>
> [*Yūsuf* (12): 24]

So He informed us that he turned evil and indecency away from him and this proves that he committed neither. As for His saying,

وَلَقَدْ هَمَّتْ بِهِۦ ۖ وَهَمَّ بِهَا لَوْلَآ أَن رَّءَا بُرْهَٰنَ رَبِّهِۦ ۚ

> «She wanted him and he would have wanted her had he not seen the Clear Proof of his Lord»
>
> [*Yūsuf* (12): 24]

The word 'desire' (*hamm*) is a generic noun (*ism jins*) and it falls into two categories as Imām Aḥmad said, 'Desire is of two types: a desire that is merely thoughts, and a desire that one commits and persists in.' It is established in the *Ṣaḥīḥ* that the Prophet (ﷺ) said,

> When a servant desires to commit a sin, nothing is recorded against him, if he then leaves that sin for the sake of Allāh, one good deed is recorded for him, if he commits that sin, one sin is recorded for him, if he leaves that sin, but not for the sake of Allāh, no sin or reward is recorded for him.[63]

So Yūsuf (*ʿalayhis-salām*) had a desire which he abandoned for the sake of Allāh and this is why Allāh turned him away from evil and indecency by virtue of his sincerity. Hence, this 'turning away' occurs when the cause for committing sin is present, i.e. desire, yet contending with this is one's sincerity to Allāh. So Yūsuf (*ʿalayhis-salām*) did nothing except good deeds for which he would be rewarded for, Allāh, Exalted is He, says,

إِنَّ ٱلَّذِينَ ٱتَّقَوْاْ إِذَا مَسَّهُمْ طَيْفٌ مِّنَ ٱلشَّيْطَٰنِ تَذَكَّرُواْ فَإِذَا هُم مُّبْصِرُونَ ﴿٢٠١﴾

> «As for those who have *taqwā*, when they are bothered by visitors from Satan, they remember and immediately see clearly»
>
> [*al-Aʿrāf* (7): 201]

As for what is reported that he untied his lower garment and they both got into the position for intercourse at which point he saw the image of Yāʿqūb biting his hand, and the likes of these reports, none of them have been told us by Allāh or His Messenger. Hence

[63] The author, may Allāh have mercy upon him, has quoted the ḥadīth in meaning. It is recorded by Bukhārī [#7501] and Muslim [#128-130]

such reports were taken by the Muslims from the Jews who are the greatest liars against the Prophets and the most severe in accusing them.

As for His saying,

﴿ وَمَآ أُبَرِّئُ نَفْسِىٓ ۚ إِنَّ ٱلنَّفْسَ لَأَمَّارَةٌۢ بِٱلسُّوٓءِ إِلَّا مَا رَحِمَ رَبِّىٓ ۚ إِنَّ رَبِّى غَفُورٌ رَّحِيمٌ ﴿٥٣﴾

«I do not say that my self was free from blame, the self indeed commands to evil acts - except for those my Lord has mercy on»

[*Yūsuf* (12): 53]

these are the words of the wife of al-ʿAzīz as is clearly proven by the Qur'ān,

وَقَالَ ٱلْمَلِكُ ٱئْتُونِى بِهِۦ ۖ فَلَمَّا جَآءَهُ ٱلرَّسُولُ قَالَ ٱرْجِعْ إِلَىٰ رَبِّكَ فَسْـَٔلْهُ مَا بَالُ ٱلنِّسْوَةِ ٱلَّٰتِى قَطَّعْنَ أَيْدِيَهُنَّ ۚ إِنَّ رَبِّى بِكَيْدِهِنَّ عَلِيمٌ ﴿٥٠﴾ قَالَ مَا خَطْبُكُنَّ إِذْ رَٰوَدتُّنَّ يُوسُفَ عَن نَّفْسِهِۦ ۚ قُلْنَ حَٰشَ لِلَّهِ مَا عَلِمْنَا عَلَيْهِ مِن سُوٓءٍ ۚ قَالَتِ ٱمْرَأَتُ ٱلْعَزِيزِ ٱلْـَٰٔنَ حَصْحَصَ ٱلْحَقُّ أَنَا۠ رَٰوَدتُّهُۥ عَن نَّفْسِهِۦ وَإِنَّهُۥ لَمِنَ ٱلصَّٰدِقِينَ ﴿٥١﴾ ذَٰلِكَ لِيَعْلَمَ أَنِّى لَمْ أَخُنْهُ بِٱلْغَيْبِ وَأَنَّ ٱللَّهَ لَا يَهْدِى كَيْدَ ٱلْخَآئِنِينَ ﴿٥٢﴾ ۞ وَمَآ أُبَرِّئُ نَفْسِىٓ ۚ إِنَّ ٱلنَّفْسَ لَأَمَّارَةٌۢ بِٱلسُّوٓءِ إِلَّا مَا رَحِمَ رَبِّىٓ ۚ إِنَّ رَبِّى غَفُورٌ رَّحِيمٌ ﴿٥٣﴾

«The king said, 'Bring him to me straight away!' But when the envoy came to him, he said, 'Go back to your master and enquire of him what happened about the women who cut their hands. My Lord has knowledge of their cunning guile.' He said, 'What was this past affair of yours when you solicited Yūsuf?' Then they said, 'Allāh forbid! We know no bad of him.' The governor's wife then said, 'The truth has now emerged. Indeed I tried to seduce him then and he has simply told the honest truth. In this way he may know at last that I did not dishonour him behind his back and that Allāh most surely does not guide the deviousness of the dishonourable. I do not say that my self was free from blame, the self indeed commands to evil acts - except for those my Lord has mercy on'»

[*Yūsuf* (12): 50-53]

All of these are the words of the wife, for Yūsuf was still in prison at that time not yet having had an audience with the king, but in his absence his innocence was finally established upon which the king said,

وَقَالَ ٱلْمَلِكُ ٱئْتُونِي بِهِۦٓ أَسْتَخْلِصْهُ
لِنَفْسِيۖ فَلَمَّا كَلَّمَهُۥ قَالَ إِنَّكَ ٱلْيَوْمَ لَدَيْنَا مَكِينٌ أَمِينٌ ﴿٥٤﴾

«...'Bring him to me straight away so I may draw him very close to me.' When he spoke to him, he declared, 'Today you are trusted, established in our sight'»

[*Yūsuf* (12): 54]

Many exegetes mentioned these words[64] to be the words of Yūsuf, and some of them only mentioned this opinion. This opinion is totally false and has no evidence to support it, indeed the evidences prove the opposite. These matters have been detailed in other places.

The point of this discussion is to show that all that is contained in the story of Dhū-n-Nūn for which he could be censured for, is all forgiven, and furthermore, Allāh altered it all to good deeds and raised his ranks. He was in a much better state after coming out of the belly of the whale and his repentance than he was before. Allāh, Exalted is He, says,

فَٱصْبِرْ
لِحُكْمِ رَبِّكَ وَلَا تَكُن كَصَاحِبِ ٱلْحُوتِ إِذْ نَادَىٰ وَهُوَ مَكْظُومٌ ﴿٤٨﴾ لَّوْلَآ
أَن تَدَٰرَكَهُۥ نِعْمَةٌ مِّن رَّبِّهِۦ لَنُبِذَ بِٱلْعَرَآءِ وَهُوَ مَذْمُومٌ ﴿٤٩﴾ فَٱجْتَبَٰهُ رَبُّهُۥ
فَجَعَلَهُۥ مِنَ ٱلصَّٰلِحِينَ ﴿٥٠﴾

«So wait steadfastly for the judgment of your Lord and do not be like the Companion of the Fish when he called out in absolute despair. Had a blessing from his Lord not overtaken him, he would have been thrown up on the naked shore, for he was at fault. But his Lord chose him and made him one of the righteous»

[*al-Qalam* (68): 48-50]

This was different to his state when he was in the belly of the whale,

---

[64] i.e. the words of [*Yūsuf*: 53],

وَمَآ أُبَرِّئُ نَفْسِىٓ ۚ

«I do not say that my self was to blame...»

فَٱلْتَقَمَهُ ٱلْحُوتُ وَهُوَ مُلِيمٌ ﴿١٤٢﴾

«Then the fish devoured him and he was to blame»

[*as-Ṣāffāt* (37): 142]

So in this state he was blamed, but he was not in this state when taken out of the belly of the whale, hence his condition after saying,

لَّآ إِلَٰهَ إِلَّآ أَنتَ سُبْحَٰنَكَ إِنِّى كُنتُ مِنَ ٱلظَّٰلِمِينَ ﴿٨٧﴾

«None has the right to be worshipped save You; glory be to You, far removed are You from any imperfection; I have been amongst the wrong-doers»

[*al-Anbiyā'* (21): 87]

was better than his state before. What is taken into consideration is the perfection of the end state, not what may have occurred in the beginning. Actions are by their conclusions.

[2.15 Deeds are by their conclusion]

Allāh, Exalted is He, created man and took him out of the belly of his mother knowing nothing. Then He taught him and transferred him from a state of deficiency to a state of perfection, hence it is not permissible to judge the worth of man based on his initial state, rather on his final state. Yūnus (*'alayhis-salām*), and other Prophets, in their final states were in the most perfect of states.

It is from this perspective that those who thought the Angels better than the Prophets and righteous erred. They compared the perfection of the Angels with the initial stages of the righteous and their deficiencies, were they to have compared the two after the righteous entered Paradise and their having attained the pleasure of the All-Merciful and the removal of all defects, when they are in the state that,

وَٱلْمَلَٰٓئِكَةُ يَدْخُلُونَ عَلَيْهِم مِّن كُلِّ بَابٍ ﴿٢٣﴾ سَلَٰمٌ عَلَيْكُم بِمَا صَبَرْتُمْ فَنِعْمَ عُقْبَى ٱلدَّارِ

«Angels will enter in to welcome them from every gate: 'Peace be upon you because of your steadfastness! How wonderful is the Ultimate Abode!'»

[*al-Ra'd* (13): 23-24]

-were they to have made the comparison in this state the excellence of this state over the state of all other objects of creation would have been clear.

As for what some people presume, that one who is born into Islām and never leaves it is better than one who was a disbeliever and then accepted Islām, this is not correct. What is considered is the conclusion, whichever of the two has more *taqwā* of Allāh at the end is the better of them. It is known, for example, that the Forerunners from amongst the Muhājirūn and Anṣār - i.e. those who accepted Islām after having been disbelievers - are better than those who came after them who were born into Islām, be they of their own offspring or others. Indeed someone who has tasted evil and known it and then tastes good and knows it, could well discern the good better, love it more, and hate the evil more than those who have not tasted evil. Indeed the one who has known nothing save good could come across evil and not recognise it and either fall into it or not reject it with the same fervour as the one who has previously experienced it.

It is for this reason that 'Umar bin al-Khaṭṭāb said, 'Islām will only be loosened knot by knot by those who are born into Islām, never having known the *Jāhiliyyah*.' This is true, for the perfection of Islām comes about through enjoining the good and prohibiting the evil, this in turn is perfected through undertaking *Jihād* in His way. Whoever is born into goodness and does not know anything else could quite possibly not be aware of evil and its dire consequences whereas the one who has experienced evil would. Hence this person may not undertake the required *Jihād* whereas the one who knows would. This is why the Companions, may Allāh be pleased with them all, had greater *Īmān* and *Jihād* than those who came after them, because of their understanding both the good and evil, because of their complete love for the good and hatred of the evil, having experienced the excellence of Islām and the filth of disbelief. It is for this reason that the one who has experienced poverty and illness appreciates health, security, and sufficiency more than the one who has not, and works harder to preserve it. In this respect it is said,

Opposites bring out the beauty of their opposites

And,

By their opposites do things become clear

'Umar bin al-Khaṭṭāb, may Allāh be pleased with him, would say, 'I am not one who spreads corruption and neither does corruption deceive me.' The sound heart desires good and not evil and this can only fully come about by knowing both the good and evil, whoever does not know evil has an aspect of deficiency in him.

This does not mean that everyone who has experienced disbelief and sin is necessarily more knowledgeable of it or necessarily despises it more than one who has not. The doctor has more knowledge of disease than the one afflicted with it, the Prophets, may Allāh shower peace and blessings upon them, are doctors of religion and hence they are the most knowledgeable of people with regards what will correct or corrupt the hearts, even though they may not have experienced evil as the people have.

What is meant here is that are to be found people who have a great aversion to evil by virtue of their having experienced both evil and good that may not be found in others. The one who was a polytheist, a Jew or a Christian, and then accepted Islām could have more love and desire of Islām, and more hatred of disbelief than the one who does not know the reality of disbelief and Islām. This is because the former had previously lived in darkness, sin, doubts, and falsity whereas the latter is merely blindly following others in his praise of something or censure of something else.

For example, one who has experienced hunger followed by satiation, or illness followed by health, or fear followed by safety will be more desirous and appreciative of satiation, health, and safety than the one who has not. Likewise whoever enters the ranks of the People of innovation and sin followed by Allāh guiding him to sincerely repent from this and nourishing him with *Jihād* in His way, would explain the state of the innovators, boycott them, and strive against them more than the one who has not. Nu'aym bin Ḥammād al-Khuzā'ī, who used to be a Jahmī, said, 'I am harsh against them because I used to be one of them.'[65] Allāh, Exalted is He, says,

لِلَّذِينَ هَاجَرُوا۟ مِنۢ بَعْدِ مَا فُتِنُوا۟ ثُمَّ جَٰهَدُوا۟
وَصَبَرُوٓا۟ إِنَّ رَبَّكَ مِنۢ بَعْدِهَا لَغَفُورٌ رَّحِيمٌ ﴿١١٠﴾

«But to those who migrated after they were persecuted and then did *Jihād* and remained steadfast, to them your Lord is All-Forgiving, Most Merciful»

[*an-Naḥl* (16): 110]

[65] adh-Dhahabī, *Siyar* [10/597]

This verse was revealed concerning a group of the Companions who were put to trial by the polytheists with respect their religion, then Allāh turned towards them in forgiveness and they migrated to Allāh and His Messenger, performed *Jihād* and showed patience and constancy.[66]

'Umar bin al-Khaṭṭāb and Khālid bin al-Walīd, may Allāh be pleased with both, used to be from the most stringent of people in opposing Islām, yet when they accepted Islām they exceeded many of those who had accepted Islām before them. Indeed 'Umar bin al-Khaṭṭāb by virtue of his *Īmān*, sincerity, truth, knowledge, and insight was the most removed of the Companions from submitting to his desires, and the best of them save Abū Bakr, may Allāh be pleased with them all.

All of this, and other matters, go to show that consideration is to be taken with the conclusion, not the commencement.

[2.16 Allāh loves those who repent]

As regards what is mentioned in some of the Judeao-Christian reports that, 'Allāh said to Dāwūd, "As for your sin, I have forgiven it, but as for love, this will never return.' Even if this were authentic, it cannot be considered to be legislation for us for the religion of Muḥammad (ﷺ) comes with a repentance that was not meted out to those who came before us, it was for this reason that he said,

> I am the Prophet of mercy and I am the Prophet of repentance.[67]

[66] al-Wāḥidi, *Asbāb an-Nuzūl* [p. 282], *Rūḥ al-Ma'ānī* [7/340] and *al-Muḥarrar al-Wajīz* [3/425]

[67] at-Tirmidhī, *ash-Shamā'il* [#369] and Aḥmad [#23443, 23445] on the authority =

Through him, Allāh lifted many of the difficulties and constraints placed on those who came before us. Allāh, Exalted is He, said in His Book,

إِنَّ ٱللَّهَ يُحِبُّ ٱلتَّوَّٰبِينَ وَيُحِبُّ ٱلْمُتَطَهِّرِينَ ﴿٢٢٢﴾

«Allāh loves those who turn in repentance and loves those who purify themselves»

[*al-Baqarah* (2): 222]

He informs us that He shows more joy at the repentance of His servant than one who finds something he has lost that he had dire need of.[68] So if this is the joy and love that Allāh displays at repent-

=

of Ḥudhayfah.

Similar aḥādīth are recorded on the authority of Jubayr by Bukhārī and Muslim; and Abū Mūsā by Aḥmad [#19525, 19621, 19651]

It was declared ṣaḥīḥ by ibn Ḥibbān [#6315]; as-Suyūṭī [#2701] and al-Albānī, *Ṣaḥīḥ al-Jāmi'* [#1473]

[68] The author, *al-Istighfār* [p. 66] says, 'This is why it is said that repentance is a station that accompanies the servant throughout his entire life, and everyone is in need of it. The whole of creation must repent and repent continuously. Allāh, Exalted is He, says

إِنَّا عَرَضْنَا ٱلْأَمَانَةَ عَلَى ٱلسَّمَٰوَٰتِ
وَٱلْأَرْضِ وَٱلْجِبَالِ فَأَبَيْنَ أَن يَحْمِلْنَهَا وَأَشْفَقْنَ مِنْهَا وَحَمَلَهَا
ٱلْإِنسَٰنُ ۖ إِنَّهُۥ كَانَ ظَلُومًا جَهُولًا ﴿٧٢﴾ لِّيُعَذِّبَ ٱللَّهُ ٱلْمُنَٰفِقِينَ
وَٱلْمُنَٰفِقَٰتِ وَٱلْمُشْرِكِينَ وَٱلْمُشْرِكَٰتِ وَيَتُوبَ ٱللَّهُ
عَلَى ٱلْمُؤْمِنِينَ وَٱلْمُؤْمِنَٰتِ ۗ وَكَانَ ٱللَّهُ غَفُورًا رَّحِيمًا ﴿٧٣﴾

«Indeed We offered the trust to the heavens and the earth and the mountains, but they declined to bear it and feared it; but man [undertook to] bear it. Indeed he was unjust and ignorant. It was so that Allāh may punish the hypocrites, men and women, and the polytheists, men

=

ance, how can it be said that His love will not return?

وَهُوَ ٱلْغَفُورُ ٱلْوَدُودُ ﴿١٤﴾ ذُو ٱلْعَرْشِ ٱلْمَجِيدُ ﴿١٥﴾ فَعَّالٌ لِّمَا يُرِيدُ ﴿١٦﴾

«He is the Ever-Forgiving, the All-Loving, the Possessor of the Throne, the All-Glorious, the Doer of whatever He desires»

[*al-Burūj* (85): 14-16]

His love is in proportion to the efforts that the servant undertakes in trying to draw closer to Allāh after having repented. If the servant strives more after his repentance, the love that Allāh bestows him will be greater than what was bestowed him before, the opposite is also true; the recompense is of the same type as the action,

وَمَا رَبُّكَ بِظَلَّٰمٍ لِّلْعَبِيدِ ﴿٤٦﴾

«Your Lord does not wrong His servants»

[*Fuṣṣilat* (41): 46]

The Ṣaḥīḥ records that the Prophet (ﷺ) said,

=

and women, and that Allāh may accept repentance from the believers, men and women»

[*al-Aḥzāb* (33): 72-73]

The objective and fulfilment of every believer is repentance. Allāh, Exalted is He, says to the best of the Prophets (ﷺ) and to the best of creation after the Prophets,

لَّقَد تَّابَ ٱللَّهُ عَلَى
ٱلنَّبِيِّ وَٱلْمُهَٰجِرِينَ وَٱلْأَنصَارِ ٱلَّذِينَ ٱتَّبَعُوهُ فِى
سَاعَةِ ٱلْعُسْرَةِ مِنۢ بَعْدِ مَا كَادَ يَزِيغُ قُلُوبُ فَرِيقٍ

«Allāh has already forgiven the Prophet and the Muhājirūn and the Anṣār who followed in the hour of difficulty...»

[*at-Tawbah* (9): 117]

> Allāh says, 'Whosoever has mutual animosity with a friend (*Walī*) of Mine then I declare war on him. My servant does not draw close to Me with anything as he does by carrying out what I have made obligatory upon him. My servant continues to draw near to Me by performing optional deeds such that I love him. And when I love him, I am his hearing by which he hears, his sight by which he sees, his hand with which he strikes and his leg with which he walks. Were he to ask of Me, I would surely give him and were he to ask Me for refuge, I would surely grant it to him. I am never so hesitant to do something as I am to take the soul of my believing servant, he dislikes death and I Dislike to harm him but he must die.'[69]

It is known that the best of the *Awliyā'* after the Prophets are the Forerunners amongst the Muhājirūn and the Anṣār. The love that our Lord bestowed them after their having repented and accepted Islām was from the greatest of loves and each time they drew closer to Him through performing optional deeds, after having performed the obligatory deeds, this love increased. Allāh, Exalted is He, says,

عَسَى ٱللَّهُ أَن يَجْعَلَ
بَيْنَكُمْ وَبَيْنَ ٱلَّذِينَ عَادَيْتُم مِّنْهُم مَّوَدَّةً ۚ وَٱللَّهُ قَدِيرٌ ۚ وَٱللَّهُ غَفُورٌ رَّحِيمٌ

> «It may well be that Allāh will restore the love between you and those of them who are now your enemies. Allāh is All-Powerful. Allāh is Ever-Forgiving, Most Merciful»
> [*al-Mumtaḥinah* (60): 7]

This verse was revealed with regards the polytheists who opposed Allāh and His Messenger such as people amongst the Confederates

[69] Bukhārī [#6502] and ibn Ḥibbān [#347]

like Abū Sufyān bin Ḥarb[70], Abū Sufyān bin al-Ḥārith, al-Ḥārith bin Hishām, Suhail bin ʿAmr, ʿIkrimah bin Abū Jahl, Ṣafwān bin Umayyah and others. All of these were people who, after hating Allāh and His Messenger, came to love them in varying degrees, some more than others. It is established in the Ṣaḥīḥ that Umm Muʿāwiyah, Hind, the wife of Abū Sufyān, said,

> 'O Messenger of Allāh! By Allāh there was no family on the face of this earth that I wished to have disgraced more than yours, but today there is no family that I wish to be honoured more than yours. And the Messenger said something similar.'[71]

It is known that the love one believer feels for another follows on from their love of Allāh, Exalted is He. The most trustworthy and firm handholds of faith are to love for the sake of Allāh and to hate for the sake of Allāh.[72] Loving for the sake of Allāh is from the perfection of *tawḥīd* and and loving others alongside Allāh is *shirk*. Allāh, Exalted is He, says,

وَمِنَ
ٱلنَّاسِ مَن يَتَّخِذُ مِن دُونِ ٱللَّهِ أَندَادًا يُحِبُّونَهُمْ كَحُبِّ ٱللَّهِ
وَٱلَّذِينَ ءَامَنُوٓا۟ أَشَدُّ حُبًّا لِّلَّهِ

> «Some people set up equals with Allāh, loving them as they should love Allāh. But those who have faith have greater love for Allāh»

---

[70] as-Suyūṭī, *ad-Durr al-Manthūr* [6/205]

[71] Bukhārī [#6641, 3825]

[72] The Messenger of Allāh (ﷺ) said, 'The most trustworthy and firm handhold of faith is loving for the sake of Allāh and hating for the sake Allāh.' Recorded by ibn Abī Shaybah [#34338], Aḥmad [4/286] and it is ṣaḥīḥ as per al-Albānī [#1728].

[*al-Baqarah* (2): 165]

The love that occurred between the Messenger and the believers and those who had previously opposed them was a love that was for the sake of Allāh. Whoever loves Allāh, Allāh loves him, hence it is known that Allāh loved them after their repentance just as they loved Him. How then can it be said, 'The penitent only attains forgiveness but not love'?

Now if someone were to contend with this by saying, 'But those people used to be disbelievers, not knowing that what they previously did was prohibited, but these [Muslims] know what they do is prohibited but still do it!' The response to this is from two angles:

The first: This is not the case, many of the disbelievers know that Muḥammad is the Messenger of Allāh yet oppose him because of jealousy and arrogance. Abū Sufyān had previously already heard about the Prophet from people such as Umayyah bin Abū as-Ṣalt and Heracles. Not only this but he also informed us that he was always convinced that the Prophet would be victorious, yet still would he oppose him until Allāh caused him to enter Islām, albeit unwillingly. However, after his enmity, many events in his life after this, such as what occurred in the Year of al-Yarmuk, show the excellence of his Islām and his love of Allāh and His Messenger. Allāh, Exalted is He says,

وَٱلَّذِينَ لَا يَدْعُونَ مَعَ ٱللَّهِ إِلَٰهًا ءَاخَرَ وَلَا يَقْتُلُونَ ٱلنَّفْسَ
ٱلَّتِى حَرَّمَ ٱللَّهُ إِلَّا بِٱلْحَقِّ وَلَا يَزْنُونَ ۚ وَمَن يَفْعَلْ ذَٰلِكَ يَلْقَ
أَثَامًا ﴿٦٨﴾ يُضَٰعَفْ لَهُ ٱلْعَذَابُ يَوْمَ ٱلْقِيَٰمَةِ وَيَخْلُدْ فِيهِۦ
مُهَانًا ﴿٦٩﴾ إِلَّا مَن تَابَ وَءَامَنَ وَعَمِلَ عَمَلًا صَٰلِحًا
فَأُو۟لَٰٓئِكَ يُبَدِّلُ ٱللَّهُ سَيِّـَٔاتِهِمْ حَسَنَٰتٍ ۗ

«...those who do not call on any other god alongside Allāh and do not kill anyone Allāh has made inviolate, except with the right to do so, and do not fornicate; anyone who does that will receive an evil punishment and on the Day of Resurrection his punishment will be doubled and he will be humiliated in it timelessly, forever; except for those who repent, have faith and work righteous deeds: Allāh will transform the wrong actions of such people into good»

[*al-Furqān* (25): 68-70]

Allāh alters their bad deeds for good deeds and good deeds lead to Allāh loving them. This alteration is not only for disbelievers who have accepted Islām for Allāh says,

إِنَّمَا ٱلتَّوْبَةُ عَلَى ٱللَّهِ لِلَّذِينَ يَعْمَلُونَ ٱلسُّوٓءَ بِجَهَٰلَةٍ ثُمَّ يَتُوبُونَ مِن قَرِيبٍ فَأُوْلَٰٓئِكَ يَتُوبُ ٱللَّهُ عَلَيْهِمْ وَكَانَ ٱللَّهُ عَلِيمًا حَكِيمًا ﴿١٧﴾

«Allāh only accepts the repentance of those who do evil in ignorance and the quickly repent after doing it. Allah turns towards such people, Allāh is All-Knowing, All-Wise»

[*an-Nisā'* (4): 17]

Abū al-'Āliyah said, 'I asked the Companions of the Messenger of Allāh (ﷺ) about this verse and they replied that whoever disobeys Allāh is ignorant and whoever repents to Allāh before his death has repented quickly.'[73]

The second: This distinction between the two types of penitent people is a distinction that has no proof in the Book or Sunnah, instead

[73] At-Ṭabarī [3/640] and as-Suyūṭī [2/130]

they prove that Allāh loves the penitent and shows joy at their repentance, whether they knew what they were doing was wrong or not.

[2.17 True repentance involves a person changing himself]

Whoever knows that he has committed a sin and then repents, must change himself so that his state becomes praiseworthy: if he previously hated the truth, he must now love it, and if he loved falsehood, he must now hate it. Whatever the servant has of knowing the truth, loving it, and acting by it; hating falsehood and avoiding it, all of these are matters that are beloved to Allāh and please Him. The love that Allāh bestows to His servants is in accordance to what they have of those matters that are beloved to Him. Whoever moves from a state of being detested by the Truth to a state of being beloved to Him, Allāh would change his bad deeds for good ones because he changed his state from being blameworthy to being praiseworthy and the reward is of the same type as the action.

So if the penitent person was to conform to what the Truth loves more after his repentance, the Truth would love him more, so how can it be thought that love does not return after repentance?

Through understanding this point one can also answer the doubts raised by those who say that Allāh has never commissioned a Prophet except that he was infallible before his being commissioned. This was the position of some of the Rāfiḍah and others; likewise it answers the doubts raised by those who say that Allāh has never commissioned a Prophet except that he was a believer before his being commissioned. These people think that sins are a cause of deficiency even if one has sincerely repented from them, and this is a great error on their part. This is because the censure and punishment that is meted out to the sinner is not shared at all by the penitent who has repented immediately after his sin; it is however possible that if this person delays his repentance than he could have a portion of the retribution meted out to him.

The Prophets, may Allāh send peace and blessings upon them, would never delay repentance, rather they would rush to it and compete in doing so. They would never delay and they would never persist in committing a sin, indeed they are preserved from this. Whoever amongst them did delay repentance slightly was tried by Allāh so as to serve as expiation for the delay as was done with Dhū-n-Nūn, may Allāh's peace and blessings be upon him. This according to the opinion of those who stated that he was put in the whale of the belly after being commissioned as a Prophet, as is the famous opinion; in the opinion of those who opine that this was before his prophethood, this explanation is not required.

The one who has repented from disbelief and sin could be better than one who has not fallen into disbelief or sin. If it is possible that he be better, the best is more deserving of a Prophet; Allāh informs us of the brothers of Yūsuf and their sins, yet they became the leaders of the tribes and Allāh commissioned them as Prophets. Allāh, Exalted is He, says,

فَـَٔامَنَ لَهُۥ لُوطٌۘ وَقَالَ
إِنِّي مُهَاجِرٌ إِلَىٰ رَبِّيٓۖ إِنَّهُۥ هُوَ ٱلۡعَزِيزُ ٱلۡحَكِيمُ ٢٦

«And Lūṭ believed him and said, 'I am leaving this place to follow the pleasure of my Lord...'»

[*al-ʿAnkabūt* (29): 26]

Lūṭ then believed in Ibrāhīm and then Allāh sent Lūṭ to his people. Allāh, Exalted is He, says concerning the story of Shuʿayb,

قَالَ ٱلْمَلَأُ ٱلَّذِينَ ٱسْتَكْبَرُوا۟ مِن قَوْمِهِۦ لَنُخْرِجَنَّكَ يَـٰشُعَيْبُ
وَٱلَّذِينَ ءَامَنُوا۟ مَعَكَ مِن قَرْيَتِنَآ أَوْ لَتَعُودُنَّ فِى مِلَّتِنَا ۚ قَالَ أَوَلَوْ
كُنَّا كَـٰرِهِينَ ﴿٨٨﴾ قَدِ ٱفْتَرَيْنَا عَلَى ٱللَّهِ كَذِبًا إِنْ عُدْنَا فِى مِلَّتِكُم
بَعْدَ إِذْ نَجَّىٰنَا ٱللَّهُ مِنْهَا ۚ وَمَا يَكُونُ لَنَآ أَن نَّعُودَ فِيهَآ إِلَّآ أَن يَشَآءَ
ٱللَّهُ رَبُّنَا ۚ وَسِعَ رَبُّنَا كُلَّ شَىْءٍ عِلْمًا ۚ عَلَى ٱللَّهِ تَوَكَّلْنَا ۚ رَبَّنَا ٱفْتَحْ
بَيْنَنَا وَبَيْنَ قَوْمِنَا بِٱلْحَقِّ وَأَنتَ خَيْرُ ٱلْفَـٰتِحِينَ ﴿٨٩﴾

«The ruling circle of those of his people who were arrogant said, 'We will drive you out of our city, Shuʿayb, you and those who have believed along with you, unless you return to our religion.' He said, 'What, even though we detest it? We would be inventing lies against Allāh if we returned to your religion after Allāh has saved us from it. We could never return to it unless Allāh, our Lord, so willed. Our Lord encompasses everything in His knowledge. We have put our trust in Allāh, our Lord! Judge between us and our people with truth, You are the best of judges'»

[*al-Aʿrāf* (7): 88-89]

وَقَالَ ٱلَّذِينَ كَفَرُوا۟ لِرُسُلِهِمْ لَنُخْرِجَنَّكُم مِّنْ
أَرْضِنَآ أَوْ لَتَعُودُنَّ فِى مِلَّتِنَا ۖ فَأَوْحَىٰٓ إِلَيْهِمْ رَبُّهُمْ لَنُهْلِكَنَّ
ٱلظَّـٰلِمِينَ ﴿١٣﴾ وَلَنُسْكِنَنَّكُمُ ٱلْأَرْضَ مِنۢ بَعْدِهِمْ ۚ
ذَٰلِكَ لِمَنْ خَافَ مَقَامِى وَخَافَ وَعِيدِ ﴿١٤﴾

«Those who were disbelievers said to their Messengers,

'We will drive you from our land unless you return to our religion.' Their Lord revealed to them, 'We will destroy those who do wrong and we will leave you in the land to live in after them. That is the reward of those who fear My station and fear My threat'»

[*Ibrāhīm* (14): 13-14]

So when it becomes known that consideration is given to the perfection of the conclusion and this perfection is only attained through repentance; every servant is in dire need of repentance and it is obligatory upon the first and the last. Allāh, Exalted is He, said,

لِّيُعَذِّبَ ٱللَّهُ ٱلْمُنَٰفِقِينَ وَٱلْمُنَٰفِقَٰتِ وَٱلْمُشْرِكِينَ وَٱلْمُشْرِكَٰتِ وَيَتُوبَ ٱللَّهُ عَلَى ٱلْمُؤْمِنِينَ وَٱلْمُؤْمِنَٰتِ ۗ وَكَانَ ٱللَّهُ غَفُورًا رَّحِيمًا ﴿٧٣﴾

«This was so that Allāh might punish the men and women of the hypocrites and the men and women of the polytheists, and turn towards the men and women of the believers. Allāh is Ever-Forgiving, Most Merciful»

[*al-Aḥzāb* (33): 73]

Allāh, Glorious is He, informs us of the repentance of Ādam, Nūḥ, and those who came after them until the Seal of the Messengers, Muḥammad (ﷺ). From amongst the last verses to be revealed to him, or the last verses to be revealed to him, were,

إِذَا جَآءَ نَصْرُ ٱللَّهِ وَٱلْفَتْحُ ﴿١﴾ وَرَأَيْتَ ٱلنَّاسَ يَدْخُلُونَ فِى دِينِ ٱللَّهِ أَفْوَاجًا ﴿٢﴾ فَسَبِّحْ بِحَمْدِ رَبِّكَ وَٱسْتَغْفِرْهُ ۚ إِنَّهُۥ كَانَ تَوَّابًۢا ﴿٣﴾

«When Allāh's help and victory have arrived and you have

> seen the people entering Allāh's religion in droves, then glorify your Lord's praises and ask His forgiveness, He is the Ever-Returning»
>
> [*an-Naṣr* (110): 1-3]

The Two Ṣaḥīḥs record the ḥadīth of 'Ā'ishah, may Allāh be pleased with her, that the Prophet (ﷺ) would frequently say in his bowing and prostration,

«سُبْحَانَكَ اللَّهُمَّ رَبَّنَا وَبِحَمْدِكَ اللَّهُمَّ اغْفِرْ لِي»

> Glory be to You, O Allāh, our Lord, far removed are You from any imperfection, all praise and thanks are due to You. O Allāh! Forgive me.

Thereby implementing the Qur'ān.[74]

Before this verse, Allāh revealed,

لَّقَد تَّابَ ٱللَّهُ عَلَى
ٱلنَّبِيِّ وَٱلْمُهَٰجِرِينَ وَٱلْأَنصَارِ ٱلَّذِينَ ٱتَّبَعُوهُ فِي
سَاعَةِ ٱلْعُسْرَةِ مِنۢ بَعْدِ مَا كَادَ يَزِيغُ قُلُوبُ فَرِيقٍ
مِّنْهُمْ ثُمَّ تَابَ عَلَيْهِمْ إِنَّهُۥ بِهِمْ رَءُوفٌ رَّحِيمٌ ﴿١١٧﴾

> «Allāh has turned towards the Prophet and the Muhājirūn and the Anṣār, those who followed him at the time of difficulty, after the hearts of a group of them has almost deviated, then He turned towards them - He is All-Gentle, Most Merciful to them»
>
> [*at-Tawbah* (9): 117]

Bukhārī records the ḥadīth that the Prophet (ﷺ) would say,

[74] Bukhārī [#794, 817, 4293, 4967, 4968] and Muslim [#484]

> O People! Turn to your Lord in repentance, for by the One in whose hand is my soul, I ask Allāh's forgiveness and turn to him in repentance more than seventy times.[75]

Muslim has the ḥadīth on the authority of al-Agharr al-Muzanī that the Prophet (ﷺ) said,

> A shadow crosses my heart and I ask Allāh's forgiveness one hundred times a day.[76]

The Sunan have the ḥadīth on the authority of ibn 'Umar who said,

> We would count the Messenger of Allāh (ﷺ) saying,
>
> «رَبِّ اغْفِرْ لِي وتُبْ عَلَيَّ إِنَّكَ أَنْتَ التَّوَّابُ الغفُورُ»
>
> 'My Lord! Forgive me and turn to me, You are the Oft-Returning, the Forgiving'
>
> one hundred times in one sitting.'[77]

The Two Ṣaḥīḥs record the ḥadīth on the authority of Abū Mūsā that the Prophet (ﷺ) would say,

---

[75] Bukhārī [#6307] and at-Tirmidhī [#3259]

[76] Muslim [#2702] and Abū Dāwūd [#1515]

[77] Abū Dāwūd [#1516] and at-Tirmidhī [#3434] on the authority of ibn 'Umar. Similar aḥādith are recorded on the authority of Abū Hurayrah, Ḥudhayfah, Abū Mūsā by Aḥmad; 'Ā'ishah by Bukhārī, *Adab al-Mufrad* [#619]; Anas, Khubāb and as-Sā'ib by an-Nasā'ī, *'Amal* [#461-463]
The ḥadīth is ṣaḥīḥ and declared so by al-Baghawī [#1289], ibn Ḥibbān [#927] and al-Albānī [#556]

«اَللّٰهُمَّ، اَغْفِرْ لِي خَطِيئَتِي وَجَهْلِي، وَإِسْرَافِي فِي أَمْرِي، وَمَا أَنْتَ أَعْلَمُ بِهِ مِنِّي، اَللّٰهُمَّ، اَغْفِرْ لِي جِدِّي وَهَزْلِي، وَخَطَئِي وَعَمْدِي، وَكُلُّ ذَٰلِكَ عِنْدِي»

O Allāh! Forgive me my error, my ignorance, my transgression in my affairs and all that which You know better than I. O Allāh! Forgive my jesting, my solemnity, and my mistakes - both intentional and unintentional - for all of them are from me.

«اللَّهُمَّ اغْفِرْ لِي مَا قَدَّمْتُ، وَمَا أَخَّرْتُ، وَمَا أَسْرَرْتُ، وَمَا أَعْلَنْتُ، وَمَا أَسْرَفْتُ، وَمَا أَنْتَ أَعْلَمُ بِهِ مِنِّي. أَنْتَ الْمُقَدِّمُ، وَأَنْتَ الْمُؤَخِّرُ وَأَنْتَ عَلَىٰ كُلِّ شَيْءٍ قَدِيرٌ»

O Allāh! Forgive my past and future sins, what I did secretly and what I did openly, and all that which You know better than I. You are the one who brings forward and leaves behind and You are the Omnipotent.[78]

The Two Ṣaḥīḥs record the ḥadīth on the authority of Abū Hurayrah who asked the Messenger of Allāh about what he said in his period of silence between the opening *takbīr* for prayer and his recitation, he replied,

«اللَّهُمَّ بَاعِدْ بَيْنِي وَبَيْنَ خَطَايَايَ كَمَا بَاعَدْتَ بَيْنَ الْمَشْرِقِ وَالْمَغْرِبِ. اللَّهُمَّ نَقِّنِي مِنْ خَطَايَايَ، كَمَا يُنَقَّىٰ الثَّوْبُ الأَبْيَضُ مِنَ الدَّنَسِ، اللَّهُمَّ اغْسِلْنِي مِنْ خَطَايَايَ بِالثَّلْجِ وَالْمَاءِ وَالْبَرَدِ».

[78] Bukhārī [#6398, 6399] and Muslim [#2719]

> I say: O Allāh! Distance my sins from me in the same way as You have distanced the east from west. O Allāh! Cleanse me of my sins in the same way that a white garment is cleansed of dirt. O Allāh! Wash my sins from me with water, ice and snow.[79]

Muslim and others record that he (ﷺ) would say a similar supplication upon raising his head from the *rukūʿ*.[80]

Muslim records the ḥadīth on the authority of ʿAlī that the Prophet (ﷺ) would say in the opening supplication for prayer,

اللَّهُمَّ أَنْتَ الْمَلِكُ لَا إِلَهَ إِلَّا أَنْتَ. أَنْتَ رَبِّي وَأَنَا عَبْدُكَ،
ظَلَمْتُ نَفْسِي وَاعْتَرَفْتُ بِذَنْبِي فَاغْفِرْ لِي ذُنُوبِي جَمِيعًا إِنَّه
لَا يَغْفِرُ الذُّنُوبَ إِلَّا أَنْتَ. وَاهْدِنِي لِأَحْسَنِ الأَخْلَاقِ لَا
يَهْدِي لِأَحْسَنِهَا إِلَّا أَنْتَ، وَاصْرِفْ عَنِّي سَيِّئَهَا
لَا يَصْرِفُ عَنِّي سَيِّئَهَا إِلَّا أَنْتَ

> O Allāh! You are the King, there is none worthy of worship save You. You are my Lord and I am your servant. I have wrought evil so forgive me for none forgives sins

[79] Bukhārī [#744] and Muslim [#598]
The author, may Allāh have mercy upon him, comments on this ḥadīth thus, 'Sins lead to the heart feeling feverish, impure and weak. The heart becomes remiss and the fire of lusts is kindled within it serving to sully it; sins are to the heart what wood is to fire. This is why as sins increase, so too does the fire in the heart and its weakness. Water washes away the filth and extinguishes the fire, if this water is cold it shocks the body and revitalises its strength, this effect is heightened with snow and ice and hence is more effective in vanquishing the effects of sins.' - Quoted of him by ibn al-Qayyim, *Ighāthatu-l-Lahfān* [1/94]

[80] Muslim [#476] and Nasa'ī [1/198, 1/199]

> save You. Guide me to the best morals and manners for none guides me to them save You; turn me away from evil morals and manners for none turns me away from them save You.[81]

Muslim records the ḥadīth that the Prophet (ﷺ) would say in his *sajdah*,

> «اللَّهُمَّ اغْفِرْ لِي ذَنْبِي كُلَّهُ، دِقَّهُ وجِلَّهُ، وَأَوَّلَهُ وَآخِرَهُ وَعَلَانِيَتَهُ وَسِرَّهُ».
>
> O Allāh! Forgive me all my sins, the small and great, the open and secret, the first and last.[82]

The Sunan record the ḥadīth on the authority of ʿAlī that

> The Prophet was brought an animal to ride whereupon he praised Allāh and said,
>
> سُبْحَٰنَ ٱلَّذِى سَخَّرَ لَنَا هَٰذَا وَمَا كُنَّا لَهُۥ مُقْرِنِينَ ﴿١٣﴾ وَإِنَّآ إِلَىٰ رَبِّنَا لَمُنقَلِبُونَ ﴿١٤﴾
>
> «Glory be to Him who has subjected this to us. We could never have done it by ourselves and indeed we are returning to Our Lord»
>
> [*az-Zukhruf* (43): 13-14]
>
> Then he praised Him and exalted Him and said, "Glory be to You! I have wronged myself, so forgive me for none forgives sins save You." Then he smiled and said, "The

[81] Muslim [#771] and Abū Dāwūd [#760]

[82] Muslim [#483] and Abū Dāwūd [#878]

> Lord is well pleased with His servant when he says, 'Forgive me for none forgives sins save You,' He says, 'My servant knows that there is none who forgives sins save Me.'"[83]

Allāh, Exalted is He, says,

فَٱعْلَمْ أَنَّهُۥ لَآ إِلَٰهَ إِلَّا ٱللَّهُ وَٱسْتَغْفِرْ لِذَنۢبِكَ
وَلِلْمُؤْمِنِينَ وَٱلْمُؤْمِنَٰتِ ۗ وَٱللَّهُ يَعْلَمُ مُتَقَلَّبَكُمْ وَمَثْوَىٰكُمْ ﴿١٩﴾

> «...and ask forgiveness for your wrongdoing, and for the men and women who are believers»
>
> [*Muhammad* (47): 19]

إِنَّا فَتَحْنَا لَكَ فَتْحًا مُّبِينًا ﴿١﴾ لِّيَغْفِرَ لَكَ ٱللَّهُ مَا تَقَدَّمَ مِن ذَنۢبِكَ
وَمَا تَأَخَّرَ وَيُتِمَّ نِعْمَتَهُۥ عَلَيْكَ وَيَهْدِيَكَ صِرَٰطًا مُّسْتَقِيمًا ﴿٢﴾

> «Truly We have granted you a clear victory, so that Allāh may forgive you your earlier sins and any later ones»
>
> [*al-Fatḥ* (48): 1-2]

The Two Ṣaḥīḥs record the ḥadīth concerning the intercession, in which 'Īsā says,

> Go to Muḥammad, a servant whose past and future sins have been forgiven by Allāh.[84]

The Ṣaḥīḥ records the ḥadīth that

[83] Abū Dāwūd [#2602] and at-Tirmidhī [#3446].

At-Tirmidhī said that it was ḥasan ṣaḥīḥ and it is was declared ṣaḥīḥ by al-Albānī, *Ṣaḥīḥ at-Tirmidhī* [#2742, 2743].

[84] Bukhārī [#44, 7410, 7440, 7509, 7515] and Muslim [#193]

> The Prophet (ﷺ) would stand [in prayer] until his feet would swell and it was asked of him, 'Why do you do this when Allāh has forgiven your past and future sins?' He replied, 'Should I then not be a grateful servant?'[85, 86]

One can also ask for forgiveness and repent for leaving the best course, so whoever moves to a state better than the one he was in previously could repent from his previous state; however censure and threat can only exist for sin.[87]

Allāh knows best.

---

[85] Bukhārī [#1130, 4836, 6471] and Muslim [#2819]

[86] Here the author digresses to give an example of the interpretations given by those who hold the Prophets to be sinless. This discussion is relegated to Appendix 6.

[87] The author, *al-Istighfār* [p. 64] says, 'To be totally correct, the punishment for sins is of two types, torment which can be removed by many good deeds; or decrease in ranking and prevention from something one deserves. Allāh, Exalted is He, expiates the sins of the sinner as He says,

إِن تَجۡتَنِبُواْ كَبَآئِرَ مَا تُنۡهَوۡنَ عَنۡهُ نُكَفِّرۡ
عَنكُمۡ سَيِّـَٔاتِكُمۡ

> «If you avoid the major sins which you are forbidden, We will expiate your [lesser] sins»
>
> [*an-Nisā'* (4): 31].

Sometimes He expiates them by putting a person through tribulation, in which case his ranking stays the same or even increases, and at other times He expiates them because of good deeds that person has done.'

CHAPTER THREE

‘Does the mere acknowledgement of sin combined with *tawḥīd* lead to its forgiveness and the alleviation of difficulty, or is something else required?’

WITH REGARDS THE QUESTION, ‘Does the mere acknowledgement of sin combined with *tawḥīd* lead to its forgiveness and the alleviation of difficulty, or is something else required?’ we answer by saying:

What leads to forgiveness of sins, along with *tawḥīd*, is repentance;[1] for example Allāh will not forgive *shirk* unless it be repented

[1] The conditions for repentance are as follows: sincerity, feeling remorse for that sin, repenting, and not persisting in the sin,

وَٱلَّذِينَ إِذَا
فَعَلُواْ فَٰحِشَةً أَوۡ ظَلَمُوٓاْ أَنفُسَهُمۡ ذَكَرُواْ ٱللَّهَ فَٱسۡتَغۡفَرُواْ
لِذُنُوبِهِمۡ وَمَن يَغۡفِرُ ٱلذُّنُوبَ إِلَّا ٱللَّهُ وَلَمۡ يُصِرُّواْ عَلَىٰ
مَا فَعَلُواْ وَهُمۡ يَعۡلَمُونَ ١٣٥ أُوْلَٰٓئِكَ جَزَآؤُهُم مَّغۡفِرَةٞ
مِّن رَّبِّهِمۡ وَجَنَّٰتٞ تَجۡرِي مِن تَحۡتِهَا ٱلۡأَنۡهَٰرُ خَٰلِدِينَ
فِيهَاۚ وَنِعۡمَ أَجۡرُ ٱلۡعَٰمِلِينَ ١٣٦

=

from as He, Exalted is He, says in two places,

إِنَّ ٱللَّهَ لَا يَغْفِرُ أَن يُشْرَكَ بِهِۦ وَيَغْفِرُ مَا دُونَ
ذَٰلِكَ لِمَن يَشَآءُ ۚ وَمَن يُشْرِكْ بِٱللَّهِ فَقَدْ ضَلَّ ضَلَٰلًۢا بَعِيدًا

«Allāh does not forgive anything being associated with Him but He forgives whoever He wills for anything other than that»

[*an-Nisā'* (4): 48, 116]

Any sin, other than *shirk*, is forgiven if repented from, but if not, it is up to Allāh, if He wishes, He will forgive it and if He wishes, He will not. Allāh, Exalted is He, says

۞ قُلْ يَٰعِبَادِىَ ٱلَّذِينَ أَسْرَفُوا۟ عَلَىٰٓ أَنفُسِهِمْ لَا تَقْنَطُوا۟ مِن
رَّحْمَةِ ٱللَّهِ ۚ إِنَّ ٱللَّهَ يَغْفِرُ ٱلذُّنُوبَ جَمِيعًا ۚ إِنَّهُۥ هُوَ ٱلْغَفُورُ ٱلرَّحِيمُ

«Say: 'My servants, you who have transgressed against yourselves, do not despair of the mercy of Allāh. Truly Allāh forgives all sins, He is Ever-Forgiving, the Most Merciful'»

[*az-Zumar* (39): 53]

This verse concerns the penitent, and this is why the verse has been generalised and left unrestricted, and it has been decisively stated

---

=

«And those, who when they commit and indecent deed, or wrong themselves, remember Allāh and seek forgiveness for their sins - and who can forgive sins except Allāh? - and who do not persist in what they have done while they know. Those - their reward is forgiveness from their Lord...»

[*Āli 'Imrān* (3): 135-136]

Moreover repenting before it is too late, i.e. before the final throes of death or before the sun rises from the west. The author alludes to these conditions, barring the last, in what follows of this chapter and the next.

that He forgives all sins. In the previous verse, however, He says,

إِنَّ ٱللَّهَ لَا يَغْفِرُ أَن يُشْرَكَ بِهِۦ وَيَغْفِرُ مَا دُونَ
ذَٰلِكَ لِمَن يَشَآءُ ۚ وَمَن يُشْرِكْ بِٱللَّهِ فَقَدْ ضَلَّ ضَلَٰلًۢا بَعِيدًا

«...but He forgives whoever He wills for anything other than that»

[*an-Nisā'* (4): 48, 116]

specifying the forgiveness of all sins other than *shirk* to be dependant upon His will. Now if Allāh will only forgive *shirk* for the one who asks forgiveness, and He will forgive any other sin that person repents from, the only meaning left for this verse is that those sins, other than *shirk*, that are not repented from, Allāh will forgive them, or not forgive them, as He wills.

Acknowledgment of sin, if it includes repentance, combined with *tawḥīd*, leads to forgiveness. When sin is forgiven, its punishment is averted for forgiveness is a shield protecting one from the evil of that sin.

Some people say that *al-ghafr* (forgiveness) means *as-satar* (covering) reasoning that *maghfirah* (forgiveness) and *al-Ghaffār* (the Oft-Forgiving) were only called so because of the meaning they carry of covering and hiding. They also explain the meaning of His Name, *al-Ghaffār* to be *as-Sattār* (the Coverer). This is an incomplete explanation of *al-ghafr*. The meaning of forgiveness is to shield oneself from the evil of sin such that he not be punished for it, hence the one who is forgiven is not punished for that sin. The meaning of covering does not imply this meaning, for the one whose sin has been hidden could still be punished for it in private.[2]

[2] Refer to: *al-Mufradāt* [p. 362]; *Lisān al-'Arab* [5/25]; *Mu'jam Maqāyīs al-Lugha* [4/385]

However, despite having repented, a person could still be tried with something that would serve to increase his reward and this does not negate the reality of forgiveness.

Moreover a person could think another to have repented of sin, but in reality he is merely someone who has abandoned that sin. The one who abandons is not the same as the one who has repented. A person may not commit a sin because it never occurred to him to do so, or because he was unable to, or his desire to commit it left him for a reason other than a religious one, all these reasons do not constitute repentance. It is necessary that the penitent believe that what he did was evil, that he hate that deed simply because Allāh prohibited it, and that he leave it for the sake of Allāh and not for some worldly desire or fear. Repentance is from the greatest of good deeds, and all good deeds can only be considered to be so if they are performed for the sake of Allāh and in accordance to His command. Fuḍayl bin 'Īyāḍ said concerning His saying,

ٱلَّذِى خَلَقَ ٱلْمَوْتَ وَٱلْحَيَوٰةَ لِيَبْلُوَكُمْ أَيُّكُمْ أَحْسَنُ عَمَلًا وَهُوَ ٱلْعَزِيزُ ٱلْغَفُورُ ﴿٢﴾

«He Who created life and death to test which of you is best in deed»

[*al-Mulk* (67): 2]

'The sincere and correct.' When asked what that means he replied, 'When an action is sincere but not correct, it will not be accepted. When it is correct but not sincere it will not be accepted. It will only be accepted when it is both sincere and correct; sincere that it be only for Allāh; correct that it be performed in the way taught by the Sunnah.'[3]

[3] *Tafsīr al-Baghawī* [4/369]

'Umar bin al-Khaṭṭāb would say in his supplication, 'O Allāh! Make all my deeds righteous, make them sincerely for Your face, and do not let any portion of them be for anyone else.'[4]

The discussion on repentance has been expounded in detail elsewhere.[5]

As for acknowledging ones sin, in submissiveness to Allāh, but without the intent to abandon it, then this is merely asking for forgiveness and cannot be said to be repentance. This is like a person who asks of Allāh to forgive his sin but has not repented from it, one cannot be certain of his forgiveness for he is in the position of one who is making a mere supplication. It is established that the Prophet (ﷺ) said,

> "There is no supplicant who supplicates for something that does not contain sin or the severing of kindred-relations, except that one of three things occur: either it is answered in this life; or he gets the likes of it in reward; or its equivalent in evil is averted from him." They asked, 'O Messenger of Allāh, what if we frequently supplicate?' He replied, 'Allāh increases."[6]

---

[4] Aḥmad, *az-Zuhd* [#615] on the authority of al-Ḥasan from 'Umar. Al-Ḥasan was not contemporary to 'Umar.

[5] Refer to the author's, *at-Tawbah.*

[6] Al-Maqdisī, *Targhīb at-Du'ā* [#21] on the authority of Anas.
Similar aḥādīth are also reported on the authority of Abū Sa'īd al-Khudrī by Aḥmad [#11133], 'Ubādah bin as-Ṣāmit by at-Tirmidhī [#3573] and Abū Hurayrah by Aḥmad.
At-Tirmidhī said it was ḥasan ṣaḥīḥ, al-Ḥākim said it was ṣaḥīḥ and adh-Dhahabī agreed as did al-Albānī, *Ṣaḥīḥ at-Targhīb* [#1631]

The likes of this supplication could lead to forgiveness and if not, the attainment of some other good or the aversion of some evil. Hence, in all cases it brings about benefit and this is true of all supplications.

Those amongst the scholars who said, 'Asking for forgiveness while persisting in that sin is the repentance of liars' meant one who claims to have repented, if such a person persists in his sin it becomes clear that he has not in reality repented for repentance and persistence in sin are two opposites. Persistence opposes repentance but it does not oppose the mere asking for forgiveness when divorced from repentance.

CHAPTER FOUR

'Does the acknowledgment of one sins lead to the elimination of the evil of many sins that may have been committed, or must that person bring to mind all sins in order for this to occur?'

WITH REGARDS THE QUESTION, 'Does the acknowledgment of one sins lead to the elimination of the evil of many sins that may have been committed, or must that person bring to mind all sins in order for this to occur?'

The answer to this is founded upon a number of principles:

The First Principle

Repentance for a particular sin is valid even if that person persists in committing other sins. This opinion is well known from the *Salaf* and succeeding generations. Some of the *Ahlu-l-Kalām*, such as Abū Hāshim, said that repentance for a sin was not valid if that person was persisting in committing another. Their reasoning was that if the cause for repentance does not arise from the fear of Allāh, it is invalid. Now the fear of Allāh prevents one from committing all sins, not just one or a few. This opinion was also recorded as one opinion of Aḥmad by al-Qāḍī Abū Ya'lā and ibn 'Aqīl because al-Marrūdhī reported from him that when asked about a person who had repented from a lewd sin by saying, 'Even if I fall ill [from desire] I will not repeat that sin, but I will keep on looking,' he said, 'What sort of repentance is this? Jarīr bin 'Abdullāh said, 'I asked the Messenger of Allāh (ﷺ) about the unexpected glance to which he replied,

Avert your eyes."[1] '[2]

The well-known opinion from Aḥmad and all the *Imāms* is that such repentance is valid. In this particular issue what Aḥmad meant was this repentance was not so general that it would lead to the forgiveness of all sins but only specific, he did not mean that this sin [of looking] was like the sin of one who persists in committing a major sin; all that is reported from him concerning this issue belies this understanding. To understand the words of an *Imām* in a light which conforms to what he has to say in other places is more befitting than to understand them to be contradictory, especially when one of these understandings is an innovation that none of the *Salaf* held. Aḥmad was the one who said, 'Beware of speaking in an issue for which you who have no *Imām* preceding you.' During the Trial he would say, 'How can I say what has not been said?' Aḥmad's following of the Sunnah and narrations, his intense desire to do so, and his intense dislike of opposing them is a matter that is too well known to dispute.

---

[1] Muslim [#2159] and Abū Dāwūd [#2148]

[2] i.e. the person repented from his lewd deed but vowed to persist in performing another sin, not averting his eyes.

With regards the argument that the fear of Allāh leads to the relinquishment of all sins, the answer to this is that a person may realise the vileness of one sin and not another. It is also possible that a person realise its vileness, yet his desires overcome him with regards to one sin and not the other, hence he repents from the first but not the second. This is the same case as one who performs some of the obligations and not others, the ones he does perform are accepted.

However the Mu'tazila[3] base their argument upon a corrupt principle which in its conclusion agrees with the Khawārij.[4] They both said that those who commit major sins would remain in Hellfire forever and never leave it, be it through intercession or other than it. In their view, it is not possible that one man be punished and then later rewarded. In their view all good deeds are destroyed by a major sin.

As for the Companions and *Ahlu-s-Sunnah wa-l-Jamā'ah*, their view was that those who commit major sins will come out of the Fire and have intercession accepted on their behalf and that one major sin

[3] An early sect in Islām, followers of Wāṣil bin 'Atā' who disavowed the circle of al-Ḥasan al-Baṣrī and gave precedence to intellect over the revealed texts.

[4] The author, *Majmū' Fatāwā* [7/481] says, 'The Khawārij have a number of different titles such as *al-Ḥurūriyyah, Ahl an-Nahrawān, al-'Ibādiyyah, al-Azāriqah* and *an-Najdāt.* They were the first to declare Muslims disbelievers because of sins and they made their blood lawful because of this. They were as depicted by the Prophet (ﷺ), 'Those who would kill the Muslims and leave the idolaters.' They ruled 'Ālī and 'Uthmān bin 'Affān and those who showed them allegiance to be disbelievers...They said that people can either be believers or disbelievers, whoever does all the obligations and leaves all the prohibitions is a believer and whoever does not is a disbeliever, remaining eternally in the Fire. They then went on to rule anybody who disagreed with this belief to be disbelievers... This opinion is false and proved so by many texts of the Book and Sunnah. Allāh ordered the cutting of the hand of the thief and not his killing, if the thief was indeed an apostate because of his sin, it would have been necessary to kill him...'

will not destroy all good deeds; however it could destroy an equivalent amount of good deeds in the view of the majority of *Ahlu-s-Sunnah*. Disbelief is the only thing that destroys all good deeds and repentance is the only thing that destroys all evil deeds. When one who commits a major sin performs good deeds by which he desires the pleasure of Allāh, Allāh would reward him for this even though he be deserving of punishment for his major sin.

The Book of Allāh, Mighty and Magnificent, differentiates between the ruling of the thief, the fornicator, the believers fighting one another, and the ruling on the disbelievers. The *mutawātir* Sunnah and the *ijmāʿ* of the Companions also proves this and this issue is expounded in detail in other places.

This difference expounded upon above affects the understanding of verses such as,

إِنَّمَا يَتَقَبَّلُ ٱللَّهُ مِنَ ٱلْمُتَّقِينَ ﴿٢٧﴾

«Indeed Allāh only accepts from those who have *taqwā*»
[*al-Māʾidah* (5): 27]

In the view of the Khawārij and Muʿtazilah, good deeds will only be accepted from one who is always in a state of *taqwā* and hence never commits a major sin. In the view of the Murji'ah[5] this verse means that good deeds will be accepted from that person who avoids

[5] The author, *Majmūʿ Fatāwā* [7/190] says, '[The *Murji'ah*] erred in two fundamental matters: They thought that *Īmān* was merely belief and knowledge and is not accompanied by action at all, and this is the greatest of their errors; and they thought that whoever had been ruled to be a disbeliever, to remain in Hellfire forever, by the Legal law could only have been so if there was no belief or knowledge in his heart. In this they opposed what is witnessed, the intellect, the Legal Law, and what those of sound *fiṭrah* have agreed upon...'

shirk for they were of the view that those who commit major sins fall within the definition of '*muttaqīn*'. In the view of *Ahlu-s-Sunnah wa-l-Jamā'ah*, Allāh accepts the deeds of those who have *taqwā* in that deed they performed, that deed which was done sincerely for Him and in compliance to His command. So whoever has *taqwā* in that deed he performed, Allāh will accept it from him even if he is disobeying Him in other matters; whoever does not have *taqwā* in the action he performed, it will not be accepted of him, even though other deeds of his may well be.

Hence repenting from some sins and not others, is like performing some good deeds and not others, provided that what was left was not a condition for the validity of what was done; such as faith which is the condition for the validity of all other deeds. Allāh, Exalted is He says,

وَمَنْ أَرَادَ الْآخِرَةَ وَسَعَىٰ لَهَا سَعْيَهَا وَهُوَ مُؤْمِنٌ فَأُولَٰئِكَ كَانَ سَعْيُهُم مَّشْكُورًا ﴿١٩﴾

«But as for anyone who desires the Hereafter and strives for it with the striving it deserves, being a believer, the striving of such people will be gratefully acknowledged» [*al-Isrā'* (17): 19]

مَنْ عَمِلَ صَالِحًا مِّن ذَكَرٍ أَوْ أُنثَىٰ وَهُوَ مُؤْمِنٌ فَلَنُحْيِيَنَّهُ حَيَاةً طَيِّبَةً وَلَنَجْزِيَنَّهُمْ أَجْرَهُم بِأَحْسَنِ مَا كَانُوا يَعْمَلُونَ ﴿٩٧﴾

«Anyone who performs righteous deeds, male or female, being a believer, We will give them a good life and We will

recompense them according to the best of what they did»
[*an-Naḥl* (16): 97]

وَمَن يَرْتَدِدْ مِنكُمْ عَن دِينِهِۦ فَيَمُتْ وَهُوَ كَافِرٌ فَأُوْلَٰٓئِكَ حَبِطَتْ أَعْمَٰلُهُمْ فِي ٱلدُّنْيَا وَٱلْءَاخِرَةِ ۖ وَأُوْلَٰٓئِكَ أَصْحَٰبُ ٱلنَّارِ ۖ هُمْ فِيهَا خَٰلِدُونَ ﴿٢١٧﴾

«As for any of you who revert from their religion and die as disbelievers, their actions will come to nothing in this world and the Hereafter. They are the denizens of the Fire, remaining in it timelessly, forever»
[*al-Baqarah* (2): 217]

The Second Principle

Whoever repents from some sins and not others, what is repented from is forgiven and what is not, is not. I know of know difference concerning this except with regards the disbeliever who accepts Islām. His acceptance of Islām includes within it, his repentance from disbelief, and this is forgiven him. But are the sins he committed while being a disbeliever forgiven him as well? Or does he have to repent from them once he has become a Muslim?[6] There are two famous opinions concerning this:

---

[6] The author, *al-Istighfār* [p. 96] says, 'The scholars have differed concerning one who has repented from disbelief, if he apostates and then again accepts Islām, do his good deeds that he previously did [while Muslim] come back? There are two opinions concerning this ensuing from the question, 'Does apostasy destroy deeds unrestrictedly or does it destroy those deeds with the condition that the person dies in his state of disbelief?' The opinion of Abū Ḥanīfah and Mālik was that the deeds are destroyed unrestrictedly whereas Shāfi'ī was of the opinion that they are only destroyed if the person dies on disbelief.'

The first: All his sins will be forgiven him due to his (ﷺ) saying,

> Islām effaces what came before it.[7]

Recorded by Muslim. Allāh, Exalted is He, says,

> قُل لِّلَّذِينَ كَفَرُوٓا۟ إِن يَنتَهُوا۟ يُغْفَرْ لَهُم مَّا قَدْ سَلَفَ
>
> «Say to those who disbelieve that if they stop, they will be forgiven what is past»
>
> [*al-Anfāl* (8): 38]

The second: Only what he repented from will be forgiven him. If he accepts Islām and he persists in committing some sins, other than disbelief, then his ruling is the same as all Muslims who commit major sins. This opinion is the one that is supported by the principles and the texts. The Two Ṣaḥīḥs record that the Prophet (ﷺ) was asked by Ḥakīm bin Ḥizām whether they would be taken to account for what they did in *Jāhiliyyah* upon which he replied,

> Whoever among you makes good his Islām, he will not be taken to account for what he did in *Jāhiliyyah*. Whoever among you does not make good his Islām, he will be taken to account for the first and the last.[8]

This text makes clear that the account for what one did in the state of *Jāhiliyyah* is only lifted if he makes good his Islām, whoever does not repent has not made good his Islām. His, Exalted is He, saying,

[7] Muslim [#121] and Aḥmad [4/199, 200, 204, 205]

[8] Bukhārī [#6921] and Muslim [#120]

قُل لِّلَّذِينَ كَفَرُوٓاْ إِن يَنتَهُواْ يُغْفَرْ لَهُم مَّا قَدْ سَلَفَ

«Say to those who disbelieve that if they stop, they will be forgiven what is past»

[*al-Anfāl* (8): 38]

proves that the one who stops from something will be forgiven what is past, it does not imply that one who stops from something will be forgiven everything else he did in the past as well, just that thing. This style of expression is in common use in the language. As for his saying,

Islām effaces what came before it

in another narration,

Islām destroys what came before it.

He said this when 'Amr bin al 'Āṣ accepted Islām and he asked him how he could have his previous sins forgiven to which he (ﷺ) said,

O 'Amr, do you not know that Islām destroys what came before it, that repentance destroys what came before it, that migration destroys what came before it?

It is known that repentance leads to the forgiveness of that sin which is repented from, not every sin.[9]

---

[9] The author, *al-Istighfār* [p.99] says, 'When [a Jew or Christian] accepts Islām, both inwardly and outwardly, his previous disbelief will be forgiven him and there is no difference of opinion concerning this. As for those sins for which he has not repented such as those sins he persists in, those sins for which he has not repented =

The Third Principle

A person could bring to mind a specific sin and repent from it, or he could just make an unrestricted repentance without bringing to mind specific sins, in this case if his intention is to make a general repentance then his repentance includes everything that he believes to be a sin. A general repentance includes within it a generic resolve to do what is commanded and leave what is prohibited combined with sorrow at having committed all that was prohibited.[10]

Were someone to hate something and also attain that object of hatred, he would feel pain. Therefore one who hates sin and does not do it, will have no reason to feel remorse. The one who does not hate sin and does do it again will have no reason to feel remorse. It is only one who commits it and hates it who will feel remorse at his deed. Aḥmad records the ḥadīth on the authority of ibn Mas'ūd that the Prophet (ﷺ) said,

Remorse is repentance[11]

=
for after entering Islām; some people said that these too would be forgiven him simply by his accepting Islām. The correct opinion, however, is that they will only be forgiven him if he repents from them...'

[10] Here the author digresses to refute sorrow and delight as understood by the philosophers. This digression has been relegated to Appendix 7.

[11] Ibn Mājah [#4252] and Aḥmad [#3568, 4012, 4014, 4016, 4124] on the authority of ibn Mas'ūd.

Similar aḥādīth are recorded on the authority of ibn 'Abbās and 'Ā'ishah by Aḥmad [#2623, 25623], Anas by ibn Ḥibbān [#612]; Wā'il bin Ḥujr and Abū Sa'īd by at-Ṭabarānī [22/101, 22/775]; and Abū Hurayrah by at-Ṭabarānī, *as-Ṣaghīr* [1/69]

Al-Ḥākim [#7612, 7613] said it was ṣaḥīḥ and adh-Dhahabī agreed, it was also declared so by ibn Ḥibbān [#612, 614] and al-Albānī, *Ṣaḥīḥ al-Jāmi'* [#6802].

After this has become clear, whoever makes a generalised repentance for all his sins, this leads to the forgiveness of all his sins even though he may not have brought to mind any specific sin he committed. The only time this does not apply is the case that there be some sins that he is committing for which he does not feel penitent due to overwhelming desire or his believing that they are good and not evil, these types of sins will not be forgiven him, but the others will.

With regards just an unrestricted repentance, meaning an unspecific, vague repentance, this does not necessitate the forgiveness of all sins committed by that person because there is nothing to suggest that he intended all his sins or just some of them. Hence, such a repentance may be a cause for the forgiveness of a particular sin just as it may lead to the forgiveness of all his sins.

Most people, when repenting, only bring to mind some of the evil they did or some of the wrong they did, and what they do not bring to mind could well be worse. It could be that they left some aspect of faith such as loving Allāh and His Messenger, and this omission is more serious than the lewd sins he may have brought to mind. There was a man at the time of the Prophet (ﷺ) called Ḥimār who was an alcoholic, each time he came to the Prophet (ﷺ) he would receive the legal punishment of whipping, then one time, while he was being whipped, one of the Companions cursed him upon which the Prophet (ﷺ) said,

> Do not curse him for he loves Allāh and His Messenger.[12]

He prohibited him from being cursed for this reason despite the

[12] Bukhārī [#6780] and Abū Yaʿlā [#176, 177]

fact that he himself cursed ten categories of people who deal with alcohol saying,

> Cursed be alcohol, the one who extracts it, the one for whom it is extracted, the one who drinks it, the one who serves it, the one who carries it, the one for whom it is carried, the one who buys it, the one who sells it, and the one who makes profit from it.[13]'

However an unrestricted cursing does not necessarily mean that every specific person who does one of these actions is also cursed. The same applies to an unrestricted declaration of disbelief or an unrestricted text dealing with a threat.[14] This is why in these cases, before the ruling is applied on any individual, the necessary pre-requisites have to be met and any obstacles have to be removed, hence for example, these rulings are not meted out to one who has repented by agreement of the Muslims, nor to one whose bad deeds are wiped out by the ocean of his good deeds etc. The punishment of sins is removed through repentance, through good deeds that efface the bad, through tribulations that serve as an expiation for them, the hardship faced in the *barzakh*, the standing on the Day of

[13] Abū Dāwūd [#3674] and ibn Mājah [#3380] on the authority of ibn 'Umar. Similar aḥādīth are recorded on the authority of ibn 'Abbās by Aḥmad [#2897]; Anas by at-Tirmidhī [#1295]; and ibn Mas'ūd by al-Bazzār [#2937]

It was declared ṣaḥīḥ by ibn as-Sakan as per ibn Ḥajr, *at-Talkhīṣ* [#2106] and al-Albānī, *Ghāyatu-l-Marām* [#60]

[14] The author, *Majmū' Fatāwā* [7/619] says, 'The stance that a particular statement constitutes disbelief [does not mean that everyone who says that statement is a disbeliever] for this could be hidden or unknown to some people. So a general statement of disbelief is made such as the saying of the *Salaf*, "Whoever says the Qur'ān is created has disbelieved and whoever says that Allāh will not be seen in the Hereafter has disbelieved" but a specific individual [who holds this belief] is not to be declared a disbeliever until the proof is established against him.' Refer also to *al-Istiqāmah* [1/163-166]

Judgment, through the supplication of the believers, and the intercession of the interceder.

Therefore, any sin that a person repents from, its consequences are lifted. If a person is facing tribulation because of sins, if he repents from some of them, that tribulation will be decreased accordingly, if he repents from all of them, the tribulation will be removed.

Most people do not make a general repentance for all their sins even though they are in dire need of this. Repentance is obligatory upon every servant in every circumstance for he will always be leaving out some aspect of something ordered or doing some aspect of something prohibited.[15]

Allāh knows best.

[15] The author, *al-Istighfār* [p. 85] says, 'Seeking forgiveness takes a person away from doing an abhorrent deed and towards doing a beloved deed, or away from a deed which is deficient to a deed which is complete. It raises a person' s rank to one which is higher and more complete. Every day, rather every hour and minute, the worshipper of Allāh, the Gnostic, increases in knowledge of Allāh and insight into His religion and servitude to the point that this carries over into his eating, drinking, sleeping, waking, speech, and action. He then sees deficiency in himself and his deeds and is therefore in need of repentance day and night, he is in need of it in all states because of the great benefit it contains, its promotion of good and repression of evil, and its aiding one in performing actions of obedience better.'

CHAPTER FIVE

'Why is it that relief comes after a person has given up all hope in creation and how can one make his heart dependant on Allāh alone?'

WITH REGARDS THE QUESTION, 'Why is it that relief comes after a person has given up all hope in creation and how can one make his heart dependant on Allāh alone?'

The cause towards actualising this is to actualise *tawḥīd*: *tawḥīd ar-rubūbiyyah* and *tawḥīd al-ulūhiyyah.*

Tawḥīd ar-Rubūbiyyah is to believe that there is no creator save Him, that there is no one besides Him who regulates all affairs, everything He wills, is, and everything He does not will, is not. So if anyone besides Allāh is asked to make something happen, someone who has no independant power to do so is being asked, even if one were to ask another to do something he is able, he can not do so without the aid of Allāh.

It is only the will of Allāh which necessitates the existence of all that He desires, whatever He wills, is, and whatever He wills, is not. As for anyone else, the fact that he may desire something does not necessitate that it come into being, in fact anything he does want only comes about due to some external factors outside of his control and if Allāh was not to aid him by means of them, he would never attain his desire. Allāh, Exalted is He, says,

لِمَن شَآءَ مِنكُمْ أَن
يَسْتَقِيمَ ﴿٢٨﴾ وَمَا تَشَآءُونَ إِلَّآ أَن يَشَآءَ ٱللَّهُ رَبُّ ٱلْعَٰلَمِينَ ﴿٢٩﴾

«...to whoever among you who wishes to go straight. But you will not will unless Allāh wills, the Lord of the worlds»

[*at-Takwīr* (81): 28-29]

إِنَّ هَٰذِهِۦ تَذْكِرَةٌ ۖ فَمَن شَآءَ ٱتَّخَذَ إِلَىٰ رَبِّهِۦ سَبِيلًا ﴿٢٩﴾
وَمَا تَشَآءُونَ إِلَّآ أَن يَشَآءَ ٱللَّهُ ۚ إِنَّ ٱللَّهَ كَانَ عَلِيمًا حَكِيمًا ﴿٣٠﴾

«...so whoever wills should take the way towards his Lord. But you will not will unless Allāh wills. Allāh is All-Knowing, All-Wise»

[*al-Insān* (76): 29-30]

فَمَن شَآءَ ذَكَرَهُۥ ﴿٥٥﴾
وَمَا يَذْكُرُونَ إِلَّآ أَن يَشَآءَ ٱللَّهُ ۚ هُوَ أَهْلُ ٱلتَّقْوَىٰ وَأَهْلُ ٱلْمَغْفِرَةِ ﴿٥٦﴾

«...to which any who wills may pay heed. But they will only pay heed if Allāh wills. He is entitled to be feared and entitled to forgive»

[*al-Muddaththir* (74): 55-56]

Someone who puts his hope in creation, it is his heart that desires something from that object, but this object of creation is unable to grant it. Moreover this action is *shirk* which Allāh will not forgive. It is from the great blessings and favours of Allāh that He has prevented the attainment of anything that the believing servants desire through committing *shirk* so that instead their hearts can devote themselves to *tawḥīd*. If the servant were then to single Him out alone for worship as well, he would achieve felicity in this life and the Hereafter.

If, however, this is a person about whom it is said,

وَإِذَا مَسَّ ٱلْإِنسَـٰنَ ٱلضُّرُّ دَعَانَا لِجَنۢبِهِۦٓ أَوْ قَاعِدًا أَوْ قَآئِمًا فَلَمَّا كَشَفْنَا عَنْهُ ضُرَّهُۥ مَرَّ كَأَن لَّمْ يَدْعُنَآ إِلَىٰ ضُرٍّ مَّسَّهُۥ

«When harm touches man, He calls on Us, lying on his side or sitting down or standing up. Then when We remove the harm from him he carries on as if he had never called Us when the harm first touched him»

[*Yūnus* (10): 12]

وَإِذَا مَسَّكُمُ ٱلضُّرُّ فِى ٱلْبَحْرِ ضَلَّ مَن تَدْعُونَ إِلَّآ إِيَّاهُ ۖ فَلَمَّا نَجَّىٰكُمْ إِلَى ٱلْبَرِّ أَعْرَضْتُمْ ۚ وَكَانَ ٱلْإِنسَـٰنُ كَفُورًا ﴿٦٧﴾

«When harm occurs to you at sea those you call on vanish - except for Him alone! But when He delivers you to dry land, you turn away. Man truly is ungrateful»

[*al-Isrā'* (17): 67]

what he has of knowledge of *tawḥīd* will serve as a proof against him. It was in this way that Allāh, Glorious is He, proved the falsity of what the polytheists were upon in their believing Him to be the creator yet worshipping others besides Him,

قُل لِّمَنِ ٱلْأَرْضُ وَمَن فِيهَآ إِن
كُنتُمْ تَعْلَمُونَ ﴿٨٤﴾ سَيَقُولُونَ لِلَّهِ ۚ قُلْ أَفَلَا تَذَكَّرُونَ
﴿٨٥﴾ قُلْ مَن رَّبُّ ٱلسَّمَٰوَٰتِ ٱلسَّبْعِ وَرَبُّ ٱلْعَرْشِ ٱلْعَظِيمِ
﴿٨٦﴾ سَيَقُولُونَ لِلَّهِ ۚ قُلْ أَفَلَا تَتَّقُونَ ﴿٨٧﴾ قُلْ مَنۢ بِيَدِهِۦ
مَلَكُوتُ كُلِّ شَىْءٍ وَهُوَ يُجِيرُ وَلَا يُجَارُ عَلَيْهِ إِن
كُنتُمْ تَعْلَمُونَ ﴿٨٨﴾ سَيَقُولُونَ لِلَّهِ ۚ قُلْ فَأَنَّىٰ تُسْحَرُونَ ﴿٨٩﴾

«Say, 'To whom does the earth belong and everyone in it, if you have any knowledge?' They will say, 'To Allāh.' Say, 'Will you not then take heed?' Say, 'Who is the Lord of the seven heavens and the Lord of the Mighty Throne?' They will say, 'Allāh.' Say, 'Will you not then fear Him?' Say, 'In whose hand is the dominion over everything, He who gives protection and from whom no protection can be given, if you have any knowledge?' They will say, 'Allāh's.' Say, 'So how have you been bewitched?'»

[*al-Mu'minūn* (23): 84-89]

وَلَئِن
سَأَلْتَهُم مَّنْ خَلَقَ ٱلسَّمَٰوَٰتِ وَٱلْأَرْضَ وَسَخَّرَ ٱلشَّمْسَ وَٱلْقَمَرَ
لَيَقُولُنَّ ٱللَّهُ ۖ فَأَنَّىٰ يُؤْفَكُونَ ﴿٦١﴾

«If you ask them, 'Who created the heavens and the earth and made the sun and the moon subservient?' They will reply, 'Allāh.' So how have they been perverted?»

[*al-'Ankabūt* (29): 61]

Verses such as these are mentioned in a number of places in the Qur'ān.

From the completion of Allāh's blessings upon His believing servants is that he afflicts them with hardship and tribulation such as would make them turn back to Him and supplicate to Him alone, making their religion sincerely for Him, putting their hope in Him, and their hearts depending upon Him alone. This leads to their having absolute reliance in Him, their tasting the sweetness of faith, and their absolving themselves of *shirk*. All of these are blessings greater than the blessings of health, security, and luxury for all of these are merely bodily blessings which both the believer and non-believer experience. As for the blessings that are achieved by those who live by *tawḥīd*, they are beyond description, and every believer has a portion of this in accordance to his faith. This is why some of the *Salaf* said, 'Son of Ādam! You have indeed been blessed when in order to fulfill a need you frequently knock on the gate of your Master.'

One of the scholars said, 'I have a need for Allāh so I invoke Him and He grants me the delight of knowing Him and the sweetness of discoursing with Him which makes me desire that my need not be swiftly answered for fear that my soul become distracted from this' because the soul only desires what it wants and when it attains this it turns away.

In some of the Judeo-Christian narrations it is mentioned, 'Son of Ādam! Tribulation brings you and I together whereas ease and luxury brings you and your soul together.'

There are many narrations carrying this meaning and experienced in reality by the believers, every believer will be able to relate to what we just said, for what we have related is part of the spiritual experience that none can truly understand except for those who have experienced it.

People have differing levels of spiritual experience, that which the believers experience when they make their *tawḥīd* for Allāh alone and direct all their attention to Him such that they make their religion sincerely for Him, they love Him and love everything else for His sake, they place their reliance in Him, declare their loyalty for His sake and enmity for His sake, they ask only of Him, they place their hope in Him alone, they fear only Him, they worship Him and ask for His aid; in all states they are with their Lord without the interference of creation and with the creation without the interference of base desires; any desire has vanished in the face of what He desires, all love has vanished in face of His love, all fear has vanished in the face of His fear, all hope has vanished in the face of His hope, none is invoked save Him - that which the believers experience cannot be truly grasped except for one who actualises the above, and all believers do this to some extent.[1]

[1] The author, *Majmū' Fatāwā* [13/199-201] says while explaining the correct understanding of *fanā'*, 'That through the worship of Allāh, the worship of anything else vanishes; through loving Him, the love of anything else vanishes; through obeying Him, the obedience of anything else vanishes; through fearing Him, the fear of anything else vanishes; through having hope in Him, hope in anything else vanishes; through relying on Him, the reliance on anything else vanishes. This is the reality of the *tawḥīd* with which Allāh sent His Messengers and revealed His Books. This is the reality of testifying that none has the right to be worshipped save Allāh, for this means to empty the heart of the worship of anything besides Allāh, leaving in its wake the worship of Him alone.

This vanishing (*fanā'*) goes hand-in-hand with remaining (*baqā'*), for the heart extinguishes the worship of other than Allāh to have remain in it the worship of Allāh alone. This is the import of the testification of faith for it is built upon negation and affirmation; there is no god in existence save Allāh and there is nothing deserving worship in existence save Him. It is obligatory that this belief take firm root in the heart, and moreover this allegiance to Allāh must be accom-
=

This is the reality of Islām with which Allāh sent the Messengers, for which the Books were revealed and it is the essence of the Qur'ān.

Allāh, Glorious is He, knows best.

=

panied with hatred and absolvement of anything that is worshipped besides Him. Allāh, Exalted is He, informs us that,

وَإِذْ قَالَ إِبْرَٰهِيمُ لِأَبِيهِ وَقَوْمِهِۦٓ
إِنَّنِى بَرَآءٌ مِّمَّا تَعْبُدُونَ ﴿٢٦﴾ إِلَّا ٱلَّذِى فَطَرَنِى فَإِنَّهُۥ سَيَهْدِينِ
﴿٢٧﴾ وَجَعَلَهَا كَلِمَةًۢ بَاقِيَةً فِى عَقِبِهِۦ لَعَلَّهُمْ يَرْجِعُونَ ﴿٢٨﴾

> «Ibrāhim said to his father and his people, 'I am free of everything you worship, except for Him who brought me into being, who will certainly guide me,' He made it an on-going word among his descendants so that perhaps they might turn back»
>
> [*az-Zukhruf* (43): 26-28].'

Refer also to *al-Istiqāmah* [2/142-144] and *Majmū' Fatāwā* [10/337+]

APPENDIX ONE

Digression: Hope and Fear as Understood by the *Sūfīs* and *Ahlu-l-Kalām*

THE WORSHIPPER WHO is in such a state that his desire is to see the Face of Allāh and to look on at it, is also in a condition that combines hope and fear, dread and desire. He desires to attain his goal and dreads losing it. Allāh, Exalted is He, says

إِنَّهُمْ كَانُوا۟ يُسَٰرِعُونَ فِى ٱلْخَيْرَٰتِ
وَيَدْعُونَنَا رَغَبًا وَرَهَبًا ۖ وَكَانُوا۟ لَنَا خَٰشِعِينَ ﴿٩٠﴾

«They outdid each other in good deeds, supplicating to Us in yearning and awe»

[*al-Anbiyā'* (21): 90]

تَتَجَافَىٰ جُنُوبُهُمْ
لْمَضَاجِعِ يَدْعُونَ رَبَّهُمْ خَوْفًا وَطَمَعًا وَمِمَّا رَزَقْنَٰهُمْ
يُنفِقُونَ ﴿١٦﴾

«Their sides eschew their beds as they supplicate to their

Lord in fear and ardent hope...»

[*as-Sajdah* (32): 16]

It is unimaginable that the supplicant, who is supplicating to Allāh, be it the supplication of worship or the supplication of request, ever be devoid of hope and fear, dread and desire.

As for what has been mentioned from one of the Shaykhs that he considered hope and fear to be the state of the general masses [of Muslims and not the elite], it is possible to explain his words such that they are taken to mean [that the elite], those whose desire is only to draw closer to Allāh, desire the Face of Allāh and the bliss of looking on at Him and there is no object of creation from which they would experience bliss. This group also hopes in the attainment of this objective and fears losing it, and hence they too are in a state that combines hope and fear, but what it is that they hope for, and fear losing, is dependant upon their objective.[1]

Therefore when one of them said, 'I have never worshipped You for desire of Your Paradise, nor for fear of Your Fire,'[2] he said this

---

[1] i.e. the general masses main goal, when they worship Allāh, is the attainment of reward and the removal of sin. The main goal of the elite is to draw closer to Allāh and attain His pleasure. Both groups are in a state of hope and fear, but the first hopes in reward and fears losing it whereas the second hopes in the pleasure of Allāh and fears losing it.

[2] As is related from Rābi'a al-'Adawiyyah al-Baṣriyyah, Umm 'Amr; refer to her biography in adh-Dhahabī, *as-Siyar* [8/241-243].

There is not a single person who does not fear the punishment of Hell, the Prophets and Messengers feared it and inculcated this fear in others. As for the lack of fear of the Fire that is mentioned from some of the Gnostics, the correct position is that there is a way to understand these narrations in an authentic light. Ibn al-Mubārak said; 'Umar bin 'Abdur-Rahmān bin Mahdī informed me; I heard Wahb bin Munabbih saying, 'A sage said: I am embarrassed before Allāh that I =

thinking that Paradise was a term referring to all those created matters with which one experiences joy; and that Hellfire was a term referring to all those created matters which would engender punishment. This understanding of Paradise and Hell is both deficient and extreme, rather everything that Allāh has prepared for His *Awliyā'* is part and parcel of the term 'Paradise' and this includes looking at Him. This is why the best of creation (ﷺ) used to ask Allāh for Paradise and take refuge with Him from the Fire.[3] He once asked one of his Companions what he would say in prayer to which the Companion replied, 'I simply ask Allāh for Paradise and I take refuge with Him from the Fire for I am not able to formulate the likes of your supplications or the supplications of Mu'ādh.' He (ﷺ) said,

> It is around these matters that we supplicate.[4]

A faction of the *Ahl al-Kalām* rejected that one say, 'I ask You for

---

=

worship Him for desire of the reward of Paradise - i.e. only for this - so that I end being like a bad laborer, I only work if I am paid. I am embarrassed before Allāh that I worship Him for fear of Hell - i.e. only for this - so that I end up being like a bad servant, I only work when threatened. However the love I have for Him causes me do such deeds that no other love does.' Recorded by Abū Nu'aym, *al-Ḥilyah* [4/53-54]

The explanation given to this by some of the narrators, that the worship being censured is that done just for hope of reward or just for fear of punishment, is good. These Gnostics based there argument on two points;

1) Allāh, Exalted is He, in and of Himself deserves to be worshipped.

2) The most complete form of hope and fear is that which is connected to the *dhāt* of Allāh, Mighty and Magnificent, so the greatest fear is the fear of Allāh's displeasure and being veiled from Him.

A detailed discussion of this issue can be found in ibn Rajab, *at-Takhwīf min an-Nār* [pp. 23-38]

[3] The greatest punishment of the Fire is not being able to see the Face of Allāh.

[4] Abū Dāwūd [#792] and ibn Mājah [#910, 3847] with ṣaḥīḥ sanad.

the bliss of looking at Your Face' thinking that it is not possible to take delight by looking at the Face of Allāh, reasoning that bliss can only be attained through objects of creation. This faction also erred in their understanding of Paradise just as the previous groups had erred, the difference being that the previous group desired that which is deserving of being sought whereas this group rejected it.

As for feeling the pain of the Fire, this is a necessary matter, hence those who said, 'Were He to cause me to enter the Fire, I would be content' merely stated their resolve to be content. Resolve often dissolves when faced with reality as in the case of Sumnūn who said,

There is nothing for me except You
So try me however You will

He was tried with a urinatory disease, and would roam amongst children saying, 'Supplicate for your lying uncle!'[5] Allāh, Exalted is He, says,

وَلَقَدْ كُنتُمْ تَمَنَّوْنَ ٱلْمَوْتَ مِن
قَبْلِ أَن تَلْقَوْهُ فَقَدْ رَأَيْتُمُوهُ وَأَنتُمْ تَنظُرُونَ ﴿١٤٣﴾

«You were longing for death before you met it. Now you have seen it with your own eyes»

[*Āli 'Imrān* (3): 143]

Some of those who discussed the reasons behind the various spiritual stations came to consider the station of love (*ḥubb*), contentment (*riḍā*), fear (*khawf*) and hope (*rajā*) to be stations for the general masses of the Muslims, building upon the premise of 'witnessing

[5] Refer to al-Baghdādī, *Tārīkh al-Baghdād* [9/234-237] and Abū Nu'aym [10/309-312].

the divine decree' - that whoever has come to witness the divine decree has actualised the *Tawḥīd* of Actions to the point that whatever was not vanishes and all that remains is the One who will always remain, hence such a person emerges outside the realm of matters such as [hope, fear etc.]. Such a concept requires correction from the standpoint of reality and the standpoint of the Legal Law (*Sharīʿah*).

As for the standpoint of reality, it is not possible to imagine a living being as something that is not sensory, loving that which would pleasure it and hating all that which it is averse to. Whoever says that all attainable matters are equivalent in the eyes of a living being is either ignorant, not understanding what he is saying, or arrogant and stubborn. Even if one were to assume that a person enters a state where he is no longer in control of his sanity - call it madness, extinction, cessation of being, annihilation, fainting, or frailty - despite this, he still possesses some sensation and will still have some awareness of things that cause him pleasure or things he is averse to, if he does lose sensation of some matters, he will not lose sensation of all matters.

Therefore whoever thinks that witnessing *Tawḥīd ar-Rubūbiyyah* causes one to enter the station of unification and extinction such that he no longer perceives a distinction is mistaken, rather there must be a distinction for this is a necessary matter. Therefore, even if such a person was to lose sight of the distinction laid out by the Legal Law, their still remains the distinction that is ingrained in ones nature, [and if one ignores this] then he is merely following his base desires and not obeying his Master.

This is why when this issue was discussed by Junayd[6] and his com-

[6] His biography can be found in adh-Dhahabī [14/66-70]; al-Baghdādī [7/241-249]; and Abū Nuʿaym [10/255-287].

panions, he mentioned to them the 'second distinction' - that one must distinguish between the ordered and prohibited, between that which Allāh loves and that which He detests; this along with his witnessing the decree. Whoever does not differentiate between the ordered and prohibited has left the religion of Islām.

However these people who talk about unification do not leave the distinction laid out by the Legal Law in its entirety and were they to do so they would be the worst type of disbelievers! Such people end up considering the Messengers to be on par with other than them and they end up believing in the Unity of Existence - no longer differentiating between the Creator and created. However not all members of this group end up in this gross deviation, rather they make a distinction in some aspects but not in others. Therefore they obey Allāh and His Messenger (ﷺ) sometimes and disobey them at other times, and as such they are like the sinners amongst the Muslims. These matters have been discussed at length in other places.[7]

[7] Refer to the authors, *The Decisive Criterion* [section 11.6.3], the English translation of *-Furqān bayna Awliyā ur-Raḥmān wa awliyā ash-Shayṭān.* The Decisive Criterion between the Friends of Allāh and the friends of Shayṭān; Published by Dar as-Sunnah Publishers 1421H/2000CE.

APPENDIX TWO

Digression: The Different Usages of the Word *Īmān*

IN THIS STATEMENT THEY also differentiated between the phrases '*āmana lahū*' and '*āmana bihī*'.

The first is said to the one informing as the brothers of Yūsuf said,

وَمَآ أَنتَ بِمُؤْمِنٍ لَّنَا وَلَوْ كُنَّا صَٰدِقِينَ ﴿١٧﴾

«...but you are never going to believe us now...»

[*Yūsuf* (12): 17]

And Allāh, Exalted is He, says,

فَمَآ ءَامَنَ لِمُوسَىٰٓ إِلَّا ذُرِّيَّةٌ مِّن قَوْمِهِۦ

«No one believed in Mūsā except for a few offspring among his people»

[*Yūnus* (10): 83]

and the second is said about the information. Allāh, Exalted is He, says,

وَمِنْهُمُ ٱلَّذِينَ يُؤْذُونَ ٱلنَّبِيَّ وَيَقُولُونَ هُوَ أُذُنٌ قُلْ أُذُنُ خَيْرٍ لَّكُمْ يُؤْمِنُ بِٱللَّهِ وَيُؤْمِنُ لِلْمُؤْمِنِينَ

«Among them are those who insult the Prophet, saying he is only an ear. Say, 'An ear of good for you, believing in Allāh and believing the believers...' »

[*at-Tawbah* (9): 61]

In this verse a distinction is made between his *Īmān* with Allāh (*Īmān billāh*) and his *Īmān* of the believers (*Īmān lil mu'minīn*) because the meaning is that he believes the believers when they inform him of something, but as for his *Īmān* in Allāh, it is part and parcel of his belief in Him and affirmation and acknowledgement (*iqrār*) of Him.

Allāh, Exalted is He, tells us concerning Pharaoh that he said,

فَقَالُوٓا۟ أَنُؤْمِنُ لِبَشَرَيْنِ مِثْلِنَا وَقَوْمُهُمَا لَنَا عَـٰبِدُونَ ﴿٤٧﴾

«What! Should we believe two humans like ourselves...»

[*al-Mu'minūn* (23): 47]

i.e. should we believe them? Similarly He says,

أَفَتَطْمَعُونَ أَن يُؤْمِنُوا۟ لَكُمْ وَقَدْ كَانَ فَرِيقٌ مِّنْهُمْ يَسْمَعُونَ كَلَـٰمَ ٱللَّهِ ثُمَّ يُحَرِّفُونَهُۥ مِنۢ بَعْدِ مَا عَقَلُوهُ

«Do you really hope that they would believe you when a group of them heard the Word of Allāh and then, after grasping it, knowingly distorted it?»

[*al-Baqarah* (2): 75]

فَـَٔامَنَ لَهُۥ لُوطٌ ۘ وَقَالَ
إِنِّى مُهَاجِرٌ إِلَىٰ رَبِّىٓ ۖ إِنَّهُۥ هُوَ ٱلْعَزِيزُ ٱلْحَكِيمُ ﴿٢٦﴾ وَوَهَبْنَا

«And Lūṭ believed him and said, 'I am leaving this place to follow the pleasure of my Lord...'»

[*al-'Ankabūt* (29): 26]

Concerning the second usage, Allāh, Exalted is He, says,

ٱلَّذِينَ يُؤْمِنُونَ بِٱلْغَيْبِ

«...those who have faith in the unseen...»

[*al-Baqarah* (2): 3]

ءَامَنَ ٱلرَّسُولُ بِمَآ أُنزِلَ
إِلَيْهِ مِن رَّبِّهِۦ وَٱلْمُؤْمِنُونَ ۚ كُلٌّ ءَامَنَ بِٱللَّهِ وَمَلَٰٓئِكَتِهِۦ وَكُتُبِهِۦ
وَرُسُلِهِۦ لَا نُفَرِّقُ بَيْنَ أَحَدٍ مِّن رُّسُلِهِۦ ۚ

«The Messenger has faith in what has been revealed to him from his Lord, and so do the believers. Each one has faith in Allāh, His Angels, His Books and His Messengers. We do not differentiate between any of His Messengers»

[*al-Baqarah* (2): 285]

وَلَٰكِنَّ
ٱلْبِرَّ مَنْ ءَامَنَ بِٱللَّهِ وَٱلْيَوْمِ ٱلْءَاخِرِ وَٱلْمَلَٰٓئِكَةِ وَٱلْكِتَٰبِ
وَٱلنَّبِيِّـۧنَ

«...rather, those with true devoutness are those who have faith in Allāh and the Last Day, the Angels, the Book and the Prophets...»

[*al-Baqarah* (2): 177]

i.e. affirms and acknowledges this, this usage is frequently seen in the Qur'ān.

APPENDIX THREE

Digression: Examples of Word-Pairs in the Qur'ān

ANOTHER EXAMPLE OF THIS are the words *ma'rūf* (good) and *munkar* (evil); Allāh, Exalted is He, says,

كُنتُمْ خَيْرَ أُمَّةٍ أُخْرِجَتْ لِلنَّاسِ تَأْمُرُونَ بِالْمَعْرُوفِ
وَتَنْهَوْنَ عَنِ الْمُنكَرِ وَتُؤْمِنُونَ بِاللَّهِ

«You are the best nation ever to be produced before mankind. You enjoin the right and forbid the wrong and have faith in Allāh»

[*Āli 'Imrān* (3): 110]

وَالْمُؤْمِنُونَ وَالْمُؤْمِنَاتُ بَعْضُهُمْ
أَوْلِيَاءُ بَعْضٍ يَأْمُرُونَ بِالْمَعْرُوفِ وَيَنْهَوْنَ عَنِ الْمُنكَرِ

«The men and women of the believers are friends and supporters of one another. They command what is right and forbid what is wrong»

[*at-Tawbah* (9): 71]

يَأْمُرُهُم بِٱلْمَعْرُوفِ وَيَنْهَىٰهُمْ عَنِ ٱلْمُنكَرِ

«...commanding them to do right and forbidding them from doing wrong...»

[*al-A'rāf* (7): 157]

Therefore *munkar* carries the meaning of all that Allāh detests just as *ma'rūf* carries the meaning of all that Allāh loves. In another place, Allāh says,

إِنَّ ٱلصَّلَوٰةَ تَنْهَىٰ عَنِ ٱلْفَحْشَآءِ وَٱلْمُنكَرِ

«...prayer precludes indecency and wrongdoing»

[*al-'Ankabūt* (29): 45]

Here the word *munkar* is mentioned alongside *al-faḥshā'*, so *munkar* here also carries the meaning of *al-baghī*. In another place, Allāh says,

إِنَّ ٱللَّهَ يَأْمُرُ بِٱلْعَدْلِ
وَٱلْإِحْسَٰنِ وَإِيتَآيِٕ ذِى ٱلْقُرْبَىٰ وَيَنْهَىٰ عَنِ ٱلْفَحْشَآءِ
وَٱلْمُنكَرِ

«Allāh commands justice and doing good and giving to relatives. He forbids indecency and doing wrong and tyranny...»

[*an-Naḥl* (16): 90]

Here *munkar* is mentioned alongside *al-faḥshā'* and *al-baghī.*

Yet another example of this lies with the words *al-fuqarā'* and *al-masākīn*; when one is mentioned alone it includes the meaning of the other, but when they are mentioned together they take on different meanings. However the previous examples all showed a case of where one word was more general than the one accompanying it, whereas here both words are as general as each other and take on specific meanings when accompanied with the other.

APPENDIX FOUR

Digression: *Fiqh* of War Booty

A GROUP OF THE LEGAL JURISTS thought that when property is mentioned appended to the Messenger, it means that it actually belongs to him just as property belongs to other people. Then a group of these went on to say that the war booty of Badr belonged to the Messenger (ﷺ). Others said that the *fai'* and fourth fifths of the war booty belonged to the Messenger; yet others said that one fifth of the *khumus* belonged to him; yet others said that he only deserved one fifth of the one fifth of *fai'*. These opinions can be found amongst some of the companions of ash-Shāfi'ī, Aḥmad, Abū Ḥanīfah and others, but this opinion is incorrect for a number of reasons:

From amongst these is that the Messenger of Allāh (ﷺ) never actually owned this property in the normative sense that one understands and neither could he deal with it as he pleased. Owners of property can spend their wealth as they please, to fulfill personal needs or, in the case of a king, the needs of his kingdom. This is the state of the Prophet-King like Dāwūd and Sulaymān; Allāh, Exalted is He, says,

فَٱمْنُنْ أَوْ أَمْسِكْ بِغَيْرِ حِسَابٍ ﴿٣٩﴾

«'...so bestow it or withhold it without reckoning'»
[*Ṣād* (38): 39]

i.e. give to whoever you want and hold back from whoever you want, in either case you will not be punished. However our Prophet was a Messenger-Servant, he would not give except to those he was ordered to give and he would not hold back except from those he was ordered to, hence he would never distribute and use wealth except that it be in the worship of Allāh and in obedience to Him.

From amongst these is that the Prophets are not inherited from,[8] even if a Prophet be a king. So if even those Prophets who were kings never owned their possessions in the way that non-Prophets did, then how can we say this of the elite of the Messengers, one who is a Messenger-Servant?

From amongst these is that the Prophet (ﷺ) would only spend on himself and his dependents to fulfill his basic needs, everything else he would distribute in the obedience of Allāh, this then does not correspond to what one expects from one who owns his wealth. All the wealth which he distributed is all 'belonging to Allāh and His Messenger' with the meaning that it was Allāh who ordered His Messenger to distribute this wealth and he complied, hence it is obligatory to follow him in his apportioning of this wealth just as it is obligatory to follow him in all that he commands, and whoever obeys the Messenger has obeyed Allāh.

The property that the Prophet (ﷺ) would apportion is of two types:

---

[8] Due to his (ﷺ) saying, 'We are not inherited from, all that we leave behind is charity.'

Recorded by Bukhārī [#3092, 3093, 3711, 3712, 4035, 4036, 4240, 4241, 6725-6726] and Muslim [#1758-1759]

1. That which has been specifically appointed in terms of who it goes to and how much, such as inheritance.

2. That which was distributed based upon the *ijtihād* and opinion of the Messenger (ﷺ). This is because Allāh has ordered him either with affairs that are specifically defined such as the five daily prayers or affairs that are dependant on his *ijtihād*, which itself has been commanded, and these may vary in accordance to harm and benefit.

From this distribution is that which is agreed upon and that which is differed, an example of which lies in the difference of the Legal Jurists concerning how much is necessary to be spent on wives - is the amount determined by the Legal Law or is it based upon the custom of people. The majority of Legal Jurists take to the second view and it is the correct one due to the saying of the Prophet (ﷺ) to Hind,

> Take what would suffice you and your son in a reasonable manner.[9]

He (ﷺ) also said in his famous sermon,

> Women are due their clothing and spending in the customary manner.[10]

In a similar way they differed about expiations, is the amount determined by the Legal Law or the custom of the people?

---

[9] Bukhārī [#2211, 2460, 3825, 5359, 5364, 5370, 6641, 7161, 7170] and Muslim [#1714]

[10] Muslim [#1218] and Abū Dāwūd [#1905]

So that wealth which is mentioned being adjoined to Allāh and His Messenger, it is to be distributed in the way determined by the Prophet (ﷺ) and this is why he said in the Year of Ḥunayn,

> I get nothing of this booty except the one fifth and that will be returned to you.[11]

meaning that the only thing I am allowed to distribute based upon my *ijtihād* is the one fifth allotment, and this is why he said, 'and it will be returned to you'. The remaining four fifths belong to those who attended the battle. This is why the leaders of the army would divide four fifths of the war booty amongst the participants as legislated and give the remaining one fifth to the Rightly Guided Khalīfahs who would then apportion this as they saw fit.

From the war booty of the Battle of Ḥunayn, the Prophet (ﷺ) gave some to those whose hearts he wished to reconcile to Islām. It is said that this wealth was given out of the one-fifth allotment just as it is also opined that it was given from the war booty before its being apportioned. According to this latter opinion he would then have done it because the Muslims were willing to do this.[12] Some

---

[11] i.e. it will be spent in ways that will benefit you - *'Awn al-Ma'būd* [7/360]. Recorded by Abū Dāwūd [#2694] and Aḥmad [2/184] with a ḥasan isnād. A similar ḥadīth is also reported on the authority of 'Amr bin 'Abasa by Abū Dāwūd [#2755] with a ṣaḥīḥ isnād.

[12] Bukhārī [#2307, 2308, 2539, 2540, 2583, 2584, 2607, 2608, 3131, 3132, 4318, 4319, 7176, 7177] records that, 'When the delegation from the tribe of Hawāzin came to the Messenger of Allāh (ﷺ) after having accepted Islām. They appealed to him to return their properties and captives and he said to them, 'The most beloved statement to me is the true one. You have the option of restoring your properties or your captives for I have delayed distributing them.' They said, 'We choose our captive' upon which the Messenger of Allāh got up from his gathering and praised Allāh as He deserved and then said, 'Your brothers have come to you =

people say that the war booty, before it is apportioned, does not belong to the participants, rather it is for the Imām to apportion it as he sees fit. This is explained in other places.

=
with repentance and I see it proper to return their captives to them. Whoever amongst you would wish to do that as a favour, let him do it, and whoever wishes to keep his share until we pay him from the original booty, let him do so.' The people said, 'We agree to give up our shares willingly as a favour for Allāh's Messenger.' He (ﷺ) then said, 'We do not know who amongst you has agreed and who has not, go back and discuss so that your leaders may tell us your decision.' So all of them returned to discuss and their leaders returned to tell him that they had given up their shares willingly.'

APPENDIX FIVE

Digression: The incident of the 'Satanic Verses'

HOWEVER THE QUESTION IS, can they do something that Allāh would need to correct, effacing the suggestion of Satan and making precise, and clear, His verses? There are two opinions concerning this, what is reported from the *Salaf* conforms to the Qur'ān; those who denied this possibility amongst the later scholars censured the report concerning the addition of certain verses to *Sūrah an-Najm*, "These are the heavenly cranes and their intercession is hoped for," saying that this report is not authentic. Those who said that it was said that these words were implanted into the ears of the people by Satan and the Messenger (ﷺ) did not articulate them. However this does not really answer the question, and they also said concerning His words,

إِلَّآ إِذَا تَمَنَّىٰٓ أَلْقَى ٱلشَّيْطَٰنُ فِىٓ أُمْنِيَّتِهِۦ

> «...without Satan insinuating something into his recitation while he was reciting»
>
> [*al-Ḥajj* (22): 52]

that this refers to the speech of the soul.

As for those who affirm what is reported from the *Salaf* regarding this, saying that the reports from the *Salaf* are authentic and cannot be denied and the Qur'ān itself proves this,

وَمَآ أَرۡسَلۡنَا مِن قَبۡلِكَ مِن رَّسُولٖ وَلَا نَبِيٍّ إِلَّآ إِذَا تَمَنَّىٰٓ
أَلۡقَى ٱلشَّيۡطَٰنُ فِيٓ أُمۡنِيَّتِهِۦ فَيَنسَخُ ٱللَّهُ مَا يُلۡقِي ٱلشَّيۡطَٰنُ
ثُمَّ يُحۡكِمُ ٱللَّهُ ءَايَٰتِهِۦۗ وَٱللَّهُ عَلِيمٌ حَكِيمٞ ﴿٥٢﴾ لِّيَجۡعَلَ
مَا يُلۡقِي ٱلشَّيۡطَٰنُ فِتۡنَةٗ لِّلَّذِينَ فِي قُلُوبِهِم مَّرَضٞ وَٱلۡقَاسِيَةِ
قُلُوبُهُمۡۗ وَإِنَّ ٱلظَّٰلِمِينَ لَفِي شِقَاقِۭ بَعِيدٖ ﴿٥٣﴾ وَلِيَعۡلَمَ
ٱلَّذِينَ أُوتُواْ ٱلۡعِلۡمَ أَنَّهُ ٱلۡحَقُّ مِن رَّبِّكَ فَيُؤۡمِنُواْ بِهِۦ
فَتُخۡبِتَ لَهُۥ قُلُوبُهُمۡۗ وَإِنَّ ٱللَّهَ لَهَادِ ٱلَّذِينَ ءَامَنُوٓاْ إِلَىٰ صِرَٰطٖ
مُّسۡتَقِيمٖ ﴿٥٤﴾

«We did not send and Messenger or any Prophet before you without Satan insinuating something into his recitation while he was reciting. But Allāh revokes whatever Satan insinuates and then Allāh makes precise His verses; Allāh is All-Knowing, All-Wise. So that He can make what Satan insinuates a trial for those with sickness in their hearts and for those whose hearts are hard - the wrongdoers are entrenched in hostility. So that those who have been given knowledge will know it is the truth from their Lord and have faith in it and their hearts will be humbled to Him. Allāh is the Guide of those who have faith to a Straight Path»

[*al-Ḥajj* (22): 52-54]

saying that the narrations concerning this are established in the books of ḥadīth and *tafsīr* and are in conformity to the Qur'ān.[13] Allāh abrogating the suggestions of Satan and His making precise His verses would only occur to remove something that has happened to His verses so as to differentiate truth from falsehood and to ensure that they are not mixed with foreign elements. He made what Satan had implanted a trial for those in whose hearts is a disease and whose hearts have hardened. This can only happen if what happened is something obvious that people hear, not the speech of the soul. The trial that comes about by this category of abrogation is of the same type as the trial that comes about by the other types of abrogation.[14]

However this category of abrogation goes further to prove the veracity of the Messenger (ﷺ) and his being far removed from following his base desires than the other categories. This is because when he would be enjoined with an order, then later, enjoined with an order that went against the first, he would know that both were from Allāh and would believe in both. He would accept that the second, latter, ruling was the abrogating and the former the abrogated; this would then prove his truthfulness and his saying the truth on all occasions. This is why 'Ā'ishah (*raḍiyAllāhu 'anhā*) said, 'Were Muḥammad to have hidden anything from revelation, he would have

---

[13] ibn Ḥajr, *Fatḥ* [8/439] has a valuable discussion on all the various routes of this incident and leans towards the opinion that it does have a basis. He then mentions seven explanations offered by the scholars concerning this incident, the most plausible of which, in his view, was that he (ﷺ) either said this to them by way of censure and reprimand, in the same way that Ibrāhīm said, *"rather the largest of them did this"* or that Satan uttered these words and the polytheists believed them to have been uttered by the Prophet (ﷺ).

Qāḍī 'Iyaḍ, *Muḥammad Messenger of Allāh* [pp. 299-306] has a valuable discussion on this incident, objecting to its authenticity, which the reader is strongly encouraged to refer to, as does al-Albānī, *Naṣb al-Majānīq*

[14] Refer to the author's, *al-Iklīl fī al-Mutashābih wa at-Ta'wīl.*

hidden this verse,

وَتُخْفِي فِي نَفْسِكَ مَا ٱللَّهُ
مُبْدِيهِ وَتَخْشَى ٱلنَّاسَ وَٱللَّهُ أَحَقُّ أَن تَخْشَىٰهُ

> «...while concealing something in yourself which Allāh wished to bring to light, you were fearing the people when Allāh has more right to your fear»
>
> [*al-Aḥzāb* (33): 37]'[15]

Do you not see that the one who exalts himself wishes to support everything he says, even if it be wrong? So in the Messenger (ﷺ) clarifying that Allāh made precise His verses and abrogated what Satan implanted lies a great proof of his veracity and absolution from lying, and this is the purpose of Messengership. He (ﷺ) is the truthful and the one trusted and this is why to disbelieve him is without doubt, sheer disbelief.

[15] Bukhārī [#4612, 4855, 7380, 7531] and Muslim [#177]

APPENDIX SIX

Digression: *Ta'wīl* of those who held the Prophets were sinless

THE TEXTS OF THE BOOK AND SUNNAH concerning this are many and clear, likewise the narrations concerning this from the Companions, the Tābi'īn, and Muslim scholars are many. However those who disagree with this stance interpret these texts using a method that resembles that used by the Jahmiyyah and Bāṭiniyyah in their explanation of various verses. Whoever ponders these explanations will soon see their weakness, an example of which lies in their explanation of His saying,

لِّيَغْفِرَ لَكَ ٱللَّهُ مَا تَقَدَّمَ مِن ذَنۢبِكَ

> «...so that Allāh may forgive you your earlier sins and any later ones»
>
> [*al-Fatḥ* (48): 2]

that the previous sin refers to the sin of Ādam and the later sins refer to the sins of his nation. This is clearly wrong and can be proven so from a number of different angles:

The First: Allāh had already forgiven Ādam before his descent to the earth, let alone before the year of al-Ḥudaybiyyah in which this chapter was revealed. Allāh, Exalted is He, says,

وَعَصَىٰٓ ءَادَمُ رَبَّهُۥ فَغَوَىٰ ﴿١٢١﴾
ثُمَّ ٱجْتَبَٰهُ رَبُّهُۥ فَتَابَ عَلَيْهِ وَهَدَىٰ ﴿١٢٢﴾

«Ādam disobeyed his Lord and became misled. But then his lord chose him and turned to Him and guided him»
[*ṬāHā* (20): 121-122]

فَتَلَقَّىٰٓ ءَادَمُ مِن رَّبِّهِۦ كَلِمَٰتٍ فَتَابَ عَلَيْهِ ۚ إِنَّهُۥ هُوَ ٱلتَّوَّابُ ٱلرَّحِيمُ ﴿٣٧﴾

«Then Ādam received some words from his Lord and He turned towards him. He is the Ever-Returning, the Most Merciful»
[*al-Baqarah* (2): 37]

He also said,

قَالَا رَبَّنَا ظَلَمْنَآ أَنفُسَنَا وَإِن لَّمْ تَغْفِرْ لَنَا وَتَرْحَمْنَا لَنَكُونَنَّ مِنَ ٱلْخَٰسِرِينَ ﴿٢٣﴾

«Our Lord! We have wronged ourselves. If You do not forgive us and have mercy on us, we will be among the lost»
[*al-A'rāf* (7): 23]

The Second: In your view, Ādam himself falls under your objection, he does not need to have his sin forgiven for he is a Prophet as well. If you hold that Prophets cannot commit a sin then this holds true for Ādam just as it does for Muḥammad.

The Third: Allāh does not impute a person with a sin that he never committed; He is the One who says,

وَلَا تَزِرُ وَازِرَةٌ وِزْرَ أُخْرَىٰ

«No burden-bearer can bear the burden of another»

[*al-Anʿām* (6): 164]

So it is not possible that the sin committed by Ādam or his nation be annexed to Muḥammad (ﷺ). Allāh, Exalted is He, says,

فَإِنَّمَا عَلَيْهِ مَا حُمِّلَ وَعَلَيْكُم مَّا حُمِّلْتُمْ

«...he is only responsible for what he is charged with and you are responsible for what you are charged with»

[*an-Nūr* (24): 54]

فَقَٰتِلْ فِي سَبِيلِ ٱللَّهِ لَا تُكَلَّفُ إِلَّا نَفْسَكَ

«So fight in the Way of Allāh, you are only answerable for yourself...»

[*an-Nisā'* (4): 84]

If what they presume were allowed it would be permissible to annex the sins of all the Prophets to Muḥammad (ﷺ) and it could then be said that verse,

لِّيَغْفِرَ لَكَ ٱللَّهُ مَا تَقَدَّمَ مِن ذَنۢبِكَ

«...so that Allāh may forgive you your earlier sins and any later ones»

[*al-Fatḥ* (48): 2]

refers to the sins of all the previous Prophets and their nations because on the Day of Judgement he will intercede for the whole of creation because he is the Master of the children of Ādam.

> I am the Master of the children of Ādam without boasting for Ādam and all those who came after him will be under my banner on the Day of Judgement. I am the spokesperson of the Prophets when they come in delegations and their Imām when they gather.[16]

So in this case, Ādam alone should not be specified, but the sins of the first and last should be annexed to him (ﷺ), were one to follow the logical course of their argument. If it said: but Allāh has not forgiven the sins of all the nations [hence they cannot be included in the import of the verse]. The response to this is that in a similar fashion he has not forgiven the sins of his entire nation [and hence the believers too cannot be included in the import of the verse].

The Fourth: He differentiated between his sins and the sins of the believers in His saying,

فَاعْلَمْ أَنَّهُۥ لَآ إِلَٰهَ إِلَّا ٱللَّهُ وَٱسْتَغْفِرْ لِذَنۢبِكَ
وَلِلْمُؤْمِنِينَ وَٱلْمُؤْمِنَٰتِ ۗ وَٱللَّهُ يَعْلَمُ مُتَقَلَّبَكُمْ وَمَثْوَىٰكُمْ ﴿١٩﴾

> «...and ask forgiveness for your wrongdoing; and for the men and women who are believers»
>
> [*Muḥammad* (47): 19]

So how can the sins of the believers be considered to be his sins?

The Fifth: It is established in the Ṣaḥīḥ that when this verse was revealed the Companions said to the Messenger of Allāh (ﷺ), 'This

[16] Muslim [#2278] and Abū Dāwūd [#4673]

is for you, what about us?'[17] upon which Allāh revealed the verse,

هُوَ ٱلَّذِىٓ أَنزَلَ ٱلسَّكِينَةَ فِى قُلُوبِ
ٱلْمُؤْمِنِينَ لِيَزْدَادُوٓا۟ إِيمَٰنًا مَّعَ إِيمَٰنِهِمْ ۗ وَلِلَّهِ جُنُودُ ٱلسَّمَٰوَٰتِ

> «It is He who sent down serenity into the hearts of the believers thereby increasing their faith with more faith...»
>
> [al-*Fatḥ* (48): 4]

thereby proving that the Messenger and the believers understood that

لِّيَغْفِرَ لَكَ ٱللَّهُ مَا تَقَدَّمَ مِن ذَنۢبِكَ

> «...so that Allāh may forgive you your earlier sins and any later ones»
>
> [*al-Fatḥ* (48): 2]

was specific to him.

The Sixth: Allāh has not forgiven the sins of the entirety of his nation, instead it is established that there will be members of his nation who will be punished for their sins in this world or the Hereafter; this has been reported to us via multiple routes, the Truthful and Trusted one informed us of this (ﷺ), the *Salaf* of this nation have unanimously agreed to the truth of this, and countless examples of this have been physically witnessed in this life. Allāh, Exalted is He, says,

---

[17] Bukhārī [#4172, 4834] and at-Tirmidhī [#3263]

لَّيْسَ بِأَمَانِيِّكُمْ
وَلَآ أَمَانِيِّ أَهْلِ ٱلْكِتَٰبِ ۗ مَن يَعْمَلْ سُوٓءًا يُجْزَ بِهِۦ
وَلَا يَجِدْ لَهُۥ مِن دُونِ ٱللَّهِ وَلِيًّا وَلَا نَصِيرًا ﴿١٢٣﴾

«It is not a matter of wishful thinking on your part nor of the wishful thinking of the People of the Book, anyone who does evil will be repaid for it»

[*an-Nisā'* (4): 123]

APPENDIX SEVEN

Digression: Emotions in the view of the Philosophers

WITH REGARDS TO SORROW it is said that it falls under the category of beliefs or desires or it arises from the pain that the soul feels when it does something that harms it. When the heart feels that it has done something that is harmful, one comes to know that what he did was evil and this then falls under the category of beliefs. His dislike of what he did falls under the category of desires, and his experiencing discomfort and sorrow falls under the category of feeling pain just as joy and happiness falls under the category of experiencing delight.

Those amongst the philosophers who said that delight is to attain agreeable circumstances as they truly are and pain is to attain fearful circumstances as they truly are, are wrong. Delight and pain are two states that arise as a result of attaining agreeable and fearful circumstances. Love of agreeable circumstances, like food that one craves, falls into one of three cases,

The first: love itself, exemplified by the craving for food.

The second: attaining the object of love, exemplified by eating the food.

The third: the delight that arises from this.

Hence delight is something different from craving and tasting the desired thing, rather it arises as a result of this tasting and is not actually the tasting. The same applies to something which is disliked, such as being beaten. The same applies to the delight and joy that the Gnostics feel arising from their love of Allāh; their love for Allāh is one thing, what they attain from making mention of the beloved is another, and the delight arising from this is a third.

There is no doubt that love is conditional upon having some sort of awareness of the object of love, just as desire is conditional upon having some sort of awareness of the object of desire, however the awareness that is conditional for attaining delight is different from the awareness that is conditional for attaining love; this latter matter is called attainment (*idrāk*), or spiritual realization (*dhawq*), or spiritual ecstasy (*wajd*), or achievement (*nayl*), or arrival (*wiṣāl*) and other similar terms used to describe this state of attaining the object of love. Moreover this spiritual realisation necessitates delight and delight is something that every living being senses both inwardly and outwardly.

The Prophet (ﷺ) said in the ṣaḥīḥ ḥadīth,

> He has tasted the relish of faith, the one who is pleased with Allāh as his Lord, with Islām as his religion and with Muḥammad (ﷺ) as his Prophet.[18]

The Two Ṣaḥīḥs record the ḥadīth in which he (ﷺ) said,

[18] Muslim [#34] and at-Tirmidhī [#2623]

> There are three qualities, whoever has them will experience the sweetness of faith: the one to whom Allāh and His Messenger are more beloved than anything else; the one who loves a person only for the sake of Allāh; the one who abhors to regress back to disbelief after Allāh has delivered him from it just as he would abhor being thrown in the Fire.[19]

So he (ﷺ) explained that tasting the relish of faith is for one who is pleased with Allāh as his Lord, with Islām as his religion and with Muḥammad (ﷺ) as his Prophet; but that experiencing the sweetness of faith is for the one who finds that Allāh and His Messenger are more beloved to him than anything else, to one who loves another only for the sake of Allāh and abhors to return to disbelief as he would abhor to be thrown into the Fire. So this love for faith and hatred of disbelief leads to experiencing the sweetness of faith whereas the pleasure and contentment mentioned in the previous ḥadith leads to tasting the relish of faith. This is delight, it is not the actual knowledge and belief that takes root in the heart, nor is it the actual love that is found therein, instead it is the fruit of this and a necessary consequence of it. Delight can never be found unless accompanied with love and tasting, otherwise whoever loves something but does not taste it, will not feel delight. An example of this lies in one who craves for food but never tastes it; similarly if one were to taste something he does not love, this too would not bring about any delight

[19] Bukhārī [#16, 21, 6041, 6941] and Muslim [#43]

INDEX TO QUR'ĀNIC QUOTATIONS

Ādam disobeyed his Lord and became misled.	p.211
Allāh commands justice and doing good and giving to	p.199
Allāh does not forgive anything being associated with	p.164
Allāh has helped you on many occasions, including the	p.110
Allāh has turned towards the Prophet and the	p.156
Allāh is Rich Beyond Need, the Praiseworthy	p.63
Allāh loves those who turn in repentance and	p.131, 145
Allāh only accepts the repentance of those who do evil in..	p.151
Allāh only did this for it to be good news for you and	p.76
Allāh, there is none worthy of worship save Him,	p.59
Allāh would never punish them while you were among	p.100
All praise and thanks are due for Allāh the Lord of the	p.117
All who obey Allāh and His Messenger and have awe	p.106
Among them are those who insult the Prophet, saying he	p.195
...and ask forgiveness for your wrongdoing, and for the	p.160, 213
...and Dhū-n-Nūn when he left in anger	p.33
...and Ismāʿīl, al-Yasāʿ, Yūnus and Lūṭ	p.32
And Lūṭ believed him and said, 'I am leaving	p.153, 196
...and they repudiated them wrongly and haughtily	p.99
And to ʿĀd we sent their brother Hūd. He said, 'My	p.111
...and We were not affected by fatigue	p.57
Angels will enter in to welcome them from every gate:	p.142
Any disaster that strikes you is through what your own	p.100

Anyone who performs righteous deeds, male or female	p.173
As for anyone who associates others with Allāh,	p.73
As for any of you who revert from their religion and die	p.174
As for those who have taqwā, when they are bothered	p.137
Begged forgiveness from his Lord and fell down prone	p.136
Bring him to me straight away so I may draw him	p.139
But as for anyone who desires the Hereafter and strives	p.173
But as for My servants, you will have no authority over	p.80
But to those who migrated after they were persecuted	p.144
...but you are never going to believe us now...	p.98, 194
...but you have denied the truth, so punishment	p.44
By Your might, I will mislead all of them except	p.81
...commanding them to do right and forbidding them	p.139
Do not supplicate to another god along with Allāh;	p.44
Do not worship anyone but Allāh! I am a warner	p.83
Do you really hope that they would believe you when a	p.195
...except for those who turn in repentance and have faith	p.131
Fight them until there is no more trial and the religion	p.93
Glory be to Him who has subjected this to us.	p.122, 160
Great harm has afflicted me and You are	p.57
...had it not been that he was a man who glorified Allāh	p.35
Have you seen him who has taken his whims and desires	p.79
He called out in the pitch darkness, 'There is none	p.35
He is the Ever-Forgiving, the All-Loving,	p.147
...he is only responsible for what he is charged with and	p.212
He responds to those who have faith and do righteous	p.40
He swore to them, 'I am one of those who give good	p.123
He Who created life and death to test which of you	p.166
...He Who I sincerely hope will forgive my mistakes	p.134
His Lord chose him and made him one of the righteous	p.33
How is it that there has never been a city who believed	p.34
I do not love what sets	p.80
I do not say that my self was free from blame, the self	p.138, 140

...I have my trust in Him and I turn to Him...	p.112
I only created jinn and mankind to worship Me	p.104
If Allāh helps you, no one can vanquish you.	p.76
If Allāh touches you with harm, none can remove it but	p.68
If My servants ask you about Me, I am near.	p.45
If only they had been pleased with what Allāh	p.107
If you asked them, 'Who created the heavens and the	p.87, 184
Indeed Allāh only accepts from those who have taqwā	p.172
It is He who sent down serenity into the hearts of the	p.114
It is not a matter of wishful thinking on your part nor of	p.115
It may well be that Allāh will restore the love between	p.148
Know that there is none worthy of worship save Allāh	p.109
Know that when you take any booty a fifth of it belongs	p.114
Most of them do not have faith in Allāh without	p.87
My Lord! Forgive me and give me a kingdom the like	p.136
My Lord, I am truly in need of any good You	p.49, 53
My Lord! I have wronged myself. Forgive me	p.53, 135
My Lord! I have wronged myself so forgive me	p.119, 134
My Lord, I take refuge with You from asking You	p.49, 119, 134
....my Lord is Rich Beyond Need, Generous	p.63
No burden-bearer can bear the burden of another	p.212
No, by your Lord, they are not believers until they	p.125
No one believed in Mūsā except for a few offspring	p.194
None has the right to be worshipped save You; glory be	p.121 -122 141
O mankind! Worship your Lord who created you	p.105
Or do they have partners who have laid down a religion	p.91
Our Lord! Accept this from us! You are the All-Hearing	p.120
Our Lord! Give us good in this world and good in the	p.120

Our Lord! Forgive me and my parents and the believers p.134
...Our Lord! I have settled my offspring by Your Sacred p.119
Our Lord! We have wronged ourselves. If You do not p.48, 55, 119, 123 134, 211
...prayer precludes indecency and wrongdoing p.199
Put your trust in Allāh if you are believers p.72
...rather, those with true devoutness are those who p.128, 196
Remember the Name of your Lord and devote yourself p.113
Say: 'Booty belongs to Allāh and the Messenger' p.115
Say: 'Call on those you make claims for apart from Him p.75
Say: 'He is Allāh the One... p.103
Say: 'I take refuge with the Lord of mankind p.117
Say: 'If your fathers, or your sons, or your brothers p.106, 126
Say: 'My servants, you who have transgressed against p.164
Say: 'O Disbelievers!... p.123, 104
Say: 'To whom does the earth belong and everyone in it, p.88, 184
Say, 'We have faith in Allāh and what was sent down to p.128
Say: 'What has my Lord to do with you if you p.42
Say to those who disbelieve that if they stop, they p.175, 176
She wanted him and he would have wanted her p.136
...so bestow it or withhold it without reckoning p.202
So do not supplicate to any other god along with Allāh p.41
So fight in the Way of Allāh, you are only answerable p.212
So glorify the name of your Lord, the Magnificent! p.64
So take a straight course to Him and ask His forgiveness p.116
...so that Allāh may forgive you your earlier sins and any p.210, 111, 214
So wait steadfastly for the judgment of your Lord p.121, 140

So We cast him up onto the beach and he was sick p.36
So when you have finished, work on, and to your Lord p.72, 107
...so whoever wills should take the way towards his Lord. p.51
So worship Him and put your trust in Him p.105, 112
Some people set up equals with Allāh, loving them p.74, 89,94, 106, 149
Sovereignty and praise belongs to Him p.63
Supplicate to Me and I will answer you p.43
That happened so We might avert from him all evil and p.80, 136
The believers are only those who have had faith in Allāh p.94
The Day when a wrongdoer will bite his hands and say p.92
The believers are those who have faith in Allāh and His p.86
The believers are those who hearts tremble when Allāh p.86
The king said, 'Bring him to me straight away!' p.139
The invocation of truth is made to Him alone. p.42
The men and women of the believers are friends and p.198
The Messenger has faith in what has been revealed to p.128, 196
The ruling circle of those of his people who were arrogant p.153
Their final invocation is, 'All praise and thanks p.46
Their sides eschew their beds as they supplicate to their p.188
Then Ādam received some words from his Lord and p.211
...then glorify your Lord's praise... p.61
...then the fish devoured him and he was to blame p.34 122, 141
They have taken their rabbis and monks as lords besides p.90
They outdid each other in good deeds, supplicating to Us p.188
They worship, instead of Allāh, what can neither harm p.90
This was so that Allāh might punish the men and women p.155
Those We have given the Book recognise him as they p.100
...those who do not call on any other god alongside Allāh p.151
...those who do not supplicate to another god along with p.42

Those who have faith and do not mix up their faith p.73
Those who have faith and work righteous deeds p.97
...those who have faith in the unseen... p.196
Those who have most taqwā will be far removed from it: p.102
...those who remember Allāh standing, sitting and lying p.120
Those who were disbelievers said to their Messengers, p.153
...to which any who wills may pay heed. But they will p.182
...to whoever among you who wishes to go straight. p.182
Truly We have granted you a clear victory, so that Allāh p.161
We did not send and Messenger or any Prophet before p.207
We did not wrong them; rather they wronged themselves p.55
We have not wronged them; it was they p.55
We have revealed to you as We revealed to Nūḥ p.32
We offered the trust to the heavens and the earth and the p.95
...We sent him to a hundred thousand or more. p.36
We will cast terror into the hearts of the disbelievers p.73
What! Should we believe two humans like ourselves... p.195
What they supplicate to apart from Him are female idols, p.41
Whatever booty from them Allāh has given to His p.116
When Allāh's help and victory have arrived and you p.155
When harm occurs to you at sea, those you call on vanish p.98, 183
When harm touches man, he calls on Us, p.98, 183
When he ran away to the fully laden ship p.34
When he regained consciousness he said, 'Glory be to p.135
When the servant of Allāh stood, calling to Him, p.4
..when we glorify You with praise... p.24
...while concealing something in yourself which Allāh p.172
Whoever supplicates to another god along with Allāh p.41
...without Satan insinuating something into his recitation p.206
You alone we worship and You alone we ask for help p.81, 105, 98, 110,111, 117, 118
You are the best nation ever to be produced before p.198

You are our Protector so forgive us p.53, 135
You know that no one sent these down but the Lord of p.99
You were longing for death before you met it. Now you p.191
You who have faith! Obey Allāh and obey the Messenger p.92
Your Lord does not wrong His servants p.147
Yūnus too was one of the Messengers... p.32

INDEX TO AḤĀDĪTH QUOTATIONS

A shadow crosses my heart and I ask Allāh's forgiveness	p.157
Allāh says, 'Whosoever has mutual animosity with a friend	p.148
Allāh shows more joy at the repentance of His servant	p.130
As for the rukū', magnify the Lord therein, as for the sujūd,	p.65
Avert your eyes	p.170
By Allāh, I do not grant anybody anything nor prevent	p.114
By the One in whose hand is my soul, none of you believes	p.125
Cursed be alcohol, the one who extracts it,	p.179
Do not curse him for he loves Allāh and His Messenger	p.178
Every night, when their remains the last third of the night	p.44
Faith comprises sixty odd branches, the highest of which is the	p.95
Glory be to You, far removed are You from any imperfection	p.84, 156
Glory be to You, O Allāh, our Lord, far removed are You	p.84
Go to Muḥammad, a servant whose past and future sins	p.161
Grandeur is my upper garment and Majesty is my lower garment	p.65
He has tasted the relish of faith, the one who is pleased with Allāh	p.217
I am the Master of the children of Ādam without boasting for	p.213
I am the Prophet of mercy and I am the Prophet of repentance	p.145
I bear witness that none has the right to be worshipped save Allāh	p.84
I enjoin you to have Īmān in Allāh, do you know what Īmān in	p.97
I get nothing of this booty except the one fifth and that	p.204
I have forgiven you and altered every evil deed to a good deed	p.131
I say: O Allāh! Distance my sins from me in the same way as You	p.159
It is around these matters that we supplicate	p.190
In what state does this sickness find you?	p.71

Islām destroys what comes p.176
Islām effaces what came before it p.175, 176
Islām is to testify that none has the right to be worshipped save Allāh p.97
It is absolving Allāh of all evil. p.58
It is not desirable that a servant say, 'I am better than Yūnus p.67
None of you believes until I am more beloved to him than his father p.126
O Allāh! Forgive me all my sins, the small and great p.160
O Allāh! Forgive me for my past and future [sins], p.158
O Allāh! Forgive me for my previous and later [sins], p.86
O Allāh! Forgive me my error, my ignorance, my transgression in my p.158
O Allāh! I take refuge with You from knowledge that does not p.100
O Allāh! You are the King, there is none worthy of worship p.156
O Allāh! You are the King, there is none worthy of worship save p.159
O 'Amr, do you not know that Islām destroys what p.176
O Messenger of Allāh! By Allāh there was no family on the face of p.149
People! Turn to your Lord in repentance, for p.157
Remorse is repentance p.177
Satan says, 'I destroy people through sins p.82
Say: O Allāh! I have oppressed my soul greatly and frequently p.52
Say this in your rukū' p.64
Take what would suffice you and your son in a reasonable manner p.203
That which Allāh chose for his Angels: SubḥānAllāhi wa biḤamdihī p.97
The best and most noble statements after the Qur'ān are p.97
The invocation of my brother Dhū-n-Nūn, 'None has the p.72, 38, 47
The master of asking for forgiveness [is the supplication], p.56
The most superior form of dhikr is [the statement], p.46
The most superior supplication on the Day of 'Arafah is, p.50
The most trustworthy and firm p.149
The Prophet was brought an animal to ride whereupon he praised p.160
The Prophet (ﷺ) would stand [in prayer] until his feet would swell p.162
There is no god worshipped under the expanse of the heaven p.124
There is no supplicant who supplicates for something that does p.167
There are two statements that are light upon the tongue, heavy p.61
There is none worthy of worship save Allāh, the Exalted p.78

Three are the destructive traits: miserliness that is obeyed	p.111
There are three qualities, whoever has them will experience	p.218
They made unlawful lawful for them	p.91
We were afflicted by severe poverty and so I came	p.77
We would count the Messenger of Allāh (ﷺ) saying,	p.157
What you have been given of this wealth without	p.77
When a servant desires to commit a sin, nothing is recorded against	p.137
When this verse was revealed it bore down heavily on	p.74
Whoever among you makes good his Islām,	p.175
Whoever fights so that the word of Allāh be made supreme	p.93
Whoever frequently asks for forgiveness, Allāh would appoint	p.69
Whoever is diverted by the recitation of the Qur'ān	p.49
Whoever is diverted by making dhikr of Me	p.49
Whoever says, 'I am better than Yūnus bin Matta' has lied	p.67
Whoever says, 'None has the right to be worshipped save Allāh'	p.81
Whoever unexpectedly saw him would stand in awe of him	p.63
Women are due their clothing and spending in the customary manner	p.203

BIOGRAPHICAL NOTES

The Companions

'Ā'ishah: bint Abū Bakr *as-Ṣiddīq*, the Mother of the Believers and most beloved wife of the Prophet (ﷺ). She reported many *aḥādīth* from the Prophet and many Companions and Successors reported from her. She died in the year 58H.

'Abdullāh bin 'Abbās: bin 'Abdul-Muṭṭalib bin Hāshim bin 'Abd Munāf al-Qurashī al-Hāshimī, the cousin of the Prophet (ﷺ) and the interpreter of the Qur'ān. He was born three years before the *Hijrah* and was called the 'Ocean of knowledge' due to his vast knowledge. He took part in the *Jihād* in North Africa in the year 27H and died in the year 68H.

'Abdullāh bin 'Amr: bin al-'Ās bin Wā'il bin Hāshim bin Su'ayd bin Sa'd bin Sahm as-Sahmī. He and his father were Companions. He was literate and attained permission from the Prophet (ﷺ) to write everything he said. He died in the year 65H.

'Abdullāh Abū Jābir: bin 'Amr bin Ḥazzām bin Thalabah al-Anṣārī al-Khazrajī as-Sulamī, amongst those who gave the pledge of *'Uqbah*. He witnessed *Badr* and was martyred at *Uḥud*.

'Abdullāh bin Mas'ūd: bin Ghāfil bin Ḥabīb al-Hadhlī Abū 'Abdur-

Raḥmān. One of the scholars amongst the Companions and he witnessed *Badr* and the following battles. He had many virtues and died in the year 32H.

'Abdullāh bin 'Umar: bin al-Khaṭṭāb al-'Adawī, Abū 'Abdur-Raḥmān, the noble Companion and scholar. He reported many *aḥādīth* from the Messenger (ﷺ) and died in the year 73H.

'Abdur-Raḥmān bin Auf: bin Awf bin Abd Awf bin al-Ḥārith al-Qurashī az-Zuhrī, Abū Muḥammad, one of the ten promised Paradise. He migrated to Abysinnia on both occasions and witnessed every battle with the Prophet (ﷺ). He was very rich and very generous when giving in the Way of Allāh. He died in the year 32H.

Abū Bakr as-Ṣiddīq: 'Abdullāh bin 'Uthmān bin Āmir al-Qurashī. The first *Khalīfah* of the Messenger (ﷺ), his companion in the cave, his closest friend and one of the ten promised Paradise. He was the first man to accept Islām and died in the year 13H.

Abū ad-Dardā': Uwaymir bin Mālik bin Zayd bin Qays al-Khazrajī al-Anṣārī. There is a difference of opinion concerning his name. He accepted Islām on the day of *Badr* and witnessed *Uḥud*. He was from the Legal Jurists and ascetics of the Companions. He died in the year 32H.

Abū Dharr al-Ghifārī: Jundub bin Junādah bin Sakn, he was of those who accepted Islām early on but delayed his migration and hence did not witness *Badr*. His virtues are many and he died in the year 32H.

Abū Hurayrah: 'Abdur-Raḥmān bin Ṣakhr ad-Dusī. His name is greatly differed over. He accepted Islām in the year 7H and reported the most ḥadīth from the Prophet (ﷺ). He died in the year 59H.

Abū Mūsā al-Ash'arī: 'Abdullāh bin Qays bin Salīm. He had a beautiful recitation and was one of the scholars amongst the Companions. He died in the year 42H or 44H.

Abū Sa'īd al-Khudrī: Sa'd bin Mālik bin Sinān bin 'Ubaid al-Anṣārī al-Khazrajī. He and his father were both Companions and he witnessed all the battles that followed *Uḥud*. He was one of the scholars amongst the Companions and reported many *aḥādīth* from the Messenger (ﷺ). He died in the year 74H.

Abū 'Ubaidah bin al-Jarrāḥ: 'Āmir bin 'Abdullāh bin al-Jarrāḥ bin Hilāl al-Qurashī al-Fahrī, one of the ten promised Paradise. He accepted Islām early on and witnessed the battle of *Badr* and the following battles. He is the trustworthy one of this nation and died as a martyr due to a plague in the year 18H at the age of fifty-eight.

'Adī bin Ḥātim: bin 'Abdullāh bin Sa'd bin al-Ḥashraj bin 'Amr al-Qays at-Ṭā'ī, Abu Ṭarīf. He was a Christian who accepted Islām and witnessed the battles of *al-Jamal*, *Ṣiffīn* and *an-Nahrawān* with 'Alī. He died in the year 68H.

Al-'Alā' bin al-Khaḍramī: al-Khazrajī. His supplications would be answered and he died in the year 21H.

'Alī bin Abī Ṭālib: bin 'Abdul-Muṭṭalib bin Hāshim al-Qurashī al-Hāshimī, the fourth Rightly Guided *Khalīfah* and one of ten promised Paradise. He accepted Islām at the age of thirteen and was famous for his chivalry, bravery and knowledge. He married Fāṭimah, the daughter of the Prophet (ﷺ) and was martyred in the year 40H.

'Amr bin al-'Ās: bin Wā'il al-Qurashī as-Sahmī. He accepted Islām during the year of *Ḥudaybiyyah* and was the one who conquered Egypt. He died in the year 43H.

Anas bin Mālik: bin an-Naḍar bin Ḍamḍam al-Anṣārī al-Khazrajī, the servant of the Messenger (ﷺ). He witnessed *Badr* but was not of age to actually participate. He died in the year 93H.

Al-Barā'a bin Mālik: bin an-Naḍr al-Anṣārī. He witnessed *Uḥud* and gave the pledge of allegiance under the tree. He was martyred in the year 20H on the Day of *Tustor*.

'Imrān bin Ḥusain: al-Khuzā'ī al-Ka'bī Abū Nujaid. He accepted Islām during the year of *Khaybar* and reported some *aḥādīth* from the Prophet (ﷺ). He died in the year 52H.

Jābir bin 'Abdullāh: bin 'Amr bin Ḥarrām al-Anṣārī as-Sulamī, he witnessed the second pledge at *'Uqbah* while he was still a child. It is said that he witnessed *Badr* and *Uḥud* and he reported many *aḥādīth* from the Messenger (ﷺ). He died in the year 74H.

Khālid bin al-Walīd: bin al-Mughīrah al-Makhzūmī al-Qurashī Abū Sulaymān. He was a great warrior and military leader and was given the nickname, 'Sword of Allāh.' He died in the year 21H.

Khubaib bin 'Adī: bin Mālik bin 'Āmir al-Awsī al-Anṣārī. He witnessed *Badr* and was martyred during the lifetime of the Prophet (ﷺ) when he was captured by the polytheists in Mecca.

Mu'ādh bin Jabal: bin 'Amr bin Aws al-Anṣārī al-Khazrajī, Abū 'Abdur-Raḥmān, one of the foremost Companions known for his knowledge of legal rulings and the Qur'ān. He was present at the pledge of *'Uqbah* and witnessed *Badr* and the following battles and was martyred due to a plague in the year 17H or 18H.

Mu'āwiyah: bin Abū Sufyān bin Ṣakhr bin Ḥarb bin Umayyah bin 'Abd Shams al-Qurashī al-Amawī. He accepted Islām in the year of the Conquest and witnessed *Ḥunain* and *al-Yamāmah*. He was one of the scribes who would write the revelation and died in the year 60H.

Al-Mughīrah bin Shu'bah: bin Abū 'Āmir bin Mas'ūd ath-Thaqafī, Abū 'Abdullāh. He witnessed *Hudaybiyyah*, *al-Yamāmah* and the conquests of Syria and Iraq. He died in the year 50H.

Qatādah: ibn an-Nu'mān bin Zayd al-Anṣārī al-Awsī, Abū 'Amr, he witnessed the pledge of *'Uqbah*, *Badr* and every other battle that the Prophet (ﷺ) fought. He died in the year 23H.

Sa'd bin Abī Waqqās: Sa'd bin Mālik bin Ahīb bin 'Abd Munāf al-Qurashī az-Zuhrī Abū Isḥāq bin Abī Waqqās. One of the ten who were promised Paradise and one whose supplications were answered. He was the last of the ten to pass away in the year 55H.

Sa'īd bin Zayd: bin 'Amr al-Adawī al-Qurashī. He witnessed all the battles except for *Badr* and was one of the ten promised Paradise. He died in the year 51H.

Safīnah: He was a Persian slave who was bought by Umm Salamah and subsequently freed. He then devoted himself to serving the Prophet (ﷺ).

Salmān: al-Fārisī Abū 'Abdullāh, the servant of the Messenger (ﷺ). The first battle he witnessed was *al-Khandaq* and he was present at all following battles. He died in the year 36H.

Shaddād bin Aws: bin Thābit al-Anṣārī al-Khazrajī, Abū Ya'lā. He was famous for his knowledge and wisdom and died in the year 58H.

Ṭalḥah: bin 'Ubaydullāh bin 'Uthmān bin 'Amr al-Qurashī, Abū Muḥammad, one of the ten promised Paradise. He witnessed *Uḥud* and the following battles. He died in the year 36H.

'Umar bin al-Khaṭṭāb: Abū Ḥafs 'Umar bin al-Khaṭṭāb bin Nufayl al-Qurashī al-'Adawī, the second Rightly Guided *Khalīfah* and one of the ten promised Paradise. He accepted Islām five years before the *Hijrah* and his acceptance was a great victory for the Muslims. He witnessed every battle that the Prophet (ﷺ) witnessed. He was martyred in the year 23H.

'Uthmān bin 'Affān: *Dhu an-Nurayn* 'Uthmān bin 'Affān bin Abū al-'Ās bin Umayyah al-Qurashī al-Amawī, the third Rightly Guided *Khalīfah* and one of the ten promised Paradise. He was known for his generosity and freely giving in the Way of Allāh. He was married to two daughters of the Prophet (ﷺ), Ruqayyah and after her death, Umm Kulthūm. He was martyred in the year 35H.

Az-Zubair: bin al-Awām bin Khuwaylid bin Asad al-Qurashī al-Asadī, Abū 'Abdullāh. He migrated to Abysinnia on both the migrations there and accompanied the Messenger on all his military expeditions. He was one of the ten promised Paradise and died in the year 36H.

The Successors

'Āmir bin 'Abd Qais: 'Āmir bin 'Abdullāh al-Quḍayrī, famously know as 'Āmir bin 'Abd Qais al-Baṣrī. He was known for his knowledge and piety and died in the year 55H.

Al-Awzā'ī: 'Abdur-Raḥmān bin 'Amr bin Muḥammad, Abū 'Amr, one of the great scholars of his time. He was well versed in ḥadīth, *fiqh* and the military expeditions undertaken by the Prophet (ﷺ). The Muslims have agreed as to his excellence and being an *Imām*. His *fiqh* dominated Spain for a time and he died in the year 158H.

Ad-Ḍaḥḥāk: bin Muzāhim al-Hilālī, Abū al-Qāsim al-Khurasānī, the *Imām* of *tafsīr*. He was trustworthy and precise and a student of Sa'īd bin Jubair. He died in the year 105H.

Fuḍayl bin 'Iyāḍ: bin Mas'ūd at-Tamīmī, Abū 'Alī, the *shaykh* of Mecca and one of the righteous worshippers. He was trustworthy and precise, noble, having *wara'* and narrated many *aḥādīth*. He died in the year 187H.

Al-Ḥasan al-Baṣrī: Al-Ḥasan bin Abū al-Ḥasan al-Anṣārī. He was trustworthy and precise, noble and famous. He was a great scholar and narrated many *aḥādīth*. He died in the year 110H close to the age of ninety.

Sa'īd bin al-Musayyab: bin Ḥazn, Abū Muḥammad. He excelled in ḥadīth and *fiqh*, and was known for his worship and asceticism. He was one of the 'Seven Legal Jurists' of Madīnah and Imām Aḥmad regarded him to be the most virtuous of the Successors.

He was trustworthy and precise and narrated many *aḥādīth*. He died in the year 94H.

Ash-Sha'bī: 'Āmir bin Sharāḥīl ash-Sha'bī al-Ḥumayrī, Abu 'Amr, the *Ḥāfiẓ*, Legal Jurist and poet. He died in the year 103H.

Sufyān ath-Thawrī: bin Sa'īd bin Masrūq, Abū 'Abdullāh ath-Thawree, one of the great *Imāms* and worshippers of this nation. He was titled 'The Leader of Believers in Ḥadīth' and was well versed in *tafsīr*. He was the teacher of Abū Ḥanīfah and Mālik amongst others and died in the year 161H.

'Urwah: bin az-Zubair bin al-'Awām al-Asadī, Abū 'Abdullāh. He was trustworthy and precise, a Legal Jurist, a scholar, and he narrated many *aḥādīth*. He died in the year 94H.

Az-Zuhrī: Muḥammad bin Muslim bin 'Ubaydullāh al-Qurasahī, Abū Bakr, one of the *Imāms* of this nation. He was one of the most knowledgeable people of his time of ḥadīth and the Qur'ān. He was trustworthy and precise and narrated many aḥādīth. He died in the year 124H.

Others

Abū al-'Abbās bin 'Aṭā': Aḥmad bin Muḥammad bin Sahl bin 'Aṭā' al-Admī, from the *shaykhs* of the *Ṣufis*. He died in the year 309H or 311H.

Abū Dāwūd: Sulaymān bin al-Ash'ath bin Isḥāq bin Bashīr, Abū Dāwūd as-Sijistānī, the *Imām*, *Ḥāfiẓ* and author of the famous *Sunan*. He died in the year 275H.

Abū Ḥāmid al-Ghazālī: Muḥammad bin Muḥammad al-Ghazālī aṭ-Ṭūsī, Abū Ḥāmid, he excelled in many sciences and authored a number of works such as *Iḥyā Ulum ad-Dīn* and *Tahāfat al-Falāsifah*. He was known for his worship and asceticism and died in the year 505H.

Abū Ḥātim al-Bustī: see ibn Ḥibbān.

Abū Ḥanīfah: Nu'mān bin Thābit at-Tamīmī al-Kūfī, one of the great *Imāms* of this nation and the earliest of the Four *Imāms*. He commenced his studies in philosophy and scholastic theology, but later abandoned them to study *fiqh*. He died in the year 150H.

Abū Jahl: 'Amr bin Hāshim bin al-Mughīrah al-Makhzūmī al-Qurashī, one of the greatest enemies of the Prophet (ﷺ). He was killed at *Badr* in the year 2H.

Abū Nu'aym: The great *Ḥāfiẓ* and *Muḥaddith* of his age, Aḥmad bin 'Abdullāh bin Aḥmad bin Isḥāq bin Mūsā bin Mahrān al-Asbahānī *as-Ṣūfīs*. He died in the year 430H at the age of ninety-four.

Aḥmad: bin Muḥammad bin Ḥanbal bin Hilāl ash-Shaybānī, Abū 'Abdullāh, the *Imām* of the *Sunnah* and author of the famous *Musnad*. He was known for his knowledge of ḥadīth, *fiqh*, and his *taqwā* and asceticism. He died in the year 241H.

Bukhārī: Muḥammad bin Ismā'īl bin Ibrāhīm bin al-Mughīrah, Abū 'Abdullāh. He was born in the year 194H and became one of the *Imāms* of ḥadīth and was nicknamed 'The Leader of the Believers in Ḥadīth.' He died in the year 256H.

Dāwūd adh-Ẓāhirī: bin 'Alī bin Khalaf al-Aṣbahānī, Abū Sulaymān, the *Imām* of the *ẓāhirī* School of Thought and one of the *Mujtahids*. He died in the year 270H.

Ibn al-'Arabī: *Muḥiy ad-Dīn* Muḥammad bin 'Alī bin Muḥammad bin 'Arabī at-Ṭā'ī, Abū Bakr, the heretical *Ṣūfis*. He authored a number of works containing explicit disbelief and many scholars actually called him a disbeliever. He died in the year 638H.

Ad-Dāruquṭnī: 'Alī bin 'Umar bin Ahmad, the *Imām* of his era in hadīth, knowledge of the defects of *aḥādīth* and author of the famous *Sunan*. He was well versed in the various recitations of the Qur'ān, *fiqh*, language and poetry. He died in the year 385H.

Iblīs: see Shayṭān.

Ibn Ḥibbān: Abū Ḥātim Muḥammad ibn Ḥibbān al-Tamīmī al-Bustī, the *Ḥāfiẓ*, *Mujtahid* and author of the famous *Ṣaḥīḥ ibn Ḥibbān*. He died in the year 354H.

Ibn al-Jawzī: 'Abdur-Raḥmān bin 'Alī bin Muḥammad, Abū al-Faraj al-Qurashī at-Tamīmī, the *Ḥāfiẓ* and *Imām*. He was a prolific writer and authored around three hundred works. He died in the year 587H.

Isḥāq bin Rāhawayah: al-Ḥanẓalī at-Tamīmī al-Marwazī, Abū Ya'qūb, the scholar of Khurasān of his time and one of the *Mujtahid Imāms*. He taught Aḥmad, Bukhārī, Muslim, at-Tirmidhī, an-Nasā'ī and others. He died in the year 238H.

Al-Junaid: bin Muḥammad az-Zujjāj, Abū al-Qāsim. He was a Legal Jurist who followed the school of Abū Thawr and was known for asceticism. He died in the year 297H.

Ka'b bin al-Ashraf: at-Ṭā'ī, a poet from the days of *Jāhiliyyah*. He incited many people against the Prophet (ﷺ) and the Muslims, and the Prophet (ﷺ) ordered him killed. Five of the *Anṣār* left to kill him and killed him in the year 3H.

Khiḍr: He is the companion of Moses, it is said that he was a Prophet or a righteous servant - however the majority are of the opinion that he was a Prophet. This is because the realities behind his actions can only be known through revelation and because a person does not learn or follow except one who is above him and it is not possible that a non-prophet be above a Prophet. His name and life are greatly differed over and this difference is detailed by ibn Kathīr. Refer to: *'Tafsīr al-Qurṭubī'* [11/16] and *'al-Bidāyah wan Nihāyah'* [1/355].

Al-Layth bin Sa'd: bin 'Abdur-Raḥmān al-Fahmī, Abū al-Ḥārith, the *Imām* of Egypt in ḥadīth, *fiqh* and language. He was trustworthy and precise and narrated many *aḥādīth*. Ash-Shāfi'ī regarded him to be a better jurist than Mālik. He died in the year 175H.

Mālik bin Anas: ibn Mālik ibn Abū 'Amr al-Asbāhī. The *Imām* of

Madīnah in his time, one of the great *Imāms* of Islām and author of the famous *Muwaṭṭa*. His virtues are many and the scholar's praise of him is abundant. He died in the year 179H.

Ma'rūf al-Karkhī: bin Fairoz, Abū Ma'fūẓ, one of the *shaykhs* famous for asceticism and one whose supplication would be answered. He died in the year 200H.

Muḥammad bin 'Alī al-Ḥakīm at-Tirmidhī: From the great scholars of Khurasān who authored some famous works and was devoted to ḥadīth. He died in the year 320H.

Al-Mukhtār bin Abū Ubaid: bin Mas'ūd ath-Thaqafī, Abū Isḥāq, who claimed Prophethood for himself. He was killed by Muṣ'ab in the year 67H.

Musaylamah: bin Thumāmah bin Kabīr bin al-Ḥanafī al-Wā'ilī, Abū Thumāmah, the great liar. He initially accepted Islām, then apostated and claimed Prophethood for himself and gained a following. He was fought by the Muslims and was killed in the year 12H.

Muslim: bin al-Ḥajjāj bin Muslim al-Qushayrī, Abū al-Ḥusain an-Naisābūrī, the *Ḥāfiẓ* and one of the great *Imāms* of this nation. He is the author of the Ṣaḥīḥ which is the most authentic book of ḥadīth after Bukhārī. He died in the year 261H.

Najdah al-Ḥurūrī: bin 'Āmir al-Ḥanafī. He was one of the *Khawārij* who was unique, even amongst them, because he thought that it was obligatory to kill anyone who held an opposing view to him. He was killed in the year 69H.

Sahl bin 'Abdullāh: bin Yunūs Abū Muḥammad at-Tustorī, one of the

Ṣūfīs scholars. He died in the year 283H.

Ash-Shāfi'ī: Muḥammad bin Idrees bin al-'Abbās bin Shāfi'ī al-Hāshimī al-Qurashī, Abū 'Abdullāh, the *Mujaddid* of his era and one of the great *Imāms* of this nation. He died in the year 204H.

Shayṭān: Also called *Iblīs*. He is a Jinn and the enemy of mankind, devoted to leading them astray in any way that he can. The word Shayṭān is derived from the verb *shaṭana* which means to be distant, and indeed Shayṭān is distant from all good.

Ṭalḥa al-Asadī: bin Khuwaylid bin Nawfal. He initially accepted Islām at the hands of the Prophet (ﷺ) and then apostated, claiming Prophethood for himself. Many of the Arabs followed him and Abū Bakr sent Khālid bin Walīd to him who fought him. Ṭalḥa was defeated and fled to Syria where he eventually accepted Islām again. It is said that he was martyred at *Nahāwund* in the year 21H.

At-Tirmidhī: Muḥammad bin 'Īsā bin Sawrah bin Mūsā bin ad-Ḍaḥḥāk as-Sulamī at-Tirmidhī, the *Imām*, *Ḥāfiẓ* and the author of the famous *Sunan*. He was trustworthy and precise and one of the students of Bukhārī. He died in the year 279H.

GENERAL INDEX

'Abdullāh Ibn 'Abbās, 69, 78, 111, 177, 179
'Abdullāh bin 'Amr, 85, 176
'Abdullāh ibn 'Umar, 57, 111, 157, 179
'Abdullāh bin Mas'ūd, 71, 74, 85, 177
'Abdur-Raḥmān bin Maḥdī, 189
'Abdur-Raḥmān 'Alī, ash-Shaykh, 71, 93
Abī Asim, 82, 124, 125
Abī Shaybah, 149
abrogated, 208, 209
Abū Bakr as-Ṣiddīq, 52, 77, 101, 145
Abū Barzā, 85
Abū Dāwūd, 56, 65, 69, 84, 86, 88, 114, 125, 126, 157, 160, 161, 170, 179, 190, 204, 213
Abū ad-Dardā', 93,
Abū al-'Āliyah, 151
Abū Dharr al-Ghifārī, 183,
Abū Hanīfah, Imām, 115, 174, 201
Abū Hatim, 125
Abū Hāshim, 138, 169
Abū Hushī, 200
Abū Hurayrah, 74, 85, 95, 111, 145, 157, 158, 177,
Abū Mūsā al-Ash'ārī, 157
Abū Nu'aym, 49, 191, 192
Abū Sa'īd al-Khudrī, 49, 77, 167, 177
Abū Sufyān, 149
Abū Ṭālib, 102; Allāh did not accept his deeds, 102, 103
Abū Umāmah, 124
Abū Ya'lā, 51, 82
achievement (*hayl*), 245
actualisations, 87
Ādam, Prophet of Allāh, 32, 48, 67, 121, 122, 123, 211, 212, 213; his wife, 134; sin of Ādam, 210; his repentance, 155
'Adi bin Hātim, 91
Ahlu-l-Ḥadīth, 95, 171, 172, 173,
Aḥl lul Kalām, 13, 46, 169, 190, 192
Aḥl lus-Sunnah, 171, 172, 173
Aḥmad ibn Hanbal, Imām, 69, 78, 81, 85, 91, 101, 145, 148, 167, 170, 171, 174, 177, 201,
'Ā'ishah, 156, 157, 177, 208
al-Albānī, 47, 49, 82, 85, 85, 124, 145, 146, 148, 157, 160, 167, 177, 179, 208,
alcohol, 179
Allāh; mentioned frequently through out the book.
'Alī ibn Abī Tālib, 70, 78, 98, 181,

160, 171,
'Amr bin 'Abasa, 204
'Amr bin al-'Āṣ, 176
Anas ibn Mālik, 71, 97, 157, 167, 177, 179
Angels, 35; descended, 76; chose for His angels, 78, 97; perfection of the angels, 141; also see Jibra'īl,
apostate, 178
asbāb, 71
asceticism, 27
Ash'ārīyah, 13
'Aṭā', 171
attainment (*idrāk*), 217
Attributes of Allāh, the King, 56; *al-Jalāl*, *al-Ikrām*, 62; most beautiful Names, 77, 92 ; rich beyond need, 63; to know Him, 61; *ilāh*, 57; godly Attributes, 64; *Kibriya*, 65; negates evil or defect, 66; Will, 67, 181; Face, 89, 167, 191, 192; *ḍhāt*, 191; action, 189, 190, 191 decree, 69; lofty Attributes, 77; Creator of everything, 87, 193, Allāh shows more joy, 130; Lord, 117; also see Allāh
arrival (*wisāl*), 117
Ayyūb, Prophet, 32, 51
Awliyā', 108, 128, 190; see *walī*,
Battle, *badr*, 201; *Ḥunayn*, 204; *al-Huḍaybiyyah*, 211
Baqhāqī, 49, 51, 59
Bukhārī, 23, 40, 52, 56, 57, 60, 67, 74, 77, 79, 93, 94, 97, 114, 125, 126, 131, 137, 145, 148, 149, 156, 175, 177, 198, 209
barzakh, 179
al-Baghdādī, 192-193
al-Baghawi, 47
al-baghī, 199
baqa, 186
al-Bazzār, 27, 111, 179
Bāṭiniyyah, 210
beneath the throne, 35

cause of his sins, 170; cause of his trial, 35
Christians, 99, 141; did with Christ, 126, 129; people of the book, 99, 144; accepts Islām, 176; Christian narrations, 185; refutations of Christianity, 13
Companions, 145; put to trial, 145; best of *Awliyā'* the after the Prophets, 148; *Anṣār*, 142, 148,156; *Muhājirūn*, 142, 148, 156;
contentment (*riḍā*), 191
cursed ten categories of people,179

Daḥriyyah, 133
al-Darimī, 49
al-Daylamī, 125
Dāwūd, Prophet of Allāh, 32, 48, 130, 131; Prophet-King, 201
Day of Judgement, 100, 131, 179, 212
desire overcomes him, 164 ; destructive traits, 216
adh-Dhahabī, 16, 18, 47, 65, 69, 124, 144, 177
disbelief is the only thing, 165; eternally in the fire, 165, 171
Du'ā, 4, 7, 44; meaning of *du'ā*, 40, 41, 42, 43, 44; conditions of the

supplicant, 45; supplication, 77; manners of asking, 51; supplication comprises of, 84; types, 77, 86; condition, 78; opening, 56; *ṣalāh* is *du'ā*, 43
Ḍhikr, 57, 86; low voice, 15; supplication to Allāh, 19; superior form, 46; recitation of the Qur'ān, 49; best, 50, 51 ; end of the gathering, 116; completing ablution, 84; end of the prayer, 84; in *rukū'*, 158; opening *takbīr* for prayer, 168; *sajdah*, 160; frequently, 68; in the heart, 68; the meaning of *Tahlīl*: *'Lā ilāha illAllāh'*, 46, 51, 57, 58, 60, 65, 119; *Tasbīḥ*: *'SubḥānAllāh'*, 57, 58, 60, 61, 119; *ta'ẓīm*, 59, 62; *Taḥmīd*: *'Al-ḥamdulillāh'*, 46, 58, 59, 119; *Takbīr*: *'Allāhu Akbar'*, 58, 62, 118, 119; expiation for, 85; remembrance of Allāh, 26; hearts find, 57
Dhū-l-Nūn, 6, 70, 54, 121, 122, 123, 153; confessed, 124; forgiven, 140; See also Yūnus

enslavement, 78

al-Fahsha' -199
fai', 200
fanā, 186
fear of Allāh leads to the relinquishment of all sins, 172, 192; fearing His punishment, 48
fitrah, 166, 172
forgiveness, 164, 176; shield, 165
Fuḍayl ibn 'Iyād, 166
al-Fuqarā', 198

al-Ghaffār, 165
al-Ghafr, 165
Gnostics, 180, 217
good deeds, 177
Greek, 13

al-Hākim, 47, 85, 177
Hākim bin Hizān, 175
Hamār, 178
hamm (desire), 136; evil and lust, 137; desire overcome him, 164;
al-Ḥasan al-Baṣrī, 177, 181
al-Ḥaythamī, 124
hardship faced in the *barzakh*, 179
Heart, 95; freedom of the heart, 76; coming from the heart, 79; heart is the king, 95; sound heart desires good, 143 heart extinguishes, 187; heart finds tranquillity, 57; action of the heart; 94
Hell-fire for ever, 132, 171, 192; pain of the fire, 191; fire of lust, 159; greatest punishment of the fire, 190
hope (*rajā*), 186, 192; takes on a number of forms, 70; should be placed in, 71; places his hope, 72
Ḥudhafah ibn Yamān, 49, 146
Ḥulūliyyah, 21

Iblīs, 99; arrogant, 45; devils, 111; beloved to the devils, 111; satan said, 81; devils of jinn, 145; satan spoke, 123; deceived, 123; visitors from satan, 137; suggestion

of satan, 206; uttered, 206
Ibn 'Abbās, 'Abdullāh, 69, 78, 111, 177, 179
Ibn Ḥajr 'Asqalānī, 19, 20, 22, 49, 208, 179
Ibn Ḥibbān, 47, 69, 81, 85, 146, 148, 177
Ibn Jawzī, 124
Ibn Kathīr, 14, 22, 28, 37
Ibn Mājah, 47, 71, 177
Ibn Mas'ud, 'Abdullāh, 71, 74, 85, 177
Ibn Mubārak, 189
Ibn Qayyim, 14, 15, 71, 159
Ibn Rajab, 22, 22, 23, 24, 27, 45, 125, 169
Ibn as-Sakān, 179
Ibrāhīm, Prophet of Allāh, 32, 53, 208; nation of Ibrāhīm, 80; *al-Khalīl*, 78, 79, 134
Ibn Taymiyyah, 7; his teachers, 16; his student, 17; the praise of the scholars for him, 18; his saying, 24; his death, 27; his works, 28
idolaters, 171
ihsān, 97
ikhlās, 103; misdirected intentions, 108, 109, 110; perform a good deed and enter Hell, 312; deeds are by their conclusion, 141, 142, 143, 144, 145
ijmā', 165
ijtihād, 21, 156, 203
Ittiḥādiyyah, 21
imān, 96-107, 194-195; explanation of *imān*, 94-101; sixty odd branches, 95; increase, 46; root in the heart, 98; is a light, 171; sweetness of faith, 217-218; *imān al-mutlaq*, 96
iqrār, 143-144, 195
intercession, 161, 171; intercessors, 88, 106; between them, 91
'Isā, Prophet of Allāh, 32, 33, 161; Christians do with Christ, 94
Isti'faf, 110
Istighfār, 152-162, 165; see also repentance
Istighna', 77

Jahmiyyah, 8, 100, 133, 210; to be disbelievers, 101; denied the Names and Attributes, 133; harsh against them, 144
Jarīr bin 'Abdullāh, 170
jāhiliyyah, 142-143, 175
Jews, 144; greatest liars, 138; Judeo Christian narrations, 180; accept Islām
Jibra'īl, the Angel of Revelation, 78, 97, 105; see also angel
Jihād, 8, 26, 98, 134, 144; against the soul, 26; against the disbelievers and hypocrites, 26; word of Allāh made supreme, 95; takes precedences over, 126; martyrdom, 14, 27; war booty, 116, 201, 203, 204, 205; see *al-Mujāhid*
Junayd, 192

Khālīd bin Wālīd, 145
Khalīfāh, 204
khawārij, 165, 166, 171, 172

khawf, 191

legal punishment of whipping, 160
Love (*ḥubb*), 71-72, 191-192; Lord loves to be loved, 24; his master, 25; object of love, 75, 76; loving of Allāh, 89; foundation of every action, 90; action of the heart, 126; desireable love, 76; for the sake of Allāh, 49, *shirk* in ones love, 88;
Lūṭ, Prophet of Allāh, 31, 148 196

madhhabs, 22; Imāms, 19, 21, 22, 170, 205, 213; footsteps of the Imām, 19; Ḥanbalīs, 22; Mālik, 174 Shāfi'ī, 22
Mālik ibn Anas, Imām, 120, 146, 181, 174, 205
maghfirah, 173
Magicians and fortune tellers, 112
al-Manāwī, 82
al-Marrūdhī, 169
ma'rūf, 198-199;
al-Mizzī, 20, 23 244
Mu'adh ibn Jabal, 190
Muḥmmad, Messenger of Allāh, 99, 100, 101, 102, 145, 150, 210, 211, 211, 216, 217; Messenger-Servant, 113, 202, distributor, 114; beloved, 125; seal of the Messengers, 67, 155; past and future sins forgiven, 160; master of creation, 213; obligation to obey him, 92, 93, 94; Prophet of mercy, 145; given the choice, 113; honour of him, 99; elite of the Messenger, 201; spokesperson of the Prophets 213; Imām; 213
Muḥammad bin Qalāwūn, 16
Muḥmmad ibn Sulaymān, 78
al-Mujāhid, 22; see also *Jihād*
munkar, 198-199
al-Mundhirī, 111
Mūsā, Prophet of Allāh, 49, 53, 55, 135; supplicated, 47, 48, 49; sent to pharaoh, 99; repented, 135, 136
Muslim, 74, 77, 79, 86, 88, 93, 97, 95, 98, 131, 137, 144, 156, 170, 175, 209, 217, 233,
Mu'tāzilah, 13, 101, 172
muttāqqīn, 172, 173
mutāwātir, 172
Murji'āh, 172

nationalism, 93
an-Nisā'ī, 71, 85
Nūḥ, Prophet of Allāh, 20, 12, 48, 134; repentance of Nūḥ, 155;

Ostentation, 112

Paradise, 132, 189, 190, 191; denied the reality, 133
Persisting in performing, 162
Philosophers, 162
Prophets, infallibility, 127, 128, 129, 130, 152; greatest chosen servants, 124; whoever curses the Prophets is killed, 129; doctors of Religion, 143; Prophets to the sinless, 162

Qadariyyah, 208

Qaḍi ʿIyād, 237
Qaḍi Abū Yalā, 170, 178
Qarāmiṭa, 133
qiyās, 19
Qur'ān, mentioned frequently through out the book.
Rabia'a al-ʿAdāwiyyah al-Baṣrīyyah, 189
Rāfiḍah, 13, 152; *Rawāfiḍah*, 21 see also Shiʿā
Repentance, 131, 132, 133; of Ādam, 155; of Mūsā 60; of Yūnus, 47; of Nūḥ, 155; Muḥmmad, 99, 100, 101; repentance is obligation, 180; punishment for sin, 162; see *Istighfār*
Reliance, hope and fear, 69; see also *at-Tawakkul*

Salāf, 97, 101, 129, 130, 131, 132, 169, 170, 179, 206, 207, 214; say the Qur'ān is created, 172
Satanic verses, 207; implanted a trial, 209
as-Sattār, 165
al-Shāfiʿī, Imām, 22, 113, 175, 201
Shiʿā, 133
Sharīʿah, 192
shirk, 46, 71, 72, 73, 78, 88, 92, 93, 94, 95, 96, 97, 98, 182, 183, 184, 185, 186; Allāh will nor forgive *shirk*, 58; free of *shirk*, 73; forms of *shirk*, 72; committing shirk, 72; form of shirk, 81; *shirk* by ones own soul, 111; ostentation and conceit, 110, 111, 112, 113; unless it be repented, 163; is forgiven if repented from, 164; unification; 187; unity of existence, 193
sins combined with *tauḥīd*, 163; other than *shirk*, 164; has been hidden, 165; vileness, 171; major, 172; persists, 176; punished, 156
Sham, 12; Damascus, 12, 20, 27;
Shuʿayb, Prophet of Allāh, 153
sincere, 129; feeling remorse, 163
Soul, 109; the soul inclines towards, 82; speech of the soul, 206, 208; joys of the soul, 28; pain of the soul, 216;
spirital ecstasy (*wajd*), 217
spirital express, 185, 186
spirital realization (*dhawq*), 217
submissiveness to Allāh, 168
ṣūfi, 13, 9; spiritual unveiling, 108; hope and fear understood by the ṣūfis, 188, 189, 190, 191, 194, 195
Sulaymān, Prophet of Allāh, 32, 63, 136, Prophet-King, 113, 114, 115, 116, 117, 201
Sufyān bin ʿUyaynah, 51
supplication, see *duʿā*
as-Suyūṭī, 49, 82, 144, 148, 151
sweetness of faith, 213

at-Ṭabarānī, 59, 90, 91, 124, 177
at-Ṭabārī, 35, 151
Tabiʿīn, 210
tajsīm (anthropomorphism), 21
Taqlīd, 56; *taqlid* of the scholars, 93

taqwā, 107, 142,
at-Tawakkul, 71, 75, 76, 94, 95, 104, 105, 106, 107, 108, 109, 110, 111, 112; whoever depends upon an object, 75, 76; at-*Tawakkul* is that your heart, 78;
Ta'wīl, 210
taubah, 166; from disblief, 173
tawḥīd, 25, 26, 70, 75, 76, 94, 95, 104, 105, 106, 106, 107, 108, 109, 110, 111, 112; lead to forgiveness, 163; opens the door to good, 34; *al-Ilāhiyyah*, 47, 57, 70, 85, 124; *al-Ulūhiyyah*, 85, 112, 119, 181; *ar-Rubūbiyyah*, 85, 112, 113, 114, 115, 116, 117, 118, 119, 120, 121, 122, 123, 124, 125, 126, 127, 181; testifying to *tawḥīd*, 79, 80, 81, 82; wisdom mentioning *tawḥīd* alongside forgiveness, 82, 83, 84, 85, 86; understanding *tawḥīd*, 87, 88, 89, 90, 91, 92; His specific Lordship, 118;
at-Tirmidhī, 91, 126, 131, 145, 217
trial, 171, 208; tribulations, 185
Umm 'Amr, 189
Umm Mu'āwiyah, Hind, the wife of Abū Sufyān, 149
'Umar ibn al-Khaṭṭāb, 49, 103, 125, 142, 143, 145, 167,
undesirable, 77
Uthmān ibn 'Affān, 103, 171
Ubadah ibn as-Sāmit, 189

Wahb bin Munabbih, 220
Wa'il ibn Ḥujr, 177

Yā'qūb, Prophet of Allāh, 32, 97; image of Yā'qūb, 137
Yūnus, Prophet of Allāh, 32, 55, 57; born in, 23; swallowed, 34; regained heath,36; companion of the whale, supplication of Yūnus, 47;54, 121, 122, 123; his repentance, 140; mentioned frequently through out the book; see also *Dhū-l-Nūn*
Yūsuf, Prophet of Allāh, 136; sincerely truthful, 136, had a desire, 137; in prison, 139; brothers of Yūsuf, 194

zakāt, 130

INDEX OF SECTS

AHLU'L-KALĀM: Adherents to speculative theology, people seeking to explain the articles and premises of belief and to give evidences for them based on philosophy and logic.

BĀṬINIYYAH: A sect of the Shīʿa, the followers of Ismāʿīl ibn Jaʿfar. They were of the belief that the legal texts were merely superficial expressions carrying inner meanings that oppose what is outwardly understood of them, examples lie with their explanations of Paradise, Hell and the Last Day.

ḤASHWIYYAH: A term frequently used by the innovators to refer to Ahlu'l-Sunnah, the Ahl'l-Ḥadith, those who affirmed the Attributes of Allāh. The first to use this term was ʿAmr ibn ʿUbaid al-Muʿtazilī who said that ʿAbdullāh ibn ʿUmar ibn al-Khaṭṭāb was a Ḥashwī.

JABARIYYAH: Followers of the school of Jahm ibn Ṣafwān in his belief that all actions are decreed by Allāh and man has no control over them at all, instead he is forced to do what he does.

JAHMIYYAH: Followers of Jahm ibn Ṣafwān in his denial of the Names and Attributes of Allāh.

KARRĀMIYYAH: Followers of Muḥammad ibn Karrām (d. 255H), they divided into many sub-sects and were famous for their likening of Allāh to His creation (*tashbīh*).

MUTAKALLIMŪN: Speculative Theologians, adherents to *kalām*.

MU'TAZILA: Followers of Wāṣil ibn 'Aṭā' al-Ghazzāl who abandoned the circles of Ḥasan al-Baṣrī. They negated the Attributes of Allāh for fear of likening Him to His creation, yet affirmed His Names. From amongst their beliefs was that a person who committed a major sin was neither a believer nor a disbeliever, rather of a station between the two stations, but he would be consigned to Hellfire forever. They were from the rank and file of the Mutakallimūn and gave precedence to their intellects over the divine texts.

QADARIYYAH: Those who held the belief that man has complete free will in all that he does and that Allāh has no control over him.

QARĀMIṬA: A sect holding the same belief as the Bāṭiniyyah and followers of Maymūn ibn Daysān.

FALĀSIFA: Those philosophers who promoted the 'wisdom' of the Greeks, the Greek philosophers who did not believe in the Resurrection as it is mentioned in the Book and Sunnah, nor did they affirm the Names and Attributes of Allāh. From amongst their leaders was Aristotle, the student of Plato and from amongst their latter proponents was al-Fārābī and ibn Sīnā.

GLOSSARY OF ARABIC TERMS

Āyah: pl. *āyāt*. Sign, miracle, example, lesson, verse.

'Abd: pl. *'ebād*. slave, servant, worshipper.

Abrār: righteous.

Adhān: *fiqh*: the call to prayer.

Barzakh: barrier, obstruction, an isthmus. *fiqh*: a barrier placed between a person who has deceased and this worldly life.

Bid'ah: innovation, *fiqh*: that which is newly introduced into the religion of Allāh.

Ḍa'īf: weak. A *ḥadīth* that has failed to meet the criteria of authenticity.

Dīn: religion, way of life.

Dhikr: remembrance, *fiqh*: making mention of Allāh.

Du'ā: supplication, invocation.

Farḍ: see *wājib*.

Fasād: corruption, decay, and invalidity.

Fatwā: *fiqh*: legal ruling.

Fiqh: understanding and comprehension. *fiqh*: of the rulings and legislation of Islām.

Fisq: pl. *fusūq*. Immorality, transgression, wickedness.

Fitnah: pl. *fitan*. Trial, tribulation, civil strife.

Fiṭrah: primordial nature, the harmony between man, creation and Creator.

Ghayb: the Unseen, those matters beyond our senses.

Ghubṭa: envy, referring to the permissible form of envy where the envier wishes to have the same blessings as the envied but without desiring to see them removed from the envied. This is opposed to *ḥasad*, the blameworthy form of envy where the envier wishes to see the blessings removed from the envied.

Ḥāfiẓ: pl. *ḥuffāẓ*. Ḥadīth Master, commonly referred to one who has memorised at least 100 000 *aḥādīth*.

Ḥadīth: pl. *aḥādīth*, speech, report, account. *fiqh*: a narration describing the sayings, actions, character, physical description and tacit approval of the Prophet (ﷺ).

Ḥajj: *fiqh*: pilgrimage, one of the pillars of Islām.

Ḥalāl: released. *fiqh*: permissible.

Ḥanīf: pl. *Ḥunafā*. Upright and Devout. One who leaves the false religions and beliefs for the truth and does not swerve from it. His outward rectitude reflects what is inside him.

Ḥarām: forbidden, sacred, restricted. *fiqh*: unlawful, that which the legally responsible person is rewarded for leaving and sinful for doing.

Ḥasad: see *Ghubṭa*.

Ḥasan: good. *fiqh*: a ḥadīth that has met the criteria of authenticity to a sufficient level as would allow it to be used as legal proof.

Hawā: base desires.

Ḥudūd: limits, boundaries. *fiqh*: limits ordained by Allāh, prescribed punishments.

Iḥrām: the ceremonial state of making Ḥajj or the Ḥajj garments themselves.

Imām: model, exemplar. *fiqh*: religious leader, one who leads the congregational prayer or leads a community.

Īmān: faith that also comprises a meaning of submission. Its place is the heart, the tongue and the limbs and it increases with obedience and decreases with disobedience.

Ishk: passionate love.

Isnād: chain of narration.

Jāhiliyyah: Pre-Islāmic Ignorance. Technically this refers to the condition of a people before the guidance of Allāh reaches them, or the state of a people that prevents them from accepting the guidance of Allāh.

Janābah: *fiqh*: state of major impurity.

Janāzah: *fiqh*: funeral prayer, funeral procession.

Jihād: striving in the Way of Allāh to make His Word supreme.

Jinn: another creation besides mankind who are invisible to us. They are also subject to the laws of Islām and will be judged in the Hereafter according to how they lived in this life.

Kāfir: a rejecter of faith, disbeliever.

Khalīfah: pl. *khulafā*. Successor, representative. *fiqh*: of the Prophet (ﷺ), head of the Islāmic state. Also called *Amīr al-Mu'minīn* or Leader of the Believers.

Khawf: fear.

Khuṭbah: sermon, lecture. *fiqh*: Friday sermon.

Makrūh: *fiqh*: disliked, reprehensible, that which the legally responsible person is rewarded for leaving but not punished for doing.

Mawḍu': fabricated *ḥadīth*. That *ḥadīth* which is a lie against the Prophet (ﷺ).

Muḥaddith: pl. *muḥaddithūn*. Scholar of Ḥadīth.

Mujtahid: one who performs *ijtihād*. *fiqh*: that level of scholar who can deduce independent verdicts directly from the primary Islaamic sources.

Munāfiq: hypocrite. *fiqh*: one who outwardly displays Islām but inwardly conceals disbelief. This is the worst type of hypocrisy and its possessor is the worst type of disbeliever, there are other lesser types.

Qaḍā: see qadar.

Qadar: Allāh's decree of all matters in accordance with His prior knowledge and as dictated by His wisdom.

Qiblah: *fiqh*: direction to which the Muslims pray, towards the *ka'bah*.

Rahbah: dread.

RaḍiyAllāhu 'anhu/'anhā/'anhum/'anhumā: may Allāh be pleased with him/her/them/both of them.

RahimahAllāh/RahimahumAllāh: may Allāh bestow his mercy upon him/them.

Ramaḍān: ninth month of the Islāmic calendar.

Riḍā: contentment and pleasure.

Riyā': an act of worship undertaken by someone to be seen and praised by others and not purely for Allāh.

Ruqyā: recitation used to cure an illness or disease. It can only be done in the Arabic tongue, in words whose meaning is understood, using verses of the Qur'ān or supplications of the Prophet combined with the belief that it is only Allāh who in reality gives the cure.

Sabābah: fervent longing.

Ṣabr: patience, steadfastness.

Ṣaḥīḥ: healthy, sound, authentic, correct. A *ḥadīth* that has met the criteria of authenticity and can be used as a legal proof.

Ṣalāh: *fiqh*: the second pillar of Islām, the prayer.

Salaf: predecessors, commonly employed to refer to the first three generations of Muslims.

Salafī: Linguistically, *Salafī* is an ascription to the *Salaf*. This term can often be found in the speech of the people of knowledge in many places. The term *Salafiyyah* is what the people of *ḥadīth* are upon, those who are the people of the *Sunnah* and the *Jamā'ah*. These are some of the names that are used to describe the people of the *Sunnah* and the *Jamā'ah*: *Ahl al-Ḥadīth* (The people of *ḥadīth*), *Ahl al-Sunnah wa'l-Jamā'ah*, *al-Salafiyūn*, *Atbā' al-Salaf* (The followers of the *Salaf*)

Ṣawm: *fiqh*: fasting, one of the pillars of Islām.

Shaghafah: crazed passion.

Shahādah: testification, witness. The declaration that none has the right to be worshipped save Allāh and that Muḥammad (ﷺ) is the Messenger of Allāh.

Shahwā: carnal lusts.

Sharīʿah: divine Islāmic law as ordained by Allāh.

Shaykh: old man. *fiqh*: learned person, scholar. *ṣufi*: a guide along the spiritual path.

Shayṭān: Satan, Iblīs, a devil.

Shirk: polytheism, associating partners with Allāh in matters that are exclusive to Allāh.

Sunan: a compilation of *aḥādīth*.

Sunnah: habit, customary practice, norm and usage as sanctioned by tradition. *fiqh*: the sayings, commands, prohibitions, actions, and tacit approvals of the Prophet (ﷺ).

Sūrah: chapter of the Qur'ān.

Ṣurah: image, form, face.

Ṭāghut: all that is falsely worshipped besides Allāh.

Tafsīr: elucidation, clarification, explanation. *fiqh*: of the Qur'ān.

Taqwā: fearful awareness of Allāh, pious dedication, being careful not to transgress the bounds set by Allāh.

Tawakkul: trust and absolute reliance.

Tawḥīd: the foundation stone of Islām, the absolute belief in the Oneness of Allāh - His being the sole Creator and Sustainer, His being the only One deserving worship and His being unique with respect to His Names and Attributes.

Ummah: nation, the Muslim nation.

Wuḍū': *fiqh*: ritual ablution.

Zakāh: *fiqh*: one of the pillars of Islām, an obligatory tax levied on a Muslim wealth subject to certain criteria.

Other published works of Ibn Tayimiyyah by Dar as-sunnah Publishers

Disease of the Hearts and Their Cures

This is a beautiful book, containing many benefits related to curing the heart from many sickness. It covers a wide range of topics, including ailments of the hearts, envy of the heart, sickness of the hearts, the diseases of desire and passionate love. As well as remedies to cure the heart from the Qur'ān and Sunnah. This work also includes an appendix from Ibn Qayyim al-Jawziyyah on the types of hearts. It is a very beneficial read, for everyone.

ISBN 978-19043360-9-9 | 160 Pages Paper-back

The Friends of Allāh and the friends of *Shayṭān*

In a day and age in which the devil (*Shayṭān*) has overcome the majority of mankind and knowledge of the differences between the friends of the Most Merciful and the friends of *Shayṭān* is seldom found. This is an important and a monumental volume of the author, covering a wide range of topics, tackling the subject from various different angles and thoroughly refuting those who have gone astray in this matter. An important read, in which author enlightens the reader from the traps and the plot's of *Shayṭān*.

ISBN 978-1904336-15-0 | 384 Pages Paper-back

The Creed of al-Wāsiṭiyyah

This important work on the orthodox Sunnī creed, the creed of *Ahl al-Sunnah wa'l-Jamā'ah*. It commences by listing articles of belief that every Muslim must believe in concerning Allāh, in particular His Names and Attributes and the principles which must be applied to understand them. It also discuss the [reality of the] Qur'ān, Seeing Allāh on the Day of Rising, Punishment of the grave, some description of the Last Day and the events that will occur therein, the Divine Decree, faith and what it comprises of, the Virtues and Ranking of the Companions of Allāh's Messenger (ﷺ). A must read for every Muslim.

ISBN 978-19043361-9-8 | 176 Pages Paper-back